PHARAOHS AND PYRAMIDS

A Guide Through Old Kingdom Egypt

Exemption decree of Pepi II, Dynasty VI, Coptos, (now in USA)

PHARAOHS AND PYRAMIDS

A Guide Through Old Kingdom Egypt

GEORGE HART

Foreword by Professor Barry Cunliffe

THE HERBERT PRESS

TO MY MOTHER AND FATHER
with fondest love and endless gratitude

First published in Great Britain 1991 by
The Herbert Press Ltd, 46 Northchurch Road, London N1 4EJ

Drawings by Garth Denning
Designed by Pauline Harrison

Set in Granjon
Typeset by Nene Phototypesetters Ltd, Northampton

Printed and bound in Hong Kong
by South China Printing Company (1988) Ltd

The author and publishers would like to thank the following
for permission to quote from copyright material:
The Hogarth Press for *Ionic* (p. 8) from *Collected Poems*
by C. P. Cavafy, edited by George Savidis and translated by
Edmund Keeley and Philip Sherrard; Faber & Faber Ltd for
the extract from *The Hollow Men* (p. 144) from
Collected Poems 1909–1962 by T. S. Eliot.

A CIP catalogue record for this book is available
from the British Library.

ISBN 1–871569–36–2

*Frontispiece: Deity (possibly Anhur), Dynasties III–IV,
?Saqqara. Gneiss, 21.4 cm high. The Brooklyn Museum,
58.192. Charles Edwin Wilbour Fund*

Contents

Acknowledgements

Some years ago now, Ayeshah Abdel-Haleem, now Director of Bycornute Books, approached me with the idea for a book on Egypt's 'Living Past'. Her encouragement and understanding have been instrumental in bringing this volume finally to fruition. She has my deepest gratitude. For David Herbert, publisher of this book, who perceived the need for a popularly-accessible interpretation of the Pyramid Era, I cannot find words strong enough to express my thanks and my respect. For far too long I made demands upon his patience and tolerance beyond what was reasonable – yet at no time was he ever less than courteous. Again I owe an immense debt of gratitude to my editor at the Herbert Press, Julia MacKenzie. Her tenacity and keen eye have eliminated many ambiguities and obscurities in the original manuscript.

I believe that readers will find the line drawings and site plans of monuments of great value. These illustrations have been executed with superb precision by Garth Denning, a good and reliable friend whom I first got to know sometime ago when he was an archeological illustrator at the British Museum.

To Professor Barry Cunliffe, whose thoughtfulness and help during my first time as a lecturer on a Swan Hellenic Mediterranean cruise I will always remember, I would like to express my thanks for agreeing to write the Foreword to this book.

Lastly, my thanks go out to the many loyal friends who have attended my lectures at the British Museum or who have accompanied me on tours to Egypt. Their sustained enthusiasm has been one of the most important and positive factors in my career. I hope that I have produced a book which will reward in some small way their devotion over the years.

Foreword

Everyone has a vision of Ancient Egypt whether they have visited the country or not. Inevitably it is tinged with the romantic – the swashbuckling days of the early collectors and pillagers like Belzoni, the brilliant decipherment of the hieroglyphs by Champollion that suddenly made the Egyptians accessible as a people with everyday lives, and of course the sheer fairytale adventure of Howard Carter's discovery of Tutankhamun's tomb. The story of the discovery of the Ancient Egyptians overflows with eccentric characters and bizarre events. It will continue to fire the imagination of generations of readers – deservedly so. And for the lucky few it may lead them to a life of archeology.

I must confess that for many years my own, rather ill-considered, view of Egypt was that it was remote and of little direct relevance to the development of western cultural development: the Egyptians were an alien people far more difficult to understand than the Minoans, Mycenaeans or the Romans – how wrong I was! On my first visit, on a flight from Cairo to Luxor, I suddenly realized what should have been self-evident – that to begin to understand the Egyptians, one had to experience their landscape. No amount of reading could do this. There below lay the silver band of the Nile, set in its pathetically narrow strip of black mud clothed in a brilliant, enduring green, as everything else in sight turned ochre at the red land or 'Deshret' as the Egyptians called it. It was a tiny thread of lushness set in a hostile world – a precisely defined ecological niche where life was possible.

Coming in to land at Luxor in the evening was another revelation. As the plane turned, there on the west bank where the green ended and the craggy hills of the desert-edge began, it was possible to make out the Valley of the Kings – the burial place of so many pharaohs. They lay on the edge of the world beyond which was nothing but desert where, every day without fail, the sun disappeared. In the stark clarity of it all it was possible to begin to understand how the complex belief systems of these people had begun to evolve.

The story of the Ancient Egyptians is long and vividly patterned. Their huge enduring monuments, the remarkable preservation powers of the desert sand and the sheer wealth of contemporary depiction and writing make the Egyptians the most readily accessible of the ancient peoples of the world. In this book George Hart has wisely concentrated on what can fairly be said to be the most exciting episodes in Egyptian history – the formative phases and the Old Kingdom. The story begins about 5000 BC with the earliest Neolithic settlers, the Badarians as they are known to archeologists. These communities soon developed a food-producing economy sufficiently stable to allow leisure for the production of works of art. Gradually, as the population began to grow, society became more complex and from about 3000 BC, when the King Lists begin, leaders can be identified by name. During this Early Dynastic period monumental architecture, especially tombs for the aristocracy, begin to dominate the archeological record. This was a prelude to the remarkable period known as the Old Kingdom to which the pyramids of Saqqara and Giza, the Sphinx and the great Solar boat belong. It was a phase of brilliant achievement lasting for barely 500 years. By the time it was over, about 2100 BC, Minoan civilization was only just getting under way in Crete and in distant Britain the inhabitants of Wessex had begun to build henge monuments like Avebury and the earliest earthen phase of Stonehenge.

George Hart's book provides a delightfully accessible way into the world of the early Egyptians. It is written by someone with an intimate knowledge of the land and the monuments who has long experience in communicating his enthusiasm to others. *Pharaohs and Pyramids* can be read for pleasure at home but better still should be read in the brilliant light and sharply contrasting colours of the Egyptian landscape where these great monuments to man's achievement are set.

BARRY CUNLIFFE
Professor of European Archeology
Oxford University

IONIC

That we've broken their statues,
that we've driven them out of their temples,
doesn't mean at all that the gods are dead.
O land of Ionia, they're still in love with you,
their souls still keep your memory.
When an August dawn wakes over you,
your atmosphere is potent with their life,
and sometimes a young ethereal figure
indistinct, in rapid flight,
wings across your hills.

C. P. CAVAFY

King List[*]

---

[*] (after Baines and Malek, *Atlas of Ancient Egypt*)

Time Chart

DATES BC	LABEL	MONARCHS	MONUMENTS	CONTEMPORARY EVENTS
5000–2920	**Predynastic**		Designer Pottery	Hacilar and Troy I, Anatolia
	Badarian		Cylinder Seals	Proto-Urban Jericho, Palestine
	Nagada I–III	Scorpion	Ivory figurines Gebel el-Arak knife handle Palettes Maceheads	Uruk period, Iraq (emergence of writing and script) Foundation of Susa, Iran
2920–2649	**Early Dynastic**	Narmer [Menes]	Hierakonpolis	Early Dynastic period, Iraq
	Dynasties I & II	Aha Djer Den Peribsen Khasekhemwy	Abydos cenotaphs Saqqara royal mastabas	Granite monoliths, Carnac, France Passage Grave, Maes Howe, Orkney Islands
2649–2144	**Old Kingdom**			
2649–2575	Dynasty III	Djoser	Step Pyramid at Saqqara	Royal Tombs of Ur, Iraq Amorite invasions, Levant
2575–2465	Dynasty IV	Sneferu	Meidum and Dahshur pyramids	Palace at Mari, Syria Cycladic marble figures, Aegean Islands
		Khufu [Cheops]	Great Pyramid at Giza 'Solar Boat'	
		Rakhaef [Chephren]	Giza Pyramid and Valley Temple Great Sphinx Tomb of Meresankh III	
		Menkaura [Mycerinus]	Pyramid and triad statues	

DATES BC	LABEL	MONARCHS	MONUMENTS	CONTEMPORARY EVENTS
2649–2144	**Old Kingdom**			
2465–2323	Dynasty V	Weserkaf Sahura Neweserra Wenis	Pyramids at Abusir and Saqqara Sun Temple at Abu Ghurob Rock Romb of Nefer Mastaba of Ty	
2323–2144	Dynasty VI	Teti Pepi I Pepi II	Mastaba of Mereruka Pyramid at South Saqqara	
*c.*2144	**First Intermediate Period**			
2040–	**Middle Kingdom**			Earliest palaces, Crete Indus Valley Civilization begins, Mohenjo Daro/ Harappa First phase of Stonehenge (80 sarsen stones in place), Wiltshire First Hellenic races – Achaians, Aeolians, Ionians – invade from North, Greece

Map of Egypt

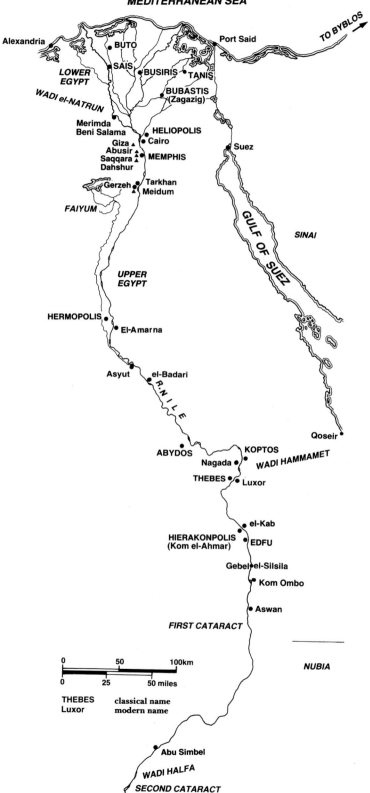

MEDITERRANEAN SEA

TO BYBLOS

Alexandria

Port Said

BUTO
SAIS
BUSIRIS
TANIS
*LOWER
EGYPT*
BUBASTIS
(Zagazig)
WADI el-NATRUN

Suez

Merimda
Beni Salama
HELIOPOLIS
Giza ▲
Abusir ▲   Cairo
Saqqara ▲   MEMPHIS
Dahshur ▲

Gerzeh ●   Tarkhan
▲ Meidum

FAIYUM

GULF OF SUEZ

SINAI

*UPPER
EGYPT*

HERMOPOLIS ●
● El-Amarna

Asyut ●   ● el-Badari

Qoseir

R. NILE

ABYDOS ●
Nagada ●
THEBES ●
● Luxor

KOPTOS
WADI HAMMAMET

● el-Kab

HIERAKONPOLIS
(Kom el-Ahmar) ●   ● EDFU

Gebel el-Silsila ●
● Kom Ombo

● Aswan

FIRST CATARACT

0   50   100km

0   25   50 miles

NUBIA

THEBES   classical name
Luxor   modern name

● Abu Simbel

WADI HALFA

SECOND CATARACT

12

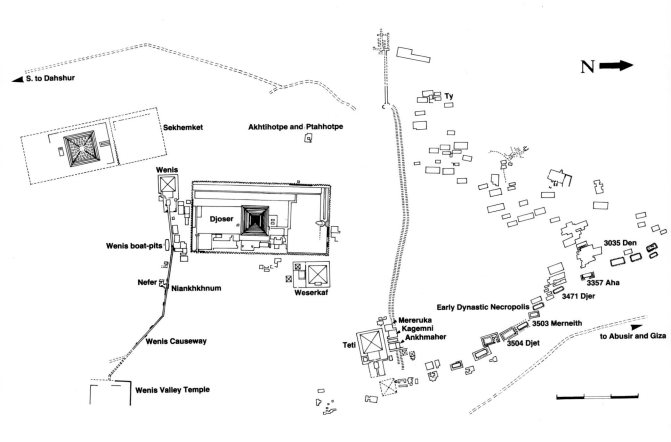

S. to Dahshur

Sekhemket

Akhtihotpe and Ptahhotpe

Ty

Wenis

Djoser

Wenis boat-pits

3035 Den

Nefer

Niankhkhnum

3357 Aha

Weserkaf

3471 Djer

Early Dynastic Necropolis

Mereruka
Kagemni
Ankhmaher

3503 Merneith

Wenis Causeway

Teti

3504 Djet

to Abusir and Giza

Wenis Valley Temple

Plan of the Saqqara Necropolis showing monuments discussed throughout the text

Introduction

Nile and Desert   The realm of the pharaohs was a land of ecological opposites: rich Nile silt and desert sands. Well over 90 per cent of Egypt consisted of the dunes, rocks and mountains flanking the Nile valley. In the Ancient Egyptian language these intractable regions were called 'Deshret' meaning the 'Red' – a colour frequently regarded as dangerous or hostile. Yet the Egyptians became experts in exploiting their deserts. The Eastern Desert between the river Nile and the Red Sea coast was pierced by arterial wadis off which lay the routes to the gold mines. The region known as Nubia beyond Egypt's southern frontier at Aswan became the most important source of gold for the pharaohs. In addition the rock strata held copper and semi-precious stones like felspar, carnelian and amethyst. Across the gulf of Suez the mines of Sinai, dominated by the Egyptians from about 2600 BC, provided abundant turquoise. The Western Desert was a vast expanse of sand crossed by a network of caravan routes that linked the prosperous oases both to the Nile valley and to the trading posts far to the south in Darfur. From these deserts came the building stone for the monuments and statues of Ancient Egypt – predominantly limestone, sandstone and granite. No civilization with the technology available 5000 years ago could have conquered the deserts of northeast Africa more successfully than the Ancient Egyptians.

However, the thriving settlements which make up the concept of Egypt as a nation were clustered along the river Nile. The southern frontier was the First Cataract at Aswan – a region where outcrops of granite form rapids in the river. In Ancient Egypt there was a dependable regime to this river which has been destroyed in the twentieth century AD by the successive dams at Aswan. Previously an annual flood of the Nile washed the fields and then receded leaving a layer of fertile silt. This gave rise to the Ancient Egyptians' name for their land which was 'Kemet' meaning the 'Black', emphasising the life-giving force of the Nile mud on which the crops were sown. They also recognized the 'Two Lands', the term by which they referred to the combination of the Egyptian Delta and the Nile valley. Environmentally these two regions were quite distinct: Lower or Northern Egypt (the Delta) where the Nile debouched in branches into the Mediterranean Sea consisted of vast arable tracts of silt criss-crossed by canals, while Upper or Southern Egypt comprised the length of the Nile from Aswan with the relatively narrow flood plain east and west of the river. The generally reliable annual inundation of the Nile resulted in bumper summer harvests of emmer wheat and barley. Famine was not unknown but as a rule Ancient Egyptian society at all levels could depend on loaves of bread as the absolute minimum at any meal. So the granaries of Egypt became strategic economic nuclei – eventually to be ruthlessly exploited by foreign overlords in the Roman and early Islamic periods.

The Egyptians   'Who were the Ancient Egyptians?' is a question that is complex and sometimes politically controversial. Certainly an indigenous northeast African people were the earliest Egyptians. Then other settlers arrived, some from Africa and some from the Middle East so that Egyptian blood became enriched through intermarriage between diverse peoples. Consequently, racial influences came from all four cardinal directions. From the north came people from Palestine and Syria, from the east came traders from Iraq, from the south came Nubian mercenaries and from the west came Libyan tribes. Archeological artefacts and historical inscriptions reflect these various racial 'inputs' into the Ancient Egyptians. In addition, the Ancient Egyptian language is a hybrid, being classified as 'Afro-Asiatic'. Also, we can mention that inter alia – Greeks, Romans, Arabs and Turks have left their imprint on the population of modern Egypt. Throughout history Africa has been a huge melting-pot of peoples: attempts to categorize the Ancient Egyptian as one exclusive racial type are at the best misguided and at the worst insidious.

Pharaohs and Gods

The eminence of the sovereign in Ancient Egyptian society derived from his supreme political power, and recognition of the ruler as a god guarded by, and related to, other deities. The five 'Great Names' which the pharaoh adopted in his titulary admirably explain his status. These titles were as follows:

'HORUS' Identification with the hawk god to whom the throne of Egypt had been awarded by a divine tribunal

'TWO MISTRESSES' Protection by the vulture Nekhbet and the cobra Wadjet, tutelary goddesses of Upper and Lower Egypt respectively

'GOLDEN HORUS' The hawk god enhanced by the most precious and incorruptible of all metals

'BELONGING TO SEDGE AND BEE' Emphasis on the political strength of the king through the heraldic symbols of Upper and Lower Egypt

'SON OF RA' Ultimate proximity to the sun god, greatest of all deities

The god-kings upheld the worship of Ra throughout the Old Kingdom. In later dynasties the sun god is still paramount as Amen-Ra 'king of the gods' or 'Aten', solar deity *par excellence* in the reign of the pharaoh Akhenaten. In addition, the vast pantheon of other gods and goddesses received donations from the royal treasury and privileges for their temples. For the ordinary Egyptians the temples were bastions from whose inner apartments they were excluded. Only on festival days when the shrines of the deities might be carried beyond the sanctuary and sacred precincts, would non-priests and non-priestesses have any significant contact with gods and goddesses.

Sources for Ancient Egypt's History

Our primary sources, released to our understanding following the discovery of the Rosetta stone in 1799 and subsequent decipherment of hieroglyphs in 1822, take the form of annals, king lists and autobiographical inscriptions. The Palermo stone (with fragments in the Petrie Museum, University College, London, and in Cairo Museum) was carved in the Old Kingdom, and on its surviving portions gives events of kings' reigns, such as the commemoration of a statue, a royal cattle census or an expedition for timber to the Lebanon. The list of Royal Ancestors found, for example, in the temple of Seti I at Abydos and the papyrus in Turin Museum known as the Royal Canon establish the succession of many pharaohs. Although, of course, a strong element of propaganda sometimes is evident in the suppression of royal names considered as unworthy – hence Seti I's list omits all Hyksos rulers, Queen Hatshepsut, Akhenaten and those pharaohs too closely associated with him, such as Tutankhamun. Tombs of courtiers give details of activities carried out on behalf of the sovereigns – in the Old Kingdom the autobiographies of the governors of Aswan, for example, are a mine of information on the relations between Egypt and its southern neighbours.

The secondary source material is quite extensive. In the fifth century BC the Greek historian and ethnographer Herodotus, who figures prominently in our discussion of the Giza pyramids in this book, visited the Nile valley. His observations comprise Book Two (dedicated to the Muse Euterpe) of his history of the wars of the Greeks and Persians. Early in the third century BC an Egyptian High Priest called Manetho was commissioned to write a history of Egypt in Greek for the benefit of the country's new rulers. His division of Egyptian history into thirty groups of ruling families (dynasties) is still in use today. Other material in cuneiform archives and Biblical literature can also be of great importance in piecing together pharaonic history.

Survey of Dynasties

The period covered in this book is the Old Kingdom or pyramid age – the years when Egypt's monuments and culture made their first major impact on history. However, it is only strictly speaking about six hundred years out of 3000 years of successive ruling families or dynasties. So probably a brief chronological survey at this point would put the pyramid era in context.

We can begin the history of Egypt under the pharaohs with the unification of Upper and Lower Egypt into a united kingdom roughly around 3000 BC. The name of the southern monarch who conquered his northern rival was Narmer or Menes, beginning Dynasty I. During the first two dynasties (Early Dynastic period) there was a significant consolidation of power by the pharaohs and organization of state bureaucracy and the labour force. Memphis became the political capital of Egypt, situated at the apex of the Nile Delta in a suitable position to control events in the Two Lands. Huge mudbrick structures serving as tombs and cenotaphs were erected at Saqqara and Abydos. The stage was set for the explosion into the massive stone architecture of Dynasties III–VI which form the nucleus of this book – Egypt in the pyramid age.

Following the fragmentation of the unified state at the end of the Old Kingdom a new monarch of Theban origin arose to weld Egypt together again under one pharaoh about 2040 BC. This inaugurates the period called the Middle Kingdom (Dynasties XI–XII). This was an era of firm centralization of royal authority culminating in the division of Egypt into three 'Departments' in the reign of Senwosret III. The same monarch imprinted Egyptian control around the Second Cataract of the Nile with a number of fortresses controlling routes to the Nubian gold mines. A loss of impetus on the part of the royal family in Dynasty XIII led to Egypt's Second Intermediate Period, when no one overall king was in control of the whole country. Then came one of the severest shocks that Egypt had ever received up to this point – it was invaded and occupied by heterogeneous groups of Bedu tribes from the Middle East, commonly referred to as the Hyksos kings.

This period of foreign domination was halted by the determined campaigns of Theban rulers which eventually saw Ahmose drive the Hyksos out from their stronghold in the eastern Delta into Palestine and then into oblivion. Egypt was now launched on its most opulent and imperialist era, known as the New Kingdom (Dynasties XVIII–XX). The pharaoh Tuthmosis III, with full power in his hands after the long usurpation of the throne by Queen Hatshepsut, built up an empire that through military occupation and diplomatic treaties stretched from the Fourth Cataract of the Nile in the Sudan to the banks of the river Euphrates in Syria. Contact with Crete and Mycenae grew in a mutual trading 'koine' and untold wealth poured into pharaohs' coffers. This was the era of the individualist monarch Akhenaten and his queen Nefertiti, of Tutankhamun and his treasures buried in the Valley of the Kings, of the immaculate art in the reign of Seti I, of the grandiose monuments of Ramesses II and of the brilliant strategist Ramesses III. But the splendour of the New Kingdom monarchs was eclipsed shortly before 1000 BC when the last Ramesside pharaoh died and a new royal family, based at Tanis in the northeast Delta, governed Egypt, with power in the south gathered into the hands of the High Priests of Amun. The last thousand years of Ancient Egyptian civilization are a gradual drift towards foreign occupation. There are still great moments and periods of revival such as Dynasty XXV when Nubian pharaohs renovated temples and preserved valuable religious documents that were decaying. Next, under the Saïte kings (Dynasty XXVI) this 'renaissance' in Egyptian art continues and a sense of pride in monuments constructed 2000 years earlier leads to the impressive exploratory excavations made into the Step Pyramid at Saqqara. But against this must be weighed the constant loss of prestige through successful foreign invaders like the Assyrians and Persians. Then in the Fourth Century BC Alexander the Great, pursuing the Persian King Darius III through the Levant, conquered Egypt. It was his general, whom he left in charge of the country in his absence, who in 300 BC began the line of Greek kings all called Ptolemy and queens variously known as Arsinoe, Berenike and Kleopatra who ruled Egypt down to 30 BC. Today, some of the most visited temples, like Edfu, belong to this period.

With the suicide of Kleopatra VII in 30 BC, Egypt became a Roman Province and was subject to the vicissitudes of the power struggles between pagans and Christians. Slowly the temples fell before the spread of Christianity and were turned into basilicas. However, it was not until the reign of the Emperor Justinian that the cult of the goddess Isis on the island of Philae was finally suppressed. So, by the time of the Arab invasions of the seventh century AD, turning Egypt into the predominantly Muslim country that it has remained ever since, the gods of the pharaohs had not been dead for long.

Historical Outline

If Ancient Egypt seems remote from our 'high-tech' society, it is worth recalling that in terms of geological time we are separated from the pharaohs merely by the equivalent of minutes. The earth came into existence about 4,500 million years ago; complex life forms began to appear on our planet about 600 million years ago, now discovered as fossils in rocks of the Cambrian era. It is *only* in the last two million years that protohominids and Homo sapiens have made their mark on earth. Most specifically for our purposes, from 12,000 BC the nomadic hunter-gatherer groups ranging across the desert edges of northeast Africa began to make settlements beside the river Nile. Gradually more communities linked themselves to the Nile's regime, and it is with the settled cultures and industries of the fifth millennium BC that our survey of sites and monuments of the Valley and the Delta starts.

Predynastic civilization c.5000–3000 BC

Meticulous excavations in cemeteries, middens, temporary camps and the barest foundations of town settlements give tantalizing vignettes of life in Egypt before the pharaohs. The Badarians of Upper Egypt cultivated barley, pulled up flax plants to weave into linen clothes and manufactured pottery of an unbelievably delicate quality. Their successors, known as the Nagada I culture, give us scant glimpses of mudbrick dwellings and storerooms, but more evidence of the skill to carve slate cosmetic palettes and of a superior flint-flaking industry. However, the subsequent culture, called Nagada II, was the immediate predecessor of pharaonic Egypt. In this period ideas and artefacts from south Iraq travelled into the Nile valley through the Eastern Desert; craftsmanship became more sophisticated with complicated designs carved on ivory knife handles and slate palettes; the coppersmith emerged as an indispensable member of the community for tools and weapons. Also, individual groups and villages gradually formed a larger society knit together by the benefits brought by artificial irrigation supplementing the annual Nile flood. Despite scant archeological evidence, there is every likelihood that Lower Egypt had extensive cultural and trade links beyond the eastern Delta into Palestine. These two highly organized spheres of north and south – 'The Two Lands' of dynastic Egyptian inscriptions – were welded under southern pressure into one state, the Egypt of the pharaohs. ('Pharaoh' means 'great house' which later was used to signify 'king'.)

The early dynasties (I and II) c.3000–2649 BC

The unification of Upper and Lower Egypt, probably achieved through a series of battles, was attributed by the Ancient Egyptians to King Meni (named Menes in Manetho's *History*, and Narmer (or, according to some, Aha) on contemporary inscriptions). The political acumen of these early rulers is reflected in the decision to found a new administrative capital for the kingdom whence control over north and south could be exercised. This was the fortified town of Memphis at the apex of the Nile Delta, known as the 'Balance of the Two Lands'. Its local god Ptah joined the national pantheon that included Ra, sun god of Heliopolis.

1. Simple Nagadan haberdashery in ivory, Fitzwilliam Museum, Cambridge

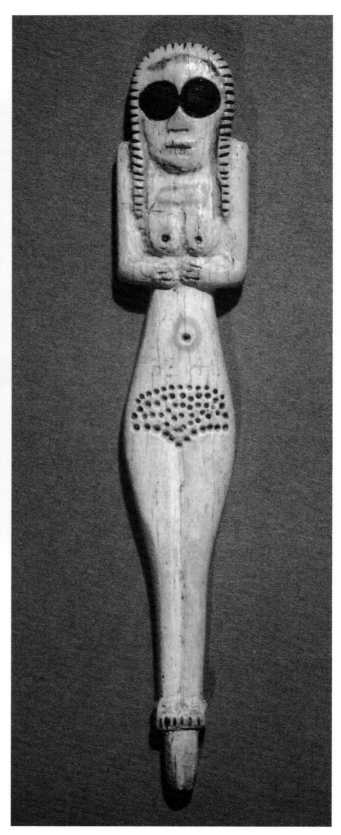

2. (above) Battered statue of the fertility-god Min,
Nagada II, Ashmolean Museum, Oxford

3. (right) Ivory female figurine with eyes of imported
lapis lazuli, Nagada II, British Museum

4. (opposite) Pot painted with distinctive ritual boat,
Nagada II, British Museum

The ancestral home of the early kings was in Upper Egypt at a place called This. Its necropolis at Abydos has a series of foundations originally supporting royal monuments identified by commemorative stelae. The structures must have been 'cenotaphs' where each ruler's name could be preserved in the hallowed precincts of his forefathers. But it is in the north, on the escarpment of the desert at Saqqara, that a series of royal tombs survive as a row of splendid 'mastabas' whose mudbrick super-structures imitate the buttresses and recesses of palace architecture (see p. 53). There was now a growing expertise in stone-cutting (limestone and granite) for royal stelae, occasional statues and lining-slabs for burial chambers.

5. (opposite) Female figure, Nagada II, Ma'mariya, north of Hierakonpolis. Terracotta, 29.3 cm high. The Brooklyn Museum, 07.447.505. Museum Collection Fund

From this we surmise that the monarchy and state became firmly consolidated: a military campaign under King Den was launched against tribes on Egypt's eastern frontier; jubilee festivals of rejuvenation for the king were held at Memphis; ceremonies were conducted for Apis, the capital's sacred bull, herald of the god Ptah. In other words, traditions of war propaganda, the cult of the god-ruler and religious rituals were established at the very beginning of Egypt's dynastic history and were destined to remain observed for 3000 years.

The Old Kingdom c.2649–2144 BC (Dynasties III–VI)

The architectural concepts of the king's chancellor Imhotpe, heralded the pyramid age with the world's first colossal edifice in stone – King Djoser's Step Pyramid at Saqqara. The six-tiered pyramid and the complex of pavilions and shrines within its buttressed boundary-wall declare in no uncertain terms the King's concern with the hereafter, but do little to amplify the meagre historical details of his reign. The first ruler of the following Dynasty (IV), King Sneferu, leaves one, however, with an impression of an expansionist foreign policy being operated by the Old Kingdom pharaohs. Sneferu's campaigns in the west and the south resulted in thousands of captives and heads of cattle as booty. Strong links were intensified between Egypt and the Lebanon where ports thrived on commerce with the Aegean and the overland Middle-Eastern trade routes: Sneferu received forty boatloads of timber from the cedar slopes of Lebanon. There are three pyramids associated with this king's name at Meidum and Dahshur, providing an intriguing puzzle about the ritual and economic logistics of building these monuments.

Khufu (2551–2528 BC), son of Sneferu, was the pharaoh for whom the Great Pyramid was raised at Giza and whom the Greek historian, Herodotos, writing 2000 years later, castigated unjustly as an archetypal tyrant. Khufu and his descendants were responsible for the apogée of pyramid construction, a phenomenon which leaves one overawed when you consider the willing acquiescence of courtiers, foremen and peasants in organizing, quarrying, dragging and raising millions of limestone blocks for the tomb of the pharaoh. Obviously other sites in Egypt were receiving resources from the royal treasury to embellish sanctuaries, for example Bubastis in the Delta, where there once stood a magnificent temple to the cat-goddess Bastet, daughter of Ra, but the main thrust was clearly to magnify Memphis and its environs (now on the outskirts of modern Cairo).

In Dynasty V a new ruling family emerged with a more pronounced allegiance towards the sun-god Ra and his priesthood. The pyramids of these pharaohs at Abusir and Saqqara today are amorphous heaps of limestone, and their sun-temples have been ruthlessly plundered for stone to make other buildings. Yet their intellectual achievements survive. The earliest compilation of hundreds of texts centring around the king's afterlife was carved on the walls of the inner chamber of the pyramid of Wenis at Saqqara. Among the pot-pourri of offering and ritual spells, these pyramid texts attempt to describe the life-force of the pharaoh in the hereafter: as a spirit dwelling with the 'Imperishable Ones' (the stars), or as an entity existing with or within the sun god himself.

On a secular level, the bureaucracy left hieratic texts itemizing rota duties for priests in mortuary temples and divisions of rations. The worries of the pharaoh and his civil servants are not unlike our own: what happens upon death of the body, job demands, and the need for financial security. The courtiers of the pyramid era, in particular, recounted their careers and leisure hours in minute detail on the walls of their mastaba tombs at Giza and Saqqara, which afford fascinating glimpses of everyday life in Ancient Egypt.

The years of Dynasty VI mark the decline of Old Kingdom Egypt. Pyramids of these kings are ill-preserved superstructures which are difficult to visit, but the interiors are again carved with valuable texts for the royal hereafter. The ninety-four-year reign of Pepi II was probably the time when the loss of royal authority over the whole of Egypt began. The death of the last ruler of this dynasty, Queen Nitokris, left Memphis and some loyal provinces under the control of nominal successors to the crown of Upper and Lower Egypt; in reality the country fragmented into power zones ruled by local noblemen. However, from the earlier reigns of Dynasty VI, fine courtiers' tombs have survived, such as the much-visited mastaba at Saqqara of Mereruka, vizier of King Teti. In general, however, tombs became less grandiose, though many are of immense historical interest.

In Dynasty VI worsening climate changes, as well as weak rulers, led to economic decline. The history of the Old Kingdom ended on a sad note, on the brink of a period of chaos.

I · DAWN

The Emergence of the Pharaonic Realm

CHAPTER I

THE PREDYNASTIC ERA

Traces of predynastic culture from the period 5000–3000 BC, are to be found from the Nile Delta through the Faiyum, the river valley beyond the First Cataract and into Nubia. Unfortunately for today's visitor, most of the dwellings and cemeteries of these early inhabitants lie beneath sand or silt. Those settlements currently being dug and documented by archeologists are, for the most part, inaccessible to outsiders while work is in progress, and subsequently make little visual impact because of the lack of imposing superstructures.

Modern scientific methods are used to give a broader picture: satellite photography to plot settlements and delineate the ancient map, machine borings into Nile mud to retrieve predynastic debris, calibrated radio-carbon dating on once-living organisms and thermoluminescence inspection of pottery, to reveal their approximate age. A new generation of excavators realize that priority must be given to urban and domestic sites, neglected for so many years in favour of the rewards of clearing the Theban necropolis or documenting magnificent temples. However, it is the museum collections in Egypt, Europe and America which give the clearest understanding of these predynastic industries and cultures (*1*).

For millenia before 5000 BC the Egyptians had been successful hunters and gatherers, abundantly supplied with birds, Nile fish and wild grains. An efficient food-collecting economy together with the modest consumption of a small population may well have bred the complacency which made Egypt resistant to changing over to agriculture until two thousand years after the earliest instances of it in the Near East and Saharan hill country. Possibly cattle herding was an indigenous development, but it was stimuli from abroad that led to the cultivation of barley and emmer wheat, and the domestication of herd animals like sheep, goats and pigs. Further foreign input into the Egyptian economy can be traced in the neolithic bifacial flint tradition of north Africa and the advanced metallurgy of western Asia. Although the flood plain either side of the Nile had roughly its modern course and dimensions, a moister climate resulted in fertile valleys in the Red Sea hills and a desert savanna with a variety of wildlife. Consequently early settlements can be found on the desert margins of the flood plain for the seasonal exploitation of game, many near quarries of flint for weapons.

The Egyptian Delta took its present appearance about 6000 years ago. Its northern edge comprises swamps, salt marshes and lagoons of brackish water, above which the middle and southern Delta are cut by branches of the Nile. There were originally three major estuaries, at Rosetta, Sebennytos and Damietta – increasing through the dynastic period to the seven or eight mouths mentioned by Greek and Roman writers. Sand-islands or 'turtlebacks' provided excellent terrain for settlements with surrounding flood land for farming crops – upon whose richness, incidentally, Homer makes Odysseus, returned at last to Ithaka, comment in his tale to Eumaeus the swineherd.

No discussion of civilization in pre-pharaonic Egypt dare ignore the pioneering dating system of Sir W. M. Flinders Petrie (1853–1942), the intrepid excavator who first put the predynastic era on the archeological map, and holder of the first chair of Egyptology in the UK, at University College, London, where his museum displays many crucial artefacts from this period. In the absence of modern scientific techniques able to elucidate an absolute, if approximate, chronology, Petrie devised a method of dating objects by comparing them to each other, in relative stages from the older to the more recent. The consecutive steps which he postulated for the predynastic period were based on the evolution of styles in pottery, discovered as containers for now-perished burial victuals. All the other artefacts (beads, knives and cosmetic containers, for example) accompanying a particular genre of pot into the grave could therefore be assigned to the same period. This system of 'sequence dating' has been a boon to Egyptologists, even though it cannot evaluate the objects concerned in terms of their manufacture in years before the present time. But it has limitations and is by no means foolproof. It is in fact a crude 'proforma' for the archeologist, giving a framework capable of subtle refinement from its rough categorization of the material evidence. Petrie himself occasionally modified his numerical compartments and, in view of his intellectual integrity, would be the first to acknowledge corrections that could be archeologically sustained.

Nevertheless, taking a series of sequence dates in combination it is possible to reconstruct the major predynastic cultures. The names given to these combined numbers are based on the Upper Egyptian sites where Petrie and his colleagues discovered similarly-classifiable artefacts in sufficient quantities to warrant those localities being perpetuated in a nomenclature of types and their stylistic development:

PETRIE'S SEQUENCE DATES	ASSEMBLAGE NAME
Periods 21–29	Badarian
30–37	Amratian
38–63	Gerzean
64–76	Semainean

The first twenty numbers (Petrie originally left thirty) are unassigned to allow inclusion of possible as yet undiscovered earlier predynastic cultures. Also, modern research has revealed that the transition from predynastic Egypt into Dynasty I occurs at the end of the Gerzean sequence, so that the Semainean assemblage is really transitional, reflecting the early dynastic era.

To complicate matters for the lay person, however, other terminologies were later formulated and are currently used for the predynastic period following the Badarian civilization. For example a system of eight categorizations under neutral numeric descriptions emerged from the extensive researches of W. Kaiser. For general purposes, because the cemeteries of Nagada, to the north of modern Luxor, have produced

such an abundance of predynastic material, some scholars prefer the
following classification scheme:

Badarian
Nagada I = Amratian
Nagada II = Gerzean
Nagada III = Transitional/Protodynastic/Semainean

The above system will be adopted here together with approximate dates
based on scientific analysis of surviving material.

The Badarians
5000–4600 B C

From this phase in the early predynastic period we can trace, through
physical remains, the development of manufactured objects into the
culture of the pharaohs. The regalia of the later dynastic kingship reveals
the continuity by its retention of several prehistoric elements, such as the
ostrich feathers on a type of royal crown and the wearing of a linen kilt
overlaid with a belted tail. However, let us concentrate on the archeological evidence from which we can elicit details of life in Upper Egypt
during Badarian times.

In addition to the site of el-Badari which provided the group name for
this culture, contemporary groups of artefacts have been found at
el-Mustagidda, Matmar, Deir Tasa, Hiw, Abadiya and in a particularly
well-stratified midden at el-Hammamiya. Living in huts or tents the
Badarians cultivated barley and emmer wheat which they harvested with
bifacial flint sickles. The grain was stored in silos lined with reeds. Their
pottery falls into two major categories: utilitarian and 'up-market'. The
former consisted of everyday serviceable bowls and cooking pots with a
coarse brownish fabric; the latter, for occasional or ceremonial use, often
had eggshell thin walls, rivalling for its fineness any pottery from the
Nile valley at any period. The polish on Badarian pottery came from the
red or black slip being burnished with a pebble before firing in the
newly-invented kiln. Sometimes a comb was drawn across the surface of
the still malleable pot to make a ripple pattern, and, as a result of being
placed upside down in ashes, an attractive bichrome outer surface could
be produced, giving black rims to red ware.

Badarians gathered flax for spinning into linen, and some of their
tailors' needles have survived. But there does not seem to have been the
general embargo on wearing animal skins – whether for climatic or
ritual reasons – that applied in the pharaonic period. The Badarians, who
had lithe physiques, slender heads, dark wavy hair and brown skins,
exhibited the love of personal adornment that permeates Egyptian life
across the millennia. For their jewellery they employed steatite, a soft
stone that could be carved into beads which were then glazed with a blue
colour to make them more attractive. Other necklaces or bangles
consisted of shells from the shores of the Red Sea. For their cosmetics the
Badarians ground green malachite or greyish galena on stone surfaces
and mixed the powder with fat or resin. Keeping this eye make-up
uncontaminated until it was applied led to the creation of ivory
containers. Bone carvings of gazelle heads must have had some amuletic
properties for the Badarian – either for attracting game to the hunters
(whose winged leaf-shaped flint arrowheads survive) or as an apotropaic

device against a creature possibly already epitomizing hostile desert forces, as it was later to do in pharaonic times, by its association with the god Seth. However, it is advisable to be cautious in trying to determine the beliefs of a culture that has left no written records, ancestral to pharaonic civilization as it may be.

It is tempting, nonetheless, to see the antecedents of the dynastic sacred animal cults in the individual burials of an ox, jackal or a ram in cemeteries bordering on those of the Badarians themselves. Their graves were predominantly oval although some large ones cut in a roughly rectangular shape were clearly for prominent members of the community. In contrast to the burial rites of the pharaonic period, Badarian corpses were contracted so that the knees met the elbows, a position less likely to symbolize a foetus than probably simulating a person harbouring warmth while sleeping on a cold night. Badarians arranged their dead with the heads facing west – dare we suppose that region was already regarded as the entrance to an underworld into which the spirit of the deceased would descend in company with an invincible guardian deity in the form of Ra as the setting sun?

Ten metres below the silt of the Nile Delta there are, no doubt, fragmentary vestiges of early prehistoric villages and cemeteries. Perhaps the standard of living was high with luxury goods imported from Palestine and Syria. In all likelihood the inhabitants of Lower Egypt looked upon the settlements beyond their eastern frontier as forming a homogeneous cultural and trading region with themselves. But archeological hypotheses based on a vacuum because sites and artefacts are missing justifiably run the risk of being dismissed. At present there is no cultural assemblage from the Delta proper which can substantiate the probabilities given above. This cautious hypothesis of a northern trading-zone linking Lower Egypt to the Near East, thereby facilitating the path of external cultural influences into the Delta, is as far as it is possible to venture into the realm of conjecture. Certainly no archeological or inscriptional evidence points to the existence of a northern confederation superior to the cultures of Upper Egypt in technology and political awareness. There is no hint that the Delta had economic dominance over the south or that it formed the sole bridge of cultural contact with the Middle East for the Nile valley. In fact – notwithstanding the likelihood that commerce between the Delta and south Iraq occurred via the Tigris–Euphrates river routes into Syria, thence into Palestine on the northern perimeter of the Lower Egypt–Levant mercantile nucleus – absolutely no Mesopotamian artefact has been discovered to date in the Delta. It would be rash, then, to suggest that the objects of definite Mesopotamian origin found in Upper Egypt owe their arrival to vigorous traders from the Delta, rather than to direct meetings between the southerners and entrepreneurs from Iraq, via alternative, southerly land and sea routes.

However, the picture is not entirely negative or resting upon supposition, as far as the north is concerned. A Neolithic culture has been discovered at a site on the margin of the western Delta called Merimda Beni Salama which can be dated to about 4900 onwards. The

Early Predynastic Culture in North Egypt

German Archeological Institute's excavations at this site in 1982 discovered an oval painted terracotta head, about 10 cm high which, although crude, is the earliest sculpture from Africa.

More information comes from the excavation of sites on the northern edge of the Faiyum, the fertile depression in the Libyan desert southwest of modern Cairo. There, an energetic and painstaking archeologist, Miss G. Caton-Thompson, working from the late 1920s onwards, has brought to notice the Faiyum A Neolithic culture flourishing approximately from 4700–4000 BC. These 'Faiyumis' were hunters using arrowheads with a concave base and their game included oxen, pigs, antelopes and – not for consumption – hippopotami, elephants and crocodiles. They seem to have trapped fish, since no fish-hooks have survived. Their underground granaries, floored with matting, gave protection to the crops harvested with highly efficient flint sickles and to the seed stored for the winter sowing. The linen industry has been attested by fragmentary pieces of textile. Unlike the Badarians, these Faiyumi communities produced a rather shapeless and undistinguished repertoire of utilitarian pottery.

Predynastic Nubia

Nubia lay south of the First Cataract of the Nile at Aswan, and was to be explored by Egyptian expeditions of the late pyramid age (*see* p. 228). Therefore we ought, albeit summarily, to survey the position of the prehistoric cultures in this region, which can be dated further back than those of Egypt proper just described.

Late Palaeolithic industries discovered in Upper Egypt at Kom Ombo (which can be taken at this early date as being on the northern edge of the Nubian sphere), and in lower Nubia, are as technologically advanced as those in Egypt or elsewhere in Africa. The grinding stones found from 15,000 BC onwards provide evidence of exploitation of wild grain, long before it was taken up in Egypt. One of these cultures, known as the Qadan (ascribed dates from 12,550 BC onwards), provides the earliest burials yet discovered in the Nile valley. The graves were shallow pits, within the occupation site, covered with stone slabs. The corpse was almost invariably orientated with the head to the east, the hands to the face and knees bent so that the heels came into contact with the upper thighs – plausibly a position for adulation of the rising sun.

The Neolithic cultures of Nubia are immediately differentiated from the Qadan industry by the appearance of pottery. The tradition of hunting game in the savannah persisted and wild grain and grasses were gathered, as the marks on surviving flint crescents witness. From 6000 BC onwards sites at Khartoum, at the confluence of the Blue and White Niles, reveal a conscious development in the local lifestyle by supplementing fish and wild game with vegetable food sources. The potters of this region were the preservers of a Sudanese–East African skill independent of northern influences and, in fact, produced bowls which at this period were more sophisticated than those of the Faiyum and Delta margin sites. An offshoot of this culture spread northwards to the Second Cataract of the Nile. Known as the 'Khartoum Variant' it flourished from 4500–3500 BC. Most characteristic of this pottery tradition was the variety of incised ripple-patterns formed by fish bones being drawn across the surface. The small funerary offering bowls which

6. Egypt today: a fellah *(peasant) works his* shaduf *to raise water from a canal to irrigate the land*

7. (overleaf) Buto: modern excavations in the temple of Wadjet reveal monuments from the New Kingdom era – remains of earlier periods are hoped for on deeper excavation

8. Early dynastic mudbrick wall at Hierakonpolis

9. Site of el-Kab with tombs of New Kingdom courtiers in the cliffs beyond

10. Egypt today: a fellah *breaks the clod to let through water to the fields, Beni Hasan*

make their first appearance in the Khartoum Variant culture are the ancestors of similar dishes which Nubians of today leave in cemeteries. Finally, lower Nubia, roughly the area between the First and Second Nile Cataracts, saw the emergence of an indigenous culture with strong ceramic affinities with Upper Egypt, whose population probably spoke not Egyptian, but a Sudanese tongue. These were the Nubians, called unimaginatively the A-group, who were the immediate southern neighbours of, and contemporary with, the civilizations of Nagadan Egypt and subsequently the earliest pharaohs.

The Nagadans of Upper Egypt 4600–3000 BC

Through the two main stages of their culture (Nagada I and II) some of the crucially formative elements emerged, which brought about a vigorous and united southern kingdom, confident enough to embark on a programme of expansion that aimed at nothing short of the domination of north Egypt.

It should be stressed, perhaps, that the Nagada I culture seems gradually to grow out of existing Badarian communities and not arrive on the scene in an outburst of immediate innovation. Towns were now more suggestive of focal fortified nuclei serving defined territorial boundaries. Today, there are modest archeological vestiges of the dwellings and storerooms used by the early Nagadans. The lower courses of walls, up to one metre high, were made of sun-dried mudbricks whose consistency was made firmer by the addition of limestone chips. But at the extant level the occupiers made no provision for a door, which indicates a higher entrance and the necessity of a step. The Nagadans were, perhaps, taking precautions against the intrusion of flood, snakes or scorpions, continual threats to family life, and which figure so prominently in the later spells of folklore medicine.

The relics of the material culture of Nagada I reveal more extensively than before the imaginative talents of Egyptian craftsmen. The potter experimented with styles that could not be classed as utilitarian, such as bi-tubular flasks, vases shaped like birds and – probably from seeing an imported prototype – a bowl standing on two human-type feet. The linear designs on pottery in a heavy off-white paint reflected the environment of Nile and desert, with crocodiles, hippopotami and hunting dogs. The stoneworker developed the slate palettes into minor *objets d'art* although they still retained their functional purpose as surfaces upon which to grind the minerals for eye paint. Thus we can delight in palettes carved as Nile turtles or hartebeest. The flint-knife industry bears witness to an advanced technology capable of pressure-flaking extraordinarily thin 35cm-long blades with finely serrated edges. The repertoire of stone which the Egyptians exploited from their deserts included granite, breccia (a composite rock) and diorite employed for disc-shaped mace-heads, which are outstanding for the precision of the hole drilled for the handle and the smoothness of their burnished surface. Of course the mace-head need not invariably have been restricted to bellicose activity, but could already have formed an integral part of a Nagadan chieftain's regalia. Similarly, there is the earliest depiction, moulded in low relief on a sherd of pottery now in the Ashmolean Museum, Oxford, of the red crown that in historic times stood for the king's jurisdiction over the Delta. These are clear indicators of a social hierarchy, in that ceremonial dress and ritual were beginning to distance successful managers of predynastic economic life from less competent, or willingly-organized, members of the community.

The Nagadans of the late fourth millennium BC (the era which we term Nagada II) were the immediate ancestors of the conquering southern armies of the first pharaoh. What, then, are the factors that distinguish these later Nagadans from their predecessors? Three developments stand out at once which together formed the cradle of dynastic civilization in Egypt: a heavier input of men with metallurgical ideas from the Middle East, the new technique of artificial irrigation, and the political union of the Upper Egyptian villages.

The increasing contact between Nile valley settlements and south Iraq and Iran can be considered first. It is highly likely that adventurous merchants sailed from the Persian gulf around the Arabian peninsula – with Bahrain and Yemen as stopping-off points – arriving on the Red Sea coast of Egypt. The modern industrial town of Qoseir marks the entrance to the Wadi Hammamat leading to Qift on the banks of the river Nile. This valley through the Eastern Desert (which is a fascinating excursion that can be made from Luxor) seems to have been the favoured route of the merchants, who have left depictions of their high-prowed boats cut into the rock of these arid mountains. Another detail showing the presence of these seafarers in the Nile valley was discovered by Flinders Petrie in the excavations of an early temple at Qift. Four-metre-high battered fragments of three statues of the fertility-god Min (even without an inscription, readily identifiable from the clear signs of the immensity of his now-missing phallus – *see 2*) bore incisions of decorative emblems. Some were inspired by the Egyptians' own environment, such as the elephants marching on desert hills, but another was unmistakably derived from a foreign motif. It shows the toothed snout of a sawfish with which the eastern sea-going merchants would have had more acquaintance than the Nile-dweller, and can also be found on monuments from the Elamite civilization of south Iran.

Perhaps nothing illustrates the contact between the East and Egypt so much as the concept of the cylinder seal and its decoration. This kind of roller seal – which the Egyptians were eventually to abandon in favour of the stamp seal in the shape of the scarab beetle – was made from steatite, glazed composition (faience), clay or, rarely, other material such as ivory. It was threaded on a length of papyrus twine running through the vertical perforation of the seal, and its incised design could be rolled across the wet clay surface of a jar stopper or other item requiring a property identification. It could also be worn as a piece of amuletic jewellery to give protection. The Mesopotamian and Elamite traders brought with them the finished products of their native glyptic industry; these early imports match those datable by the stratigraphy of Mesopotamian archeologists to the centuries just prior to 3000 BC – perfect dating as far as Egyptian chronology is concerned. The characteristic emblems carved on them include fish, human eyes and cross hatching. The Egyptian imitators of the imported prototypes then began to branch out with experimental motifs drawn from their own environment, such as

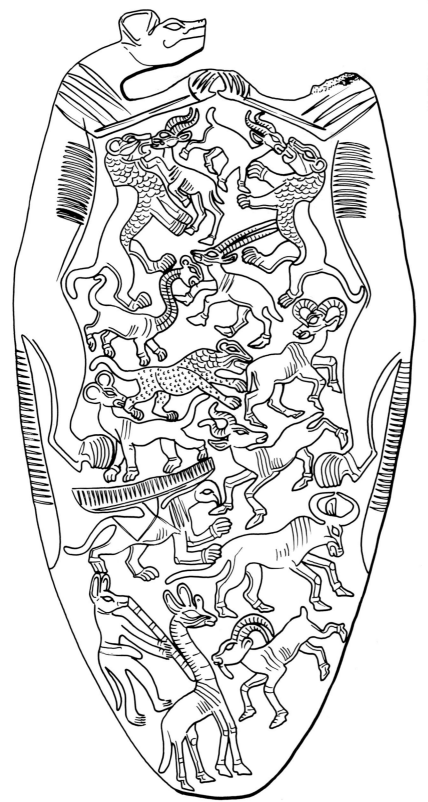

1. Animals from nature, and mythical hybrids, on a palette from Hierakonpolis, Nagada II, Ashmolean Museum, Oxford

hunting scenes, lions, crocodiles and shrines. Nevertheless, among the native Egyptian flora and fauna we occasionally find mythical creatures taken from the repertoire of foreign craftsmen. One seal, for example, displays a copy of the Mesopotamian rosette associated later with the Middle Eastern goddess Ishtar, while another depicts a griffin, a creature with a lion's body and a vulture's head, whose indisputable Elamite origins are clinched by the comb-like pair of wings emanating from its back.

From this period of Mesopotamian/Egyptian interchange the maturing skills can be seen of those craftsmen responsible for decorating the ivory handles of flint knives and for carving out of slate the cosmetic palettes which, as already mentioned, had started as the outline shapes of a variety of animals during the Nagada I period. The palettes now have reliefs cut into over 90 per cent of their surface area. Only an uncarved circle in the centre of the palette remains smooth to indicate its original purpose. The rest of the palette is a prime witness to the ability and imagination of the forerunners of those artists whose legacy was to be the large-scale reliefs in pharaonic temples and tombs. One palette with both sides crowded with natural and fabulous fauna is framed with two jackals (fig. 1). Its raised-relief designs include, in impressive confusion, lions and a leopard attacking oryxes and antelopes, an Elamite griffin about to sink its claws into a wild bull, serpentine-necked quadrupeds and a hybrid human-jackal creature playing a flute.

The Nagadan stone-carver exhibits a more orderly arrangement around the undecorated circle on the 'Lion-Hunt' palette of which fragments are in the British Museum and in the Louvre. Along the outer edges two rows of hunters, each following the falcon standards held by the leader, carry spears, maces, throwsticks, bows, arrows and lassoes. We are now looking at representations of Nagadans. They are bearded

2. Nagadans on the Lion Hunt Palette, Nagada II, British Museum

and have their hair (or wigs?) in horizontal bands of curls in which the majority wear one or two feathers (fig. 2). They wear kilts with a fox-tail hanging down from the waistband. Their main quarry are the lions which roam the Egyptian savannah. One lion hit with six arrows appears to walk away from the main scene: obviously the carver is representing a dead creature of no further threat to the hunters. But on the opposite end of the palette a lion, wounded but still in full vigour, has its claws almost into a hunter who has approached perilously close and is shown desperately trying to run to safety, aided by a companion whose bow is drawn ready to let fly an arrow. Other desert game, including a hare, an ostrich and a stag, rush along the centre of the palette pursued by jackals. The vitality of dynastic hunting scenes is already present in the Nagadan craftsman's repertoire.

What of his expertise in ivory carving? The exquisitely decorated ivory handles fitted into delicately thin flint knives bear witness to his consummate skill. He could carve animal figures, sometimes only millimetres high, that lack no crucial detail – on one knife-handle 218 creatures march in rows along both sides. His bestiary on these ceremonial knives includes storks, lions, barbary sheep, wild bulls and, probably as an amuletic device to obliterate the threat of a venomous bite, African elephants treading on the coils of snakes. Elsewhere we find ivory, hollowed into tusk-shaped tubes, incised with linear designs symbolizing the perishable thongs originally laced around them. These were containers for the resinous eye cosmetics worn by the Nagadans and placed in the tombs as objects of daily use for the afterlife. Ivory was also carved into human figurines. Formal standing statuettes discovered in the 'main deposit' of the early temple at Kom el-Ahmar (Hierakonpolis) were votive images destined to keep an individual's personality alive in a sacred enclosure. On the other hand, the informality of bandy-legged ivory dwarves – even though some were temple dedications – belongs primarily to a funerary genre and illustrates the versatility of the Nagadan craftsmen in carving these companions for the deceased. Similarly, there can be little doubt that the demand for ivory figurines of naked females, graceful or grotesque according to the competence of the sculptor, whose pubic regions at once attract the eye with emphasized dots or cross hatching, reflects the desire for sexual activity to continue in the next world (3).

Returning to the Middle Eastern influence revealed in the iconography of late predynastic Egypt, we must try to evaluate from tantalizing hints in the non-literate evidence at our disposal, to what extent foreigners were physically present in the Nile valley at this period. We can imagine eastern traders becoming impressed with the overall reliability of the Nile's regime (in contrast to the more volatile Tigris–Euphrates river system) and the resulting harvest which more than met the consumption needs of the Nagadans. The merchants might be inclined to settle, but would the indigenous population allow them to share in Egypt's prosperity? The subtle adoption of foreign motifs into the Egyptian artist's repertoire seems to suggest a secret admiration for certain alien cultural traits – would this extend to tolerating a peaceful immigration of Middle Easterners? We can have no illusions about human nature: the Nagadan would trade for lapis lazuli and obsidian with these entrepreneurs arriving from the Eastern Desert; he might upstage his fellow craftsmen and incorporate a few designs of non-Egyptian inspiration into his own panoramas on seals, knives or palettes; but he could also subscribe to the tenet of territorial exclusivity and hold that the 'gift of the Nile' was not going to become fair game for foreign exploitation without a fight. I believe that there was military confrontation, albeit brief and far from universal in scope, between invaders from the Persian Gulf and some Upper Egyptians. On what evidence is confidence in an armed conflict based?

Firstly, the Gebel el-Arak ivory-handled flint knife in the Louvre Museum (fig. 3) displays in raised relief scenes of a battle on one side and probably reconciliation on the other. Two rows of warriors wearing only phallic sheaths and armed with clubs and flint knives are engaged in a struggle in which four groups of short-haired men clearly prevail over enemies wearing headcloths. Below, boats with high sterns and prows similar to the Wadi Hammamat rock drawings are separated by corpses from boats with low curved hulls of the sort painted on Nagadan buff-coloured pottery. But whose fleet and army were victorious? The other side of the knife leaves us in no doubt: it was a Mesopotamian victory on this occasion. At the top of the handle stands a turbanned figure in a robe, holding on each side a lion 'rampant' by the throat (fig. 4). This is an uncontaminated lifting of the 'master of the animals' motif found on Mesopotamian cylinder seals. The lower design indicates that under the hero-ruler the life and the natural world familiar to Nagadans has been preserved despite the hostilities: hunting dogs, antelopes and a lion with its claws in its prey. A second proof of occasional warfare is a wall painting in a brick-lined tomb at Kom el-Ahmar. This is the earliest tomb decoration yet discovered in Egypt and the designs are crudely executed, without any of the finesse found on the palettes or ivories. Both the styles of boats described on the Gebel el-Arak knife occur in this painting, as do warriors among whom those wearing black-dotted white vests gain the upper hand. Again the victory goes to the invaders for we see a clumsily painted representation of the hero-ruler dominating two lions. This particular Mesopotamian emblem seems to be the hallmark of successful commanders of sporadic incursions into the Nile valley. Its disappearance from Egyptian iconography is likely to indicate either the absorption of the invaders into the upper echelons of Nagadan society, or their extrusion.

Metallurgy is another area in which we can observe a marked advance over previous cultures. The technological confidence that the Nagadans now had, probably stimulated by the more sophisticated metalwork exhibited by Mesopotamian traders, led to an increase in copper harpoons, daggers, needles and tools. The chisels which served the sculptor for carving palettes, cylinder seals and stone vases would more than likely have been of copper which, since it contained arsenic was a fairly tough metal, and was continuously beaten by dolorite pounders until it 'worked hard', giving a firmer cutting edge. The jewellery of the Nagadans was embellished by the metalworker's craft with rings of copper and gold, as well as beads and amulets of silver, which does not

occur in the desert mountains of Egypt and was part of a foreign merchant's inventory, possibly acquired from Anatolia.

Finally, do the settlements and cemeteries of late predynastic Egypt reveal any evidence of changes in patterns of economy or increase in political cohesion? From designs on Nagada II pottery which now displays more elaborate scenes and more human interest, we can make a few observations (4). The material for the pottery was not only the ready-to-hand Nile mud but also clay obtained from a desert source. The marl of this hand-built buff pottery was dug out from the base of desert cliffs, a task requiring more-organized labour. Noticeably, then, the pyramid structure of pharaonic society is already well beyond the embryo stage, with classes of fieldworkers, labourers and artisans, giving services or goods to managers of village economies and to the personnel

3. (left) War between Egyptians and foreigners: the Gebel el-Arak ivory knife handle, Nagada II, Louvre

4. (right) Peace – a foreign ruler dominates the forces of war and chaos: the Gebel el-Arak ivory knife handle (reverse side), Nagada II, Louvre

41

*11. (opposite) King carved in
ivory, wearing the white crown
of Upper Egypt, Dynasty I/II,
Abydos, British Museum*

in charge of local shrines. The decorations in red ochre on this pottery
are of immense help in understanding Nagadan society. Of course
abstract patterns occur in the form of whorls or mottles to suggest the
texture of the more durable stone vases, or rippled lines to imitate the
rope carriers in which such a pot could be suspended. Of more interest,
however, are the depictions of long curved-hull boats, made of papyrus
bundles, being rowed along the Nile, the principal communication route
of Ancient Egypt. Their length, and the number of oarsmen (represented
only by the oar blades jutting out from the side), seem exaggerated, but
even at this early period we should not underestimate the capability of
the riverside dockyards, which during the Old Kingdom turned out
40-metre-long wooden boats. The Nagadan crafts support two kiosks on
the centre of the deck – one with either a standard of the district or an
emblem of a local deity. In the field of the design, and so presumably on
the banks of the Nile, stand hunters with throwsticks or women with
arms making a lyre-shape above their heads as if celebrating a religious
dance in honour of a cow goddess (*see also 5*). From this evidence we can
assume that in the late Nagadan era Upper Egypt comprised a series of
settlements represented visually as heraldic devices, prototypes in fact of
the twenty-two district standards of the south in dynastic times (*see also*
fig. 5). Also, I believe that of the kiosks on the decks, one is a state cabin
for a local magnate and the other is a shrine containing the cult image of
a god or goddess. Therefore, we are seeing early depictions of the ritual
river journeys (so much a feature of later Egyptian religion) made by one
deity to the sanctuary of another district.

5. On a fragment of a slate
palette normally interpreted as
the destruction of enemy fortresses, the mattock-wielding
divine and royal emblems are
most likely to mark the found-
ing of cities, Nagada II, Cairo
Museum

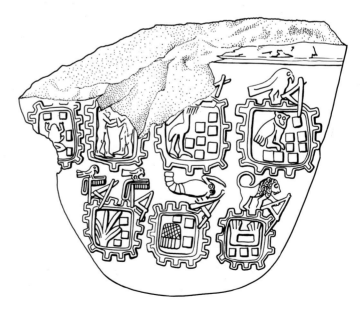

Thus, in the centuries towards the close of the fourth millennium BC,
conditions in Upper Egypt became ripe for inter-district co-operation via
the Nile link, to counteract incursions by desert Bedu tribes or friction
with more distant regions in the north that could interfere with
expanding trade contacts. Neighbouring groups of settlements, each with

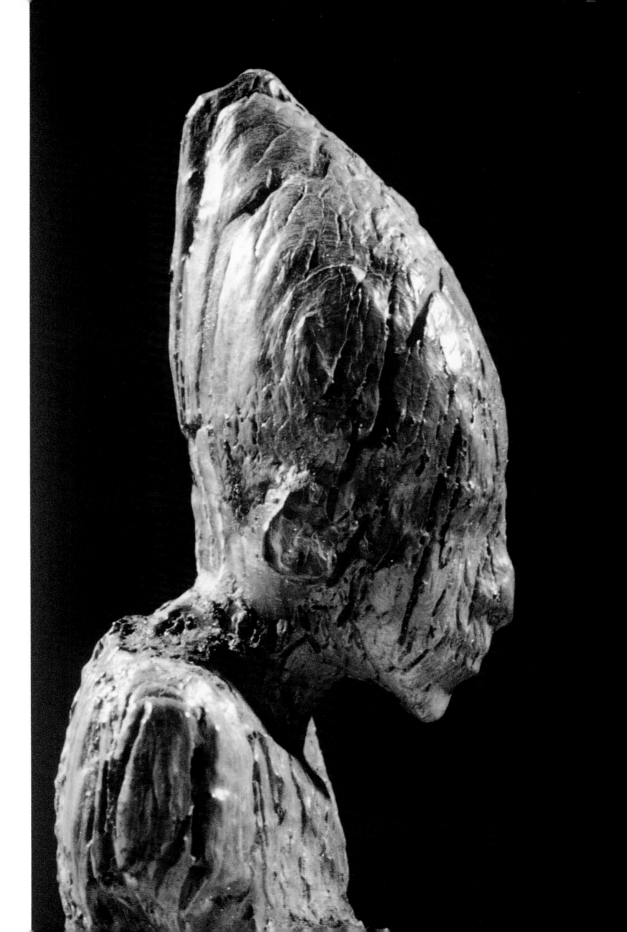

12. (top) Limestone funerary stela of Djet as Horus over his name hieroglyph within a serekh (palace enclosure), Dynasty I, Louvre

13. (above) Granite funerary stela of the Horus Raneb from his cenotaph at Abydos, Dynasty II, (now in USA)

14. (right) Granite stela of Peribsen showing erased Seth figure over his name hieroglyphs in place of the usual Horus bird, Dynasty II, Abydos, British Museum

its focal standard, might have formed larger confederations for security reasons. Religious affinities between the god of one district and the goddess of another might have led to bonds strengthening mutual efforts in times of low Nile floods and their attendant food shortages. Diverse factors obviously operated to bring about greater solidarity between Nagadan chieftains and eventually a coalition of districts under the political overlordship of one supreme commander, whose power base derived from his armed forces. But the underlying trend to joint effort between local rulers received a boost that propelled Egypt irrevocably forward along the path of unity, a course from which it has rarely deviated in its long history since the late Nagadan age.

Villagers were jolted out of the complacency of merely relying on the annual inundation of the Nile to bring water to the fields, by the advent of the first irrigational basins based on a network of canals to fill them. (This would have been instigated by Mesopotamian overlords such as the one carved on the Gebel-el-Arak knife.) Such a system enabled water to be carried to the furthest extent of the flood plain long after the inundation had receded, and further harvest yields could thereby be achieved. From an analysis of archeological excavations on predynastic sites we have proof that the Nagadans saw artificial irrigation as the mainstay of a new economic prosperity: over 140 Badarian and early Nagadan settlements were situated on the low desert spurs and agriculture only worked as a result of the yearly flood. However, only ten Nagada II sites lay on the desert edges. Where were the many others? On natural hillocks closer to the fields so that there could be continual maintenance of the new canal system feeding the fields with water all year round until the next Nile flood (6). The communities became more dependent on the skilful management of the larger workforce now required to channel the river into man-made ditches and basins kept free of silting. The district administrators of this economic boom in barley and wheat could not fail to grow more élite.

The emergence of an ambitious successful, perhaps by now native, governor of one district who was accepted by the canal barons of Upper Egypt as their overlord occurred just before 3000 BC. The final stages of the transition into the Kingdom of the Pharaohs had begun.

CHAPTER 2

THE UNIFICATION OF THE TWO LANDS

The Egyptians always maintained, on monuments and papyri, the concept of their country as two distinct lands even when they glorified the image of a combined kingdom under the rule of one pharaoh, or king. The historically crucial event of the unification of Egypt shortly before the beginning of the third millennium BC did not obscure in their minds the environmental divergencies between the Delta and the Nile valley, nor did it obliterate the memory of these northern and southern kingdoms locked in a struggle for supremacy over the whole land. At this time Lower Egypt comprised the Delta, plus a short stretch of the Nile reaching roughly to the latitude of the Faiyum; Upper Egypt dominated the flood plain to the southern frontier marked by the stark sandstone cliffs of Gebel el-Silsila. In each kingdom a stronghold near a shrine sacred to a tutelary goddess became the capital city.

The traces of the capital of north Egypt, identified buried below mounds of rubble at Tell el-Farain (or Buto) in the western Delta are woefully scant (7). However, it is known that in this period it was called Pe, and was protected by the nearby sanctuary of the cobra-goddess Wadjet. The mounds over the site have given up Saïte or later material. But exciting recent excavations in the Temple of Wadjet have revealed high-quality statuary of New Kingdom date. Future digs could surprise us with significant earlier structures and monuments. But for now the visitor has to fall back on imagination to construct the temple town of protodynastic times at present under the Delta water table.

Turning to southern Egypt we find a more extensive archeological record of its early key town and major sanctuary. The capital was on the west bank of the Nile at the site known in Arabic as Kom el-Ahmar or 'Red Mound'. This, in the language of the pharaohs, was Nekhen, possibly better known by its Greek name of Hierakonpolis or Hawk Town. Settlements on the desert edge just southwest of Nekhen mainly belong to the Nagadan era. Nekhen itself consists of a town enclosure with a temple precinct where, in a pit (known as the 'main deposit'), there were hidden, for security or reburied through later building projects, objects from the beginning of dynastic civilization, including the Scorpion mace-head and the Narmer palette discussed below (p. 47). Along the desert wadi opposite Nekhen are the ruins of a mudbrick construction with walls still 10 metres high (8). It is likely to date to the early dynastic period, probably to the reign of King Khasekhemwy, c.2650 BC, and probably represents the remains of a palace or funerary complex rather than its popular description of 'fort'. Just to the north of Nekhen on the east bank of the Nile is Nekheb, the chief sanctuary of Upper Egypt in this period and one of the most evocative sites around which to wander despite, or perhaps because of, its ruinous condition. Today, it is called el-Kab and is distinguished by a massive girdle wall that encloses an area 566 by 548 metres. Within stood the ancient shrine sacred to the vulture-goddess Nekhbet, although the extant structures on the site are of New Kingdom or later date (9). These sites, on opposite banks of the Nile, are infrequently visited by tourists but are accessible by road on a day's excursion from Luxor.

The predynastic rulers of these capitals appear as protective deities in temples and royal tombs. Thus we see the kings of pre-unification Egypt symbolized as the 'souls of Pe', falcon headed, and as the 'souls of Nekhen' with jackal heads. This vivid imagery becomes balder in Manetho's description of the precursors of the kings of the first dynasty as 'dead souls, the half-gods'.

Before we look at the surviving record of the battles leading to the unification of Egypt we must ask ourselves if it is possible to deduce any factors which might have given impetus to the struggles of about 3000 BC. It seems to me that underlying the grand strategy of welding Upper and Lower Egypt into one kingdom were ecological pressures. There is every indication that the climate became much drier during the early third millennium BC, an hyperaridity that resulted in the loss, from Egypt to Nubia, to the Saharan rainbelt and to the East African savannah, of the elephant, giraffe and rhinoceros. In addition, the flood water was covering almost a third less arable area than previously. Water for crops was now therefore at a premium and made demands on the ingenuity of the canal managers. A larger labour force and more systematic layout of channels feeding water to the fields became paramount. Co-operative expansion over local territorial divisions in the south pushed the domain of the overlord of Upper Egypt to the borders of the northern kingdom. Conflict was inescapable.

Nekhen has produced our first real historical monument of the unification era in the form of fragments from a ceremonial limestone mace-head carved with scenes of a southern ruler inaugurating a major irrigation network (fig. 6). The ruler holds a mattock and wears the white crown of Upper Egypt. He is identified by the emblems of a rosette – probably signifying the status of monarch – and a scorpion. Thus King Scorpion, dwarfing all accompanying figures, is ritually cutting open a canal of some importance (cf. 10) and worthy of commemoration on this mace-head originally dedicated in the temple at Nekhen. But there is an intrusive element into this peaceful activity: district standards are shown bearing lapwings hanged by the throat. The lapwing is the hieroglyph for 'people' – clearly King Scorpion has celebrated some conquests of regions in northern Egypt.

However many battles Scorpion fought in Lower Egypt, the credit for the total subjugation of the north must be given to King Narmer, equatable with the 'Meni' of later king lists and the 'Menes' of Manetho. The most impressive monument of the unification is a slate palette discovered in the 'main deposit' at the Nekhen temple (fig. 7). Its carving in raised relief is the prototype for the military iconography of the pharaoh for the next three thousand years. Both sides at the top display the heads of a cow goddess which flank the name of Narmer. Hieroglyphs of a 'catfish' and a 'chisel' are used to render the sounds of the royal name. This system of writing by pictures, the idea of which

6. Macehead of King Scorpion
opening the irrigation dyke,
Ashmolean Museum, Oxford

7. (below left) The Narmer
Palette (obverse), Dynasty I,
Cairo Museum

8. (below right) The Narmer
Palette (reverse), Dynasty I,
Cairo Museum

48

(but not the individual signs) came into Egypt from the East, now provides historical data: the Ancient Egyptians are communicating across the millennia. The central motif of the obverse of the palette depicts King Narmer, in the regalia of the white crown, ceremonial bull tail behind and tassels suspended down the front of his linen kilt forming a row of cow-goddess heads, menacingly raising his mace while holding a kneeling captive by the top of his hair. Above the prisoner's head a symbolic device leaves one in no doubt as to the significance of this victory: a hawk with an arm stretching from its breast grasps a rope leading below to the nose of an enemy whose body is transformed into a papyrus clump. For the hawk, read 'the god Horus', i.e. the divine manifestation of kingship, and for the papyrus understand 'north Egypt' which it heraldically represents. One can therefore interpret this emblem as Narmer conquering the Delta kingdom, an event spelt out even more emphatically on the reverse of the palette (fig. 8). There you see a parade of standards and officials, and King Narmer wearing the red crown of Lower Egypt newly subjected to his sovereignty. The purpose of the procession is to provide Narmer with an opportunity to gloat over the beheaded bodies of his northern opponents. With this gruesome scene the 'Two Lands' are united into one kingdom and pharaonic civilization launches into the construction of monuments, some of such a magnitude as to leave one, even in the space age, gasping.

CHAPTER 3

ROYAL TOMBS AND CENOTAPHS: Early Dynastic Monuments at Abydos and Saqqara

The ancestral homeland of the victorious Narmer included the region (around the modern village of El-Araba el-Madfuna) known as Abydos, a Greek corruption of the Ancient Egyptian name. A first-time visitor to this site should concentrate on the magnificent temples of Seti I and Ramessess II of Dynasty 19. However, those concentrating on the Old Kingdom, or those on a return visit who want to feel the atmosphere of remoteness, should head for the desert escarpment beyond the electricity pylons southwest of the Temple of Seti I. The mounds of sand and shattered pottery mark the spot where at the turn of the twentieth century Flinders Petrie brought archeological discipline to try to rectify the French excavator Emile Amélineau's (1850–1915) earlier 'ransacking' approach to the monuments. Archeologists have returned here recently. Already an important clay sealing has been found giving an early king list.

Beneath the sand lie the mudbrick foundations of vanished superstructures that, judging from jar sealings and finely-carved stelae, probably belonged to all the monarchs of the first dynasty and to two kings of the second dynasty (*11*). The monument of King Djer (third king, Dynasty I) was reinterpreted by the Ancient Egyptians in a later era as the burial place of the god Osiris to whom Abydos was paramountly sacred. (Murdered by his brother-god Seth, Osiris was sufficiently resuscitated by the goddess Isis (his sister/wife) for her to conceive Horus (with whom every pharaoh identified), who regained the throne of Egypt. Osiris then left the realm of Egypt to be the ruler of Duat, the underworld where all Egyptians eventually had to go.) It was the numerous pilgrims to the site who generated the vast quantity of pottery dedicated to the god and scattered all over the ground. One glance will tell how pertinent is this location's Arabic name of Umm el-Qaab – 'mother of pots'.

Hundreds of subsidiary graves for courtiers and retainers were arranged in trenches near the principal monument. We cannot escape the horrific conclusion that in the early dynastic era compulsory attendance at the afterlife court of a deceased monarch was required of many servants and artisans still in their full vigour. Nearly 600 people joined King Djer in the next world. No doubt the drain on manpower and loss of human experience and expertise available to the succeeding ruler led by the end of the early dynastic (archaic) period to the gradual decrease and abandonment of these series of mass executions. Naturally, the robbers of Ancient Egypt had a field day in this necropolis. One of them made a hiding hole in the north wall of the monument of King Djer and placed in it bracelets of gold and semi-precious stones still attached to the arm that he had wrenched off the corpse of a lady of high rank.

The royal stelae in limestone and granite labelling the ownership of the monuments have long since vanished from this site into musuem collections. For example, the Louvre possesses a stela carved with consummate precision to display the Horus name of King Djet: the hawk stands above the rectangular shape of the *serekh* or palace enclosure, in the upper section of which is the cobra that represents the royal name, while the design below consists of the buttresses of the palace wall (*12*). A later stela of Raneb is carved out of the more intractable granite (*13*). A stela now in the British Museum, from the monument of a second-dynasty ruler, gives us a tantalizing hint of religious upheaval (*14*). King Peribsen came to the throne of Egypt as the embodiment of the god Horus but then changed his allegiance to the god Seth. This deity was the ancient manifestation of chaotic forces in the cosmos and, in the cycle of legends that later grew up around Osiris, god of the Underworld, unlawful seizer of the kingship from Horus. Consequently Peribsen's name on the granite stela is surmounted in the *serekh* not by the hawk but by the heraldic animal of Seth – a quadruped with pricked ears and a forked tail. This manoeuvre displacing Horus could not have occurred without friction, and possibly even resulted in warfare within the northern confines of the newly-united kingdom. When the kingship passed to Khasekhemwy, the royal titulary boasted that the monarch was Horus *and* Seth and that the two deities were reconciled in the person of the king. Peribsen's stela, however, shows that the image of Seth subsequently became anathema at Abydos – the creature of that god has been hacked out of the raised relief in an attempt to obliterate its presence.

Although the foundations of these monuments used sun-dried mud-brick, a chamber in the structure belonging to King Khasekhemwy was dressed with limestone blocks, an indication of the growing technical expertise of the stonemason that was soon to develop into the confidence of the builders of the earliest pyramid. The sinuous terrain of Umm el-Qaab reveals little above ground of the ability of the architects of the early dynastic period here at Abydos, but a stroll across the desert directly northwards from this location will rectify that. The goal is Shunet el-Zebib, the ruined enclosure partly below drift sand (fig. 9). Its mudbrick walls, still retaining in places their original limestone plaster mantle, are over 5 metres thick and up to 18 metres high (*15*). The ramparts display on the northeast and southeast sides an architectural panorama of buttresses and recesses – the antecedents of the girdle wall of the Step Pyramid complex (Dynasty III) at Saqqara (*see* p. 58). Probably Shunet el-Zebib was a mansion for the *ka* or spirit of King Khasekhemwy and was linked in purpose to his monument at Umm el-Qaab. (The *ka* is an elusive concept peculiar to Ancient Egyptian religion. With the same appearance as the body it comes into being at a person's birth and survives their physical death. In the funerary cult it has the power to animate the mummified corpse and stone statues alike, and make use of the offering formulae and reliefs carved on the tomb walls. Perhaps the closest understanding we can get of the *ka* is that it is an indestructible life force.) The vast rectangle (123 by 64 metres) has a complicated internal pattern, although it is probable that three interlock-

9. Plan of inner apartments of Shunet el-Zebib, funerary mansion of King Khasekhemwy, Dynasty II, Abydos

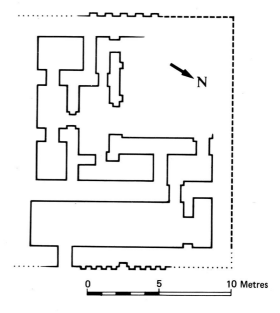

ing rooms on the east were for rituals celebrating the cycle of the three four-monthly seasons: inundation, winter sowing and summer harvest. Looking from Shunet el-Zebib to the north brings us back, perhaps too sharply, from the earliest pharaohs to modern Egypt and a living religion celebrated in the Coptic monastery.

In describing Umm el-Qaab I have deliberately chosen the neutral words 'monument' or 'structure', avoiding the seemingly obvious phrase 'royal tomb'. This is because despite the series of stelae, seal impressions and ivory and ebony labels naming the monarchs, and despite the human remains showing the area was in part sepulchral, at least for royal ladies and retainers, I believe there are cogent reasons for asserting that the kings' bodies were buried overlooking Memphis, the capital of Egypt, founded at the beginning of Dynasty I. What, then, would be the purpose of the royal monuments at Abydos? It is not too difficult to accept that, although for strategic accessibility to Upper and Lower Egypt the king would reside at Memphis near the apex of the Nile Delta, the genealogical ties with the southern residence of his ancestors would compel him to raise an edifice bearing his name in the traditional family necropolis. Thus the monuments of Umm el-Qaab would be cenotaphs to keep the royal names flourishing in the ancestral cemetery. Beside these cenotaphs the courtiers and retainers of the pharaonic southern residence were given real tombs where they were destined, as we have mentioned, to be buried on the death of the king.

So, what is the evidence that leads to this assumption and what are the arguments for royal burials at Saqqara, the necropolis on the desert escarpment overlooking Memphis? The exact location in this tomb-gorged region of the Western Desert lies in the northeastern sector. Like Umm el-Qaab, these monuments of archaic Egypt are infrequently visited so that it is possible to contemplate them without the interference of the paraphernalia of modern tourism. The route passes east of the pyramid of King Teti (Dynasty VI) and north towards the house belonging to the Inspectorate of the Egyptian Antiquities Organization. Beyond here, stretching over 1,000 metres, the desert sands have reclaimed vast portions of the ancient structures, excavated by W. B. Emery (later Edwards Professor of Egyptology at University College London) during three archeological missions between 1936 and 1956. Huge funerary structures were uncovered, datable to the reigns of all the rulers of Dynasty I with the exception of Narmer, the first pharaoh, and of Semerkhet, the penultimate king of this dynasty.

The attributions of ownership are made from inscribed material and sealings since no royal stelae survive of the sort discovered at Umm el-Qaab. Originally the monuments seemed to belong to officials of the king, because of the private names on sealings and dockets. However, it is more likely that these high-ranking courtiers were looking towards a hereafter in which they would be protected by the pharaoh and were grateful for the privilege of having their names on funerary equipment in the royal tomb. That we are dealing with tombs, and not cenotaphs, is clear from human remains found in the burial chamber. Another point worth remembering is that the monuments here at Saqqara are twice the size of the royal structures in Abydos at Umm el-Qaab: the pre-eminence of the pharaoh would preclude any official, however elevated, from raising a tomb more magnificent than that of his monarch.

The term for the rectangular, level-roofed, mudbrick tomb which now makes its earliest appearance in Egyptian funerary architecture is a 'mastaba' – a word used by Arab workmen on archeological sites in the nineteenth century to describe their shape, which they saw as a vastly inflated version of the mud benches or mastabas which were outside their village houses and were used for all kinds of social and domestic purposes (16). It is worth studying one of these royal mastabas in some detail to understand the formative centuries of mortuary buildings that were to culminate in the pyramids. But before doing this, take a walk alongside these mastabas with their mudbrick façades representing the buttresses and niches of palace walls jutting out here and there from beneath the sand. (The numbers given are from the official designations in the archeological site reports and can be used to locate the approximate vicinity on the map of Saqqara at the front of the book.) You can orientate yourself roughly 200 metres northwest of the Inspectorate house, passing the niches and buttresses of mastaba 3506, dated to the reign of King Den.

Just beyond here, above the recess of the desert escarpment at the southern end of this range of tombs, is the mastaba of King Qaa (no. 3505), the last ruler of Dynasty I. In this tomb the excavations revealed walls with coloured designs imitating the diamond-shaped patterns of the reed-mat hangings that Qaa would have had in his palace. This feature of recreating three-dimensional perishable objects in paint on tomb walls remained constant throughout pharaonic civilization. Qaa's tomb was surrounded by an enclosure wall (65 by 37 metres) and possessed on its northern side a structure of chambers and corridors with some limestone slabs for flooring. This was the prototype of the mortuary temple which was to form an integral part of the later pyramid burials.

Walking further on and following the desert-edge as it begins to project eastwards, you find the tomb (no. 3504) of King Djet (fourth king of Dynasty I). The mastaba substructure had a roofing of timber joists and planking – wood for building was never totally discarded even in the pyramid era. King Djet's tomb exhibited an impressive surrounding array of about 300 bulls' crania moulded in clay, but with real horns. On the early ceremonial palettes the bull seems to symbolize the strength of the pharaoh as it gores enemies – but this architectural translation of the imagery of the dangerous wild bull to form a protective barrier by the royal tomb is unique. (It should be mentioned that these are now reburied in the sand.)

Here at Saqqara, paralleling the practice at Umm el-Qaab, retainers were forced to join their monarch in the afterlife: sixty-two servants accompanied King Djet in tombs arranged beside his mastaba. However, no retainers seem to have been executed on the death of King Qaa so perhaps the drain on manpower, if not humanitarian considerations, eventually brought a stop to the ritual killings here at the end of Dynasty I.

Next to the mastaba of King Djet was the tomb of Queen Merneith (no. 3503) with attendant subsidiary burials for her chief shipwright, potter and metal-worker, among others. Her exceptional position among the tombs of kings suggests that she was a queen probably at some time following the death of King Djer or queen-regent on behalf of King Den until his maturity. At any rate, below the sand and mudbrick mastaba was buried one of the two royal ladies of eminence and power that we know about before the pyramid age – the other being Queen Horneith who lived slightly earlier in Dynasty I, and for whom an impressive mastaba in the Saqqara style was erected at Nagada in Upper Egypt.

About 200 metres further along to the north was the mastaba of King Djer (no. 3471), whose cenotaph at Umm el-Qaab, it will be remembered, came to be regarded as the tomb of the god Osiris. From Djer's mastaba we can proceed to the tomb of his predecessor Hor-Aha (no. 3357), hereafter referred to as Aha, the king who followed Narmer, the uniter of Egypt, onto the throne. His name means 'Horus the fighter' and may refer to his campaigns both to consolidate Narmer's achievement and to press the frontier of Egypt to the First Cataract of the Nile as Aswan. Seven hundred jar sealings with his name, vigorously portrayed in hieroglyphs as a hawk whose claws grasp a mace and shield, leave us in no doubt that this mastaba was his. Interesting features were discovered in this tomb complex which were to emerge later in the pyramid age on a different scale but with the same purpose: a large boat-shaped structure in mudbrick for housing one of the vessels required by Aha in the next world and a reconstruction in mudbrick of one of the king's estates with storerooms and granaries, ensuring that there would be no dearth of victuals in the royal hereafter.

The desert terrain now makes even more demands on the eyes to discern the elusive projections of these royal mastabas. But the tomb of King Den (no. 3035) approximately 150 metres northwest of Aha's mastaba, provided, at the time of its final excavation in 1936, the first detailed insight into the architectural complexity and magnitude of these royal monuments, as well as endowing Cairo Museum with its fullest set of early dynastic objects from a recorded archeological provenance (fig. 10). Professor Emery originally ascribed this mastaba as belonging to Hemaka, the king's chancellor, but its size and equipment militate against this and he soon became convinced that it was the tomb of the king himself. The mastaba is 57 metres from north to south and 26 metres from east to west but the mudbrick walls survive only to a height of 3.45 metres. Recesses or niches represent the style of palace walls whose thickness varies slightly either side of 4 metres. In the superstructure of King Den's mastaba were forty-five storerooms – including a group of five with interconnecting doorways that clearly formed, from over 700 wine jars discovered here to the exclusion of anything else, the everlasting royal wine cellar (fig. 10: C, D, E, F, LL). These storerooms were compactly built, the largest being 7 metres long and 2 metres wide, and generally followed the same pattern. From the desert gravel upwards there would be a sand filling upon which were laid reed mats, then the storeroom cavity itself, above which ranged diagonal log beams supporting timber planks, more reed mats and finally the mudbrick roofing. The burial chamber (fig. 10:1) of King Den was below the mastaba superstructure with its access via a stairway beginning 9 metres outside the eastern façade. Mudbrick stairs were built through the desert rock, deliberately blocked at three places by limestone portcullises lowered into position by ropes after the burial, into the precisely-cut grooves. It should be said now, at the outset of our survey of Egyptian funerary monuments, that all purposeful stratagems like stone slabs aimed at deterring tomb robbers were ineffectual. The plunderers of King Den's tomb forcibly removed the first two slabs and cut away the upper portion of the third portcullis. The burial pit itself, once roofed with timber, measured 9.5 metres by 4.9 metres and revealed two large rectangular blocks of limestone that must originally have been pillars or

10. Plan of the Mastaba of King Den at Saqqara (previously attributed to the chancellor Hemaka):

1 Burial pit
C,D,E,F,LL 'Wine cellars'

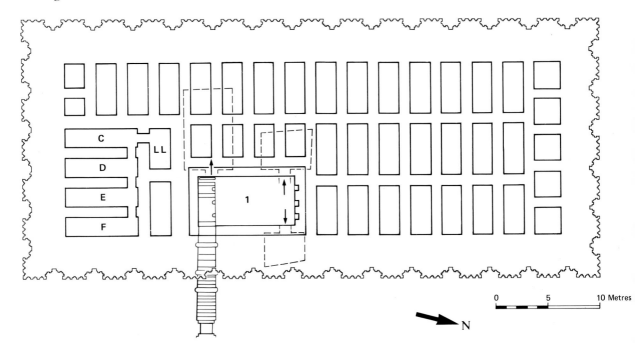

0   5   10 Metres

N

architraves. The Egyptian stonemason was finding his feet and becoming more ambitious in the early dynastic period, but no stone structure or lining of a burial chamber from this era prepares us for the colossal monuments of the subsequent Old Kingdom. Three further smaller subterranean rooms lead off from the east and west sides of the burial chamber.

Much of the royal funerary equipment and jewellery will have fallen into the hands of the robbers, but some of the magazines in the superstructure escaped their notice. Their contents, now in Cairo Museum, are our best glimpse to date of the provisions for an early pharaoh's *modus vivendi* in the hereafter. King Den was given many flint implements such as scrapers, knives and wooden sickles with flint blades. For hunting, the king had a leather quiver and about 350 bone arrows whose points could be tabulated into five distinct categories. Of great interest are forty-five discs of copper, stone, wood, horn and ivory which seem to have been for King Den to while away the hours of idleness in the next world. Wooden sticks would be fitted through the perforation in the centre so that they could be spun like tops. Some of the finest were decorated with lozenge patterns or doves and one disc, 87mm in diameter, of black steatite inlaid with pink calcite, shows a desert hunt with two masterfully carved Egyptian greyhounds (Salukis) bringing down gazelles. For notes or letters the king was furnished with a roll of papyrus – the most ancient example of the manufactured writing material synonymous with Egyptian administration.

From here one can glance towards the northern edge of the Saqqara necropolis where the mastaba of King Anedjib (no. 3038) revealed an intriguing architectural development. Behind the symbolic representation of the palace façade were some rows of mudbrick steps rising to their surviving height in an incline. Would this have been a step pyramid within the mastaba? If so, then the antecedents of King Djoser's Step Pyramid are not far to seek.

CHAPTER 4

THE FIRST PYRAMID: King Djoser's Funerary Complex at Saqqara

The Step Pyramid is undeniably the most impressive monument on the Saqqara plateau – and has been so for over 4,500 years. Towering 60 metres above the desert rock, it may not be the highest pyramid in Egypt, but in majesty it brooks no rival in its neighbourhood. It is even more overwhelming if the surrounding contemporary edifices are taken into consideration, since no surviving mortuary complex exhibits so comprehensively and on such a vast scale palaces and pavilions destined for the eternal celebration of divine kingship. Its intricate conception has been revealed largely by the architectural skills of the French archeologist Jean-Philippe Lauer, whose efforts here are proof that modern reconstruction based on archeological knowledge can enhance an ancient monument.

From later inscriptions the king for whom the Step Pyramid was built has generally gone under the name of 'Djoser' or 'holy one'; inscribed texts contemporary with his reign refer to him as 'Netjerikhet' meaning either 'godlike of body' or 'divine one of the community of gods'. There was probably a marriage linking Djoser with the last ruler of the enigmatic Dynasty II, Khasekhemwy (*17*) whose name appears with that of Netjerikhet on sealings found in galleries near the northern enclosure wall of the Step Pyramid. In Manetho's chronicle written about 2,300 years later, the following brief synopsis describes Djoser's reign: 'Tosorthros [Djoser], for 29 years, when there lived Imouthes [Imhotpe] who from his skill in medicine was regarded as Asclepios [Greek god of healing] among the Egyptians. He discovered the building technique of carved stones and also applied himself to writing.' Imhotpe then, was the architect of the Step Pyramid, the earliest large-scale man-made stone monument in the world. Manetho's claim for Imhotpe's reputation can be strikingly corroborated from an inscription discovered near the entrance colonnade of the Step Pyramid. It is carved on the pedestal of a statue of Djoser of which only the royal feet survive standing on symbols representing, under the form of lapwings and bows, the dominated enemies of the pharaoh. In the highly privileged position following the name of the Horus Netjerikhet, the hieroglyphs proclaim the name and titles of the king's architect: 'Chancellor of the king of Lower Egypt, pre-eminent after the king of Upper Egypt, hereditary prince, controller of the palace, great seer [i.e. high priest of Heliopolis], Imhotpe, builder and sculptor.' Such was the achievement of Imhotpe in raising the royal edifice that he became the embodiment of skill and wisdom for scribes, their 'patron saint' in fact, shown iconographically as seated with a papyrus unrolled across his knees (*18*). His deification as son of the god Ptah came about in response to a need for an approachable figure whose ability in magic and medicine could heal the sick. Thus over 2000 years after his death, chapels and shrines to Imhotpe were set up at Philae, Thebes and, as

11. Plan of the Step Pyramid
complex of King Djoser,
Dynasty III, Saqqara

1 Pyramid superstructure
  and shaft to Djoser's burial
  chamber
2 Southeast bastion and entrance
3 Transverse vestibule of
  colonnade
4 Southern monument
5 Approach to Robing
  Pavilion
6 *Heb Sed* court
7 Southern mansion
8 Northern mansion
9 Approach to *serdab*
10 Mortuary Temple

might be expected, in North Saqqara where his tomb was almost
certainly situated – the discovery of which is awaited with excitement,
tempered with apprehension at its probable ransacked condition. Conscious of the royal debt to Imhotpe's genius, approach the eastern
enclosure wall of Djoser's funerary complex (fig. 11).

The dimensions and monuments of the rectangular enclosure were
unsuspected until twentieth-century excavations revealed an area
measuring 544 by 277 metres, originally marked by boundary stelae
bearing the name of Netjerikhet and his two daughters Hotpe-her-nebti
and Intkawes. A 10.5-metre-high limestone wall of bastions and recesses
enclosed the pyramid complex, presenting the counterpart to the fortress
of the 'White Wall' as the ancient capital of Memphis was known (*19*).
There were originally fourteen buttresses that gave the impression of
gateways into the enclosure, but only one, the fourth, broad, deeply-
projecting bastion in the southeast corner (fig. 11:2), is a true entrance.
Beams of wood such as were used for strengthening mudbrick walls of
mastabas are imitated here in stone in the upper regions of the
reconstructed wall by small rectangular niches representing their ends.

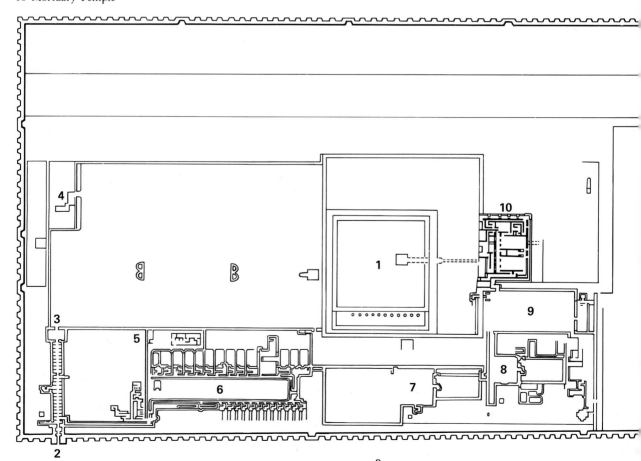

0

The stone blocks themselves have the dimensions of early dynastic mudbricks. Thus at the outset we are introduced to Imhotpe's intention of preserving the traditional styles found in mudbrick and wooden constructions within his innovatory scheme of employing, in this royal monument for eternity, the more durable material of limestone.

Walking through the entrance a visitor comes upon a narrow colonnade (20) of forty columns which at the time of their discovery, below five metres of sand, in 1925, stood less than two metres high. The fasciculated shafts (6.6 metres high) recreate bundles of reeds in masonry. Imhotpe was a bold architect and therefore the fact that these columns are not freestanding should not be seen as caution, but fidelity to an original structure, where for strength and stability the reed bundles would abut onto the side walls. We also have here an excellent example of Egyptian reluctance to abandon familiar forms, since by Djoser's reign the reed-bundle prototypes were archaic, substituted by wooden imitations in urban and temple architecture. The colonnade leads into a transverse hall (fig. 11:3) of eight columns through which the entrance into the enclosure is encouraged by a door leaf in half-open position imitated in stone.

There is no point in resisting the temptation, once in the enclosure, to photograph the Step Pyramid (fig. 11:1) unencumbered by its surrounding wall. The beige-coloured pyramid, even though now devoid of its gleaming white limestone casing dragged here from the quarries at Tura on the other side of the Nile, and despite the gash where it has been robbed of part of its superstructure on its lower southern face, still awakens a sense of wonder and incredulity (21). Could one monarch reigning for nineteen years have devoted so many units of manpower to building such a sepulchre? The answer is affirmative, and resounds from the pyramid itself where Djoser defies us to surpass his monument, a witness to Imhotpe's determination to construct a mansion worthy of a god-king. Since there will be more shocks in magnitude when the pyramids at Giza are considered, I will discuss then (p. 90) the state organization of labour that not only made Djoser's monument a viable proposition, but allowed for his other building projects, such as a shrine at Heliopolis, to progress simultaneously.

Before taking a closer look at the pyramid, cast a glance directly westward from the colonnade exit. A portion of panelled limestone wall has been reconstructed forming the eastern façade of a structure commonly called Djoser's southern tomb (fig. 11:4) (22). Forming an upper frieze, the most splendid array of nine cobras can now be seen, with their hoods puffed out ready to strike at any enemy of the king. These serpents are the sacred emblems of Wadjet, goddess of the ancient Delta kingdom and symbol *par excellence* of sovereignty. Just to the south of the cobras is a square shaft 28 metres deep, ending in a small granite chamber, the contents of which disappeared with the robbers who penetrated through the stone-lined wall on the south side. Leading off the bottom of the pit are rooms with hangings which Djoser would have been used to in his palace, imitated on the walls by means of blue tiles of glazed composition, often erroneously called faience. Carved on limestone panels in low relief, Horus Netjerikhet walks along in a stately

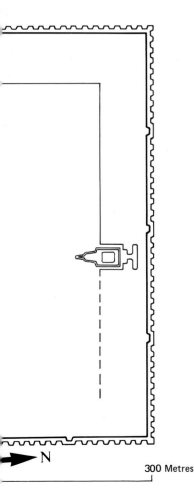

N

300 Metres

manner in the red crown of the north or, wearing the white crown of Upper Egypt in an episode from the jubilee festival (*see* p. 65), strides purposefully across a tract of land symbolizing his domain. In the upper corners of both these reliefs the god Horus manifests as a hawk protectively holding the sign of life (*ankh*) above the king, while the standard of the canine-deity Wepwawet advances in front of Djoser as a kind of talisman, keeping the royal progress free of danger.

What is the purpose, then, of this 'southern tomb'? The excavator Lauer suggested that the granite crypt held the jars containing the embalmed viscera of the king removed during the mummification process. Normally, however, these jars are in much greater proximity to the corpse itself. In my view its location provides the best explanation: Imhotpe has ingeniously created the southern cenotaph, previously as we have seen built at Umm el-Qaab at Abydos, within the enclosures at Saqqara and symbolized it as such by its proximity to the south boundary wall. All essential monuments and requirements for the spirit (or *ka*) of King Djoser have thereby been encapsulated inside a funerary complex that seems to mirror the two lands of Upper and Lower Egypt. The ancient entrance to the cenotaph was by steps and a tunnel leading from a trench situated just west of the top of the modern staircase near the wall of the cobras. It seems that a huge store of jars was being taken into the cenotaph when news was received that Djoser had died – the workforce began the task of filling in the entrance with rubble and masonry and left behind them scaffolding and an example of their haulage equipment in the form of a wooden sledge. Although the subterranean apartments of the cenotaph are too precarious to visit, it is worth climbing the stairway to the terrace along which its superstructure stretches for over 80 metres. The view straight ahead from this vantage point towards South Saqqara and Dahshur encompasses a selection of tombs of the pharaohs from the beginning of Dynasty IV until the Middle Kingdom. In the immediate vicinity to the right (i.e. west) is the dilapidated pyramid of King Wenis of Dynasty V – a monument however that is of immense value for understanding Egyptian religion, as we shall see later (chapter 11). A glance down from the terrace will reveal a well-preserved section, nearly 100 metres long, of the outer bastions of the enclosure wall.

Now wander back across the southern courtyard where you can see the vestiges of two altars between which Djoser strode as part of the jubilee festival, an event for which Imhotpe made numerous architectural provisions in this funerary complex for the king to celebrate at set intervals throughout the rest of time. Standing before the southern face of the Step Pyramid (*23*), you can trace the change in mortuary architecture that was Imhotpe's brainchild – the leap from the impressive but dimensionally low-level mudbrick royal mastaba to a gigantic stone stairway into the sky. This at any rate is how the pyramid appears to spring onto the existing panorama of funerary monuments, but we can see the stages of its evolution under the guidance of Imhotpe, who would not, of course, have been working in an architectural vacuum. Firstly, his stonemasons cut the burial chamber (fig. 12:1) and lined it with granite from Aswan. They did this at the bottom of a 7-metre square shaft that

15. (above) Funerary mansion of King Khasekhemwy, popularly known as Shunet el-Zebib ('Store-Room of the Dates'), Dynasty II, western desert at Abydos

16. (left) Egypt today: a true mastaba outside a house in a village in el-Kharga Oasis

17. Pharaoh Khasekhemwy carved in slate, Dynasty II, Hierakonpolis, Cairo Museum

18. (right) Statuette of Imhotpe, Djoser's royal architect, deified in later centuries, Late Period (c. 700 BC onwards), British Museum

had been sunk 28 metres below ground level. In the roof of the crypt there was a circular hole about 1 metre in diameter. After the burial of Djoser and his equipment they lowered into this hole a granite plug with some grooves on its edge for papyrus ropes. Despite our regret at the loss of the king's funerary apparel one cannot help feeling an illicit admiration for the robbers who, at great peril, forced their entry by dislodging this plug about 4,000 years ago. These ancient thieves, penetrating the pyramid from the northwest, left fragments of a box bearing the name of Netjerikhet on their escape route.

From the burial shaft four corridors hewn out of the desert rock lead off in the direction of the cardinal points and, by changing angles and disgorging side passages, form the nucleus of an underground network terminating in its northerly spread actually beyond the face of the pyramid itself. Blue glazed-composition tiles adorn some of the walls of Djoser's subterranean suite – a number that imitate the façade of a granary display a frieze of 'djed columns', powerful amulets meaning 'continual stability', and are on display on the upper floor of Cairo Musuem (24).

The best idea of the subsequent development of the pyramid superstructure can be gained by viewing it from a southeasterly angle, a vista which encompasses the extensive damage to the lower stages of masonry. The internal elements left exposed by the quarried-out courses of casing form the basis for our understanding of the succession of innovatory plans on the architect's drawing board. Accordingly, on the plateau surface above the royal burial chamber Imhotpe supervised the construction of a mastaba (fig. 12:3), 63 metres on its sides and 8 metres high. His materials consisted of a rubble of desert stones set in a clay mortar which served as the internal core of the monument, and well-cut limestone slabs to form a 3-metre-thick outer casing. Next, along the outside eastern edge of the mastaba, eleven shafts (fig. 12:2) were sunk to a depth of 32 metres. At the bottom of each shaft was a horizontal gallery that stretched under the mastaba in a westerly direction for 30 metres. Possibly the only way, when standing in the enclosure court, to imagine the immense effort of these excavations is to look from the pyramid's base up to half its height: this is the distance to which the labour force dug below ground and when they got there is again the length to which they tunnelled. The purpose of these shafts and galleries was both to provide burial places for members of the royal family and to act as magazines for storing vast quantities of stone vessels.

It is an interesting question why so many of these vases were incised with the names of Djoser's predecessors. On the various kinds of stone, such as porphyry, schist, calcite and diorite, are the names of pharaohs of archaic Egypt including Narmer, Djer, Djet, Den and Khasekhemwy. Were they heirlooms that he could not bear to be without in the next world? Or was their interment with him a pious reburial of vessels disturbed by the looting of royal mastabas in an early dynastic necropolis to the north? Obviously the contents of the first five shafts which were for regal burials would have included precious metals and highly-prized gemstones. Their location would be more difficult for robbers to ascertain and more inaccessible if they were incorporated below Djoser's superstructure. Thus security reasons prompted Imhotpe to extend the mastaba on its eastern side (fig. 12:4) to cover the whole series of shafts. As a defensive manoeuvre it was fruitless – two calcite sarcophagi, one containing fragments of a gilded wooden coffin in which were the bones of an 8-year-old child, are almost the only vestiges of the royal occupants of these sepulchres.

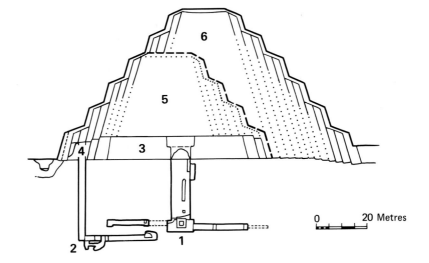

12. Cross section of the Step Pyramid of King Djoser, Dynasty III, Saqqara

1 Burial crypt
2 Subsidiary shaft
3 Original mastaba
4 Extended mastaba
5 Four-tier step pyramid
6 Final six-tier step pyramid

Approximately 4,600 years ago a conversation must have taken place between the pharaoh Djoser and his architect Imhotpe that changed the desert landscape around Memphis. The upshot was that Imhotpe should devise the most impressive stone monument that the world had ever seen, an edifice stressing in its dimensions the immutability of divine kingship and in its design embodying religious symbolism. Looking from the eastern escarpment of the Saqqara plateau, the ancient Egyptian would have seen mud ramps growing ever higher, up which the labourers dragged local desert rock. The initial result was a tower of four superimposed stages (fig. 12:5), each decreasing in area from the one below. But then Imhotpe's final plan involving overall expansion was executed and the inhabitants of Egypt's ancient capital city found themselves staring at a 60-metre-high pyramid of six steps (fig. 12:6). Its cohesion and stability were assured by the architect's attention to slanting courses of stone acting as internal buttress walls (fig. 12). Failure to angle these supports correctly in order to consolidate the superstructure accounts for the dilapidated state of later pyramids such as that of the fifth-dynasty pharaoh Wenis immediately to the south, or the heap of stones that bears the elevated description of the pyramid of Weserkaf (Dynasty V) just to the east. The Step Pyramid's original outer casing of Tura limestone produced smooth sloping sides for each of its stages. However, being of such fine quality, the stone has been prised away from the internal core mainly for post-pharaonic building projects. Thus the funerary monument in its final form can be seen above the boundary wall which, if the tomb had been left as a mastaba would have concealed it, eclipsing the natural feeling of awe that it now arouses. Imhotpe raised a sepulchre that embodies architecturally the aura of a divine monarch. It is also a colossal statement in stone of the religious belief, not found in hieroglyphic inscriptions until the end of Dynasty V, that in the afterlife Djoser's spririt would ascend to his father, the sun-god Ra, using the pyramid as a celestial ladder.

We are by no means the first to inquire into the techniques of Djoser's architect. Two thousand years after the completion of the Step Pyramid, the throne of Egypt was held by pharaohs of Dynasty XXVI whose capital was at Saïs in the Delta. They presided over a revival (actually begun in the previous dynasty) in art and architecture that looked to earlier eras for its inspiration. The cavity which can be seen at base level in front of the mid-southern face of the Step Pyramid is *not* the original entrance used at the time of Djoser's burial – that is on the northern side – but was hacked out to form a descent tunnel by Saïte workmen. Surely it was not just archeological interest that drove them to cut a gallery no less than 60-metres long and supported by a row of pillars to the edge of the burial shaft. Inevitably, the 'glint of gold' must have been at the back of their minds. Unfortunately for them, the robbers of the confused period following the Old Kingdom had already ransacked the monument. Their final effort was the clearance, to a depth of 24 metres, of limestone blocks used as filling in the central burial shaft. If you can secure official permission from the Egyptian Antiquities Organization it is this entrance and gallery that you use to look down the shaft onto the granite blocks forming the roof of King Djoser's burial chamber.

The architectural richness of the Step Pyramid complex lies not only in its central funerary hub but also in the variety of buildings along the eastern side of the enclosure. Take the three reconstructed fluted columns at the southern end (25) as your initial point of reference. In all likelihood Imhotpe has provided here a ceremonial robing hall (fig. 11:5) for Djoser who then, attired in his regalia, could move to the pavilion, instantly recognizable by the curved wall which is a rare feature of Egyptian architecture. Northward stretches the court (fig. 11:6) of the *heb sed* or jubilee festival. This celebration, a crucial element in divine kingship, was a renewal of the vigour of the monarch after a lengthy period of rule, traditionally thirty years. Its ceremonies, involving, for instance, the king striding with the sacred Apis (Hpw) bull across the field symbolizing Egypt, were held at Memphis. After the first jubilee, the festival could be celebrated at shorter intervals of two to three years. In this court Imhotpe encapsulated in stone all the shrines and state edifices that Djoser would have encountered at Memphis during the *heb sed*. On the eastern and western sides of the court are chapels with open doors carved in limestone and niches for statues of the king. However, these chapels are illusions – they are merely false façades to internal spaces filled with rubble. But in Egyptian belief these solid constructions were magically able to serve the spirit (or *ka*) of Djoser as real chapels in the eternal celebration of his festivals.

In this array of restored chapels two distinct types of sanctuary can be observed, symbolizing Djoser's allegiance to the tutelary goddesses of Upper and Lower Egypt (26). One variety exhibits an austere rectangular front terminating in a cornice which curves inward before jutting out to form a horizontal bar. Again at the beginning of the long history of Egyptian architecture a feature is met that was to endure over the millennia. This cavetto cornice represents in stone the upper stalks of reeds curving concavely below the roof in primitive shrines, in particular the *Per-Wer*, the name given to the predynastic sanctuary of the southern vulture-goddess Nekhbet. The other style sports a convex roof comparable to the shrine of Wadjet, cobra goddess of the ancient Delta kingdom. Engaged to its façade are three slender columns, from the abaci of which are carved leaves drooping on either side of a hole originally holding a banner or a horn.

Against the eastern perimeter wall stand three unfinished statues of King Djoser. It is almost disrespectful not to break away from the court for a minute to look on one of their faces already roughed out into a stern expression. This is the only above-ground opportunity to look at an image of the monarch made at the time of the pyramid itself (27).

From the north end of the *heb sed* court proceed directly to the southern mansion (fig. 11:7) which represented a palatial residence for Djoser's spirit. Its connection with the south derives from a fragment of a column in the style of the heraldic plant of Upper Egypt. Lauer has partially restored the façade with its attached fluted columns and above its doorway has introduced the ornamental freize which – in various styles – became ubiquitous in Egyptian architecture from this point on. Each individual device is called a *khekher*, circular at its base with a flame-like projection upwards (28). For the origins of this design imagine that you are looking end-on at tied bundles of reeds with projecting leaves such as existed in earlier structures to strengthen the roof. The theoretic restitution of the upper façade is for the fluted columns to stretch upward from their present height (about 3.65 metres) to an arched cornice 12 metres from the ground.

Through the door a passage leads into a chapel with three niches for statues or offerings. Black ink traces of the everyday script, known as hieratic, survive on the walls as a legacy from visitors to the Saqqara necropolis during the New Kingdom. The contents of these mild defacements will be reviewed here, including similar hieratic graffiti found on the walls of the northern mansion. One tells that two brothers, Hednakht and Panakht, who worked as scribes in the treasury and vizier's office respectively, considered the Step Pyramid complex worth an excursion in the winter of year forty-seven of the reign of Ramesses II – about 1400 years after Djoser's burial. Another graffito by the scribes Setemheb and Iahmose dscribes the northern mansion as the 'temple of Djoser' – enabling scholars to identify for certain the monarch who was called Netjerikhet on his monuments with the pharaoh named Djoser in the later king lists. Iahmose, under whose gaze lay probably 70 per cent more of the northern mansion than is now extant, lavishes praise on this monument, which he compares to the sky at the time of the sun god's rising and invokes a shower of incense and myrrh for Djoser's spirit. The last word perhaps lies with a pompous killjoy called Amenemhet. Unashamedly self laudatory, he introduces himself as a scribe 'clever of fingers ... without a rival in Memphis' and condemns such hieratic scribblings as frivolous and their authors as unworthy of a profession founded by the god Thoth.

The northern mansion (fig. 11:8) provides us with the first appearance of another architectural form. The papyrus reed, heraldic plant of Lower Egypt, is represented by three columns engaged to the building's eastern wall (29). The capitals show the bell shape of the open umbel of the papyrus plant, progenitors of the grandiose tops to the columns of the central aisle in the Great Hypostyle Hall at Karnak, built over a thousand years later. However, later columns do not follow Imhotpe's strict adherence to his prototypes in that the shafts become rounded. Here you can see the triangular stem of the *cyperus papyrus* (30) faithfully executed in limestone.

From here you can walk due west to the *serdab* court (fig. 11:9), an Egyptological term which, like mastaba, is of Arabic origin and is used to describe the closed chamber that abuts onto the northern facing of the pyramid. It should be approached from the front through the door leaves carved in stone. Two holes immediately draw your attention. Look through them and King Djoser stares back at you – or rather a plaster copy of the original limestone statue, now in Cairo Museum. The spirit of the king was thought to be able to emerge from the burial chamber and inhabit stone replicas of his body. Secure and unobserved, Djoser could view the northern precinct of his funerary monument. Carved as seated on the throne of Egypt, he wears a linen robe and holds one hand clenched across his chest (31). The massive wig is covered by the *nemes* headcloth which ends in pointed lappets – developing in subsequent dynasties into straight ends. His ceremonial false beard is almost like a ladder against the king's chin. The loss of the inlay for the statue's eyes and the rather disdainful expression of the royal mouth makes this sculpture strikingly brutal – even when you confront it in its glass cubicle in Cairo Museum.

Scrambling westward from the *serdab* you eventually locate the northern descent tunnel into the pyramid among the ruins of the mortuary temple. This cavity in the sand was the original way in (now inaccessible to the general visitor) for Djoser's funerary cortège in the twenty-seventh century BC. The surrounding wall foundations give the outline plan of the temple (fig. 11:10) where Djoser's *ka* or spirit was constantly ministered to by the mortuary priests. You can make out the bases of fluted columns at the northern end of the two major courtyards, which originally provided a portico to the inner ritual apartments. With the intensification of the cult of Ra in later pyramid complexes this important temple for the dead king's spirit is situated on the eastern face of the funerary monument so as to receive the first rays of the sun god at dawn. From Djoser's mortuary temple, however, we look northward to the pyramid field of Abusir where later, now amorphous monuments of Dynasty V serve to highlight the expertise here crystallized into magnificence by Imhotpe.

It is worth taking your time in absorbing all there is to see of the Step Pyramid and attendant buildings in the complex, since here almost the entire vocabulary of Egyptian architecture was established simultaneously. Such a self-contained and complex royal temenos (sacred precinct) was never again completed by pharaohs after him, even if it was their implicit aim. For instance, the walls of Sekhemkhet's unfinished imitation of Djoser's temenos lie southwest of the Step Pyramid, but viewing access is difficult (*32*).

Other, smaller step pyramids are to be found from this time in several places in Egypt. One, near Hierakonpolis (*33*) is late Dynasty III in date, and 18 metres square at the base, surviving now to a height of 9 metres. It could have served one of several functions: as a royal cenotaph; symbol of the primaeval mound that emerged at the beginning of time and on which the sun-god Ra stood to create the world; a power emblem of the sovereign in a region remote from the capital of Memphis – or as funerary monument for a local eminent governor. The latter could have been someone of the rank of Nedjem-Ankh (*34*), or of Sepa, whose funerary statues found with that of his wife, Neset (*35*) indicate the increasing wealth of the men of high office needed by the pharaoh to maintain the machinery of effective government.

In Dynasty IV, pyramid-making techniques were developed so that the recessed walls of the funerary monuments, which are real in Dynasties I, II and III, came to be used as decorative surfaces on tomb façades and sarcophagus sides, possibly to symbolize sanctity and permanence after death. This surface treatment has been named 'the palace façade' design (*36*), which still often included the bound lotus tops of the original prehistoric reed pavilions, possibly deriving from Mesopotamia, that Djoser's structures imitated in stone at Saqqara.

II · SUNRISE

The God-Kings of the Pyramid Age

CHAPTER 5

MONUMENTS OF KING SNEFERU

The Pyramid at Meidum

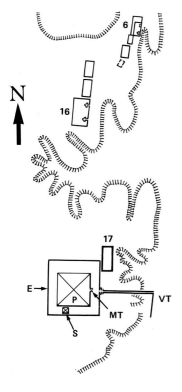

13. Sneferu's Pyramid, Dynasty IV, Meidum

P Pyramid completed by Sneferu
S Ruined subsidiary pyramid
E Original enclosure
MT Mortuary Temple
VT Vanished Valley Temple
17 Mastaba of unknown 'royal'
16 Mastaba of Nefermaat and Itet
6 Mastaba of Rahotpe and Nefret

The general approach to the pyramid of Meidum gives ample opportunity to contemplate its stark, solitary splendour (*37*). It stands like a tower fortress on the edge of the Western Desert closer to the Faiyum than to Memphis (fig. 13:P). Its situation vividly emphasizes the razor-sharp divide between the cultivation for the living and the sand for the dead, especially the view eastward that you obtain by climbing the terrace of sand and debris to the rock of the pyramid itself. The remoteness of the Meidum pyramid, southernmost of the royal sepulchres of Dynasty IV, evokes an atmosphere of melancholy in harmony with its ruined grandeur. Yet this location was once the scene of immense industry where at least nine separate gangs of labourers cut and hauled limestone blocks up mud ramps to build the pharaoh's pyramid. But under which king was this monument raised? The problems of its attribution can be mulled over as you journey (whether from Cairo or from middle Egypt) along the desert road to the pyramid's northern face.

The pyramid took its final form in the reign of Sneferu (first king of Dynasty IV, around 2600 BC) but he may not have been its inaugurator. Sneferu is the first pharaoh we meet in Egyptian history to furnish us with a well-documented reign, not just a funerary monument and a few inscriptional scraps. Although not a direct descendant of the rulers of Djoser's dynasty, Sneferu probably was of royal blood. Continuity of kingship was maintained because Sneferu married Hetpeheres, daughter of King Huni (sometimes transliterated as Hu), last monarch of Dynasty III. From this union springs the line of kings whose pyramids at Giza – on grounds of sheer magnitude alone – mark the apogee of Old Kingdom royal tombs. In his reign Sneferu campaigned beyond the confines of Egypt, capturing 18,000 prisoners and 213,000 head of cattle from Libya and Nubia. His inscriptions in the Sinai peninsula at Wadi Maghara are evidence of his pioneering determination to establish unquestionable sovereignty over the turquoise mines. Ships were built 52 metres long on his orders; forty boats laden with cedar wood returned from Lebanon. His craftsmen produced statues in gold and bronze while his builders erected fortresses, temples and palaces. But the problem we must face comes from his programme of pyramid construction: if the Meidum pyramid is his, then, during the twenty-four years given for his reign in the Turin Royal Canon, Sneferu built no less than three pyramids, the other two at Dahshur being definitely assignable to this monarch (*see* p. 87).

Can Meidum be explained as completed by Sneferu but started by Huni his predecessor? It certainly would make the surfeit of pyramids during Sneferu's kingship more comprehensible. So to begin with, can it be proved that the Meidum pyramid is older than Sneferu's monuments at Dahshur? In its original form it was a step pyramid in the tradition of

19. Limestone enclosure wall with original southeast bastion entrance into the Step Pyramid complex, Dynasty III, Saqqara

20. (overleaf) Colonnade of fasciculated columns leading westwards from the enclosure wall into the Step Pyramid temenos

that of Djoser and the unfinished monument of his successor Sekhem-khet at Saqqara. Neither pyramid at Dahshur follows this format so the Meidum pyramid is most likely the earliest of the three, its conception therefore perhaps predating Sneferu's reign. But then honesty forces the admission that no name other than that of King Sneferu can be archeologically attested on the site of Meidum. The mastabas in the necropolis for courtiers immediately to the north of the pyramid display only the titulary of Sneferu. Also, from graffiti there was no doubt in the minds of visitors to Meidum over a thousand years after its construction that Sneferu should be credited at least with the mortuary temple abutting onto the eastern face of the pyramid.

However, although there is not a shred of inscriptional evidence for the hypothesis, I would firmly argue from its structural development that King Huni initiated a step pyramid as his funerary monument at Meidum. Perhaps he was drawn this far south of Memphis in the hope of greater security for his burial equipment, away from potentially corrupt mortuary priests who, supported by centuries-old royal endowments, were able to roam the Saqqara plateau ostensibly on official duties, but also free to reconnoitre its pharaonic necropolis. Possibly Huni's architect, like Imhotpe, saw how here at Meidum a step pyramid, rising above a gently-sinuous desert slope, must demand awe from any beholder. Then, using evidence from the first scientific excavations on this site conducted by Flinders Petrie in the late nineteenth and early twentieth centuries, it can be asserted that since some limestone casing-blocks at Meidum are marked by the gang of labourers with the same rough boat device as found on blocks of Sneferu's southern pyramid at Dahshur, it was surely he and not Huni who transformed the step pyramid into the new design of a true pyramid, in the geometrical sense, with smooth sloping sides.

Although the Meidum pyramid was not destined to be the first in this style to survive, it is the earliest pyramid complex to exhibit the full repertoire of what was to be the quintessential Old Kingdom grouping of pyramid sepulchre with mortuary temple to its east, linked by a causeway to a river valley temple. However, with Sneferu's supervision and completion of the Meidum pyramid there are now more questions than answers.

Did he bury Huni in the Meidum pyramid or in the large mastaba just to the northeast? Do the mastabas of Sneferu's relatives and officials to the north indicate that it was his original intention to be buried here in the pyramid? Why, after builders had been active at Meidum for at least seventeen years, as their graffiti indicate, did Sneferu abandon this site in favour of a burial place at Dahshur? Finally, could the ultimate fate of Sneferu's pyramid at Meidum have been to stand devoid of a royal corpse and symbolize, in keeping with earlier dynasties, the monarch's southern cenotaph?

But now, having arrived in front of the northern side of the Meidum pyramid, leave speculation and face up to understanding the construction of an edifice of which even the skeletal core is impressive. Even the oblong gash in this side of the pyramid seems to deride the desperate attempts in post-pharaonic Egypt to gouge a way into the superstructure

21. (opposite above) The first view of the Step Pyramid on emerging from the entrance colonnade

22. (opposite below) Frieze of cobras decorating the southern monument of the Step Pyramid complex. The staircase leads to a fine view across South Saqqara to the pyramids of Dahshur in the far distance

in the hope of finding treasure. Yet it must be admitted that the
exploitation from antiquity into modern times of the pyramid's outer
layers as a handy quarry has left a scarred tower emerging naked from
the fallen debris of its original stone robe. From intrusive burials in this
surrounding mound of rubble it is certain that the pyramid began to
display its 'battle-worn' silhouette from the late New Kingdom. There is
always the possibility that the outer casing slipped down because of an
earth tremor. But if this is the reason for the loss of stone from the upper
courses of the pyramid, then we have to accept an accident surprisingly
systematic on all four sides.

A tunnel cut during archeological investigations revealed the building
stages that led from a stepped tomb to the first true pyramid. Above the
burial chamber an initial mastaba construction was raised on a platform
of stone resting on desert rock. Upon this six, then eventually seven,
decreasing stages were built so that the monument visible for miles
around was a pyramid of eight steps (fig. 14:4). Today, the pyramid is a
miscellany of sections from both the original and modified structure,
rising to a height originally of 94 metres; it is now broken just above the
seventh step (fig. 14:3). Over its inner core the pyramid supported six
coatings of masonry slanted at an angle for efficient bonding – the
tectonic principles of its builders were sound and its dilapidated
condition is no reflection on the competence of Sneferu's architects.

The bands of dressed masonry represent the final stages of preparing
the step pyramid, both the early and later enlarged versions, for royal
approval. The rough bands were hidden in the enlargement of the
step-pyramid phase of building, but the original dressed stone that
covered them has been looted (fig. 14:5). But then the drastic transition
was ordered: encase the sides of the step pyramid with high-quality
limestone to form four smooth sloping sides. At 51° 53′ the angle of
ascent (called the *seked* in Ancient Egyptian geometrical problems about
pyramids, in the Rhind mathematical papyrus in the British Museum)
sets the pattern for subsequent true pyramids. However, here at Meidum
the mantle of the prototype true pyramid has fallen prey to the chisels of
later generations greedy for ready-cut stone blocks.

About 30 metres up this northern side a ladder facilitates the climb to
modern metal flaps which mark the ancient entrance (fig. 14:1) to the
pyramid's internal apartments. It was not a fortuitous choice to make the
entrance on the northern face but one which had a religious significance,
as we know from Pyramid Texts later in the Old Kingdom: the pharaoh
could become an astral spirit joining the 'imperishable stars' in the sky.
There is, therefore, an exit for him from the Meidum pyramid to ascend
to the stars of the northern hemisphere. If the designer thought that by
situating the access to the burial chamber at this height, disguised by a
hopefully unscalable expanse of tightly-knit limestone blocks, robbers
would be discouraged, then he was sadly deluded. Such naive theories on
crime prevention were no match for the boldness of the ancient 'Mafiosi'
who flourished in the period of lax central authority at the end of the Old
Kingdom. By ladder-ramp you can follow their footsteps down the
57-metre-long passage through the pyramid masonry into the desert
rock. A short vertical shaft can then be negotiated via a modern twisting

stairway into the miniscule burial crypt (fig. 14:2) (5.9 by 2.65 metres) carved out at the base level of the pyramid superstructure. No sarcophagus survives to look down into, so more interest can be derived from gazing upwards at the roof, corbelled into seven steps to spread the weight of the pyramid mass away from the vulnerable burial chamber. This is a remarkably early occurrence of this architectural technique, used at its best in the Grand Gallery of the Great Pyramid (*see* p. 93), and predates the indisputably more elaborate corbelled roof of the 'tomb of Agamemnon' at Mycenae by about 1300 years (but is *later* than the corbelled tomb at Maes Howe, Scotland). Part of a timber crossbeam can be seen in one of the roof's socket holes, showing struts were inserted to strengthen the structure of the upper crypt. The signs of hacking into the southern wall of the crypt reveal a frenzied attempt by robbers to discover further chambers which might contain treasure. We can imagine their frustration if, after penetrating this far into the pyramid, they could only curse the dimensions of the crypt, too meagre to have stored any significant quantity of treasure. It is an eerie experience to extinguish all light in this crypt at the heart of the pyramid and stand for a few moments in the utter darkness, sympathizing a little perhaps with the dread of such blackness from which every pharaoh, offspring of the sun god, hoped to escape by magical force. The atmosphere can become even more frightening if you have read Sax Rohmer's thriller, *Brood of the Witch Queen*, and recall its climax of an attempt to question the spirits of the dead in a hidden chamber somewhere in the Meidum pyramid.

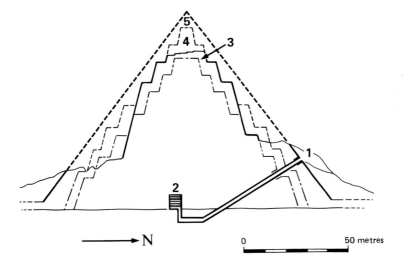

14. Cross section of the Meidum Pyramid

1 Entrance
2 Burial crypt with corbelled roof
3 Seven-tier step pyramid
4 Eight-tier step pyramid
5 Original casing of true pyramid

Debouched from the pyramid you can now survey the exterior elements of the whole complex. On the eastern side of the pyramid Flinders Petrie excavated the debris to reveal a mortuary or offering temple (fig. 13: MT). Though of much more modest dimensions than that of Djoser at Saqqara, it is situated against the slope facing the rising sun, as was to be the norm from now on, because of the increasing importance of the cult of Ra. Approaching it we are struck not so much by the building itself as by the two tall limestone stelae with curved tops in the courtyard behind it (*38*). These flank a central altar for offerings. The chapel itself should be entered, perhaps in recognition more of its historical importance as the earliest on the eastern side, than of its architectural interest. Faded black marks indicate spots where ancient tourists left graffiti, mostly in Dynasty XVIII. It is hard to understand why some of them, like Aakheprurasoneb coming here just before 1450 BC, broke into high-flown eulogy over this part of the complex. Indeed the mortuary temple, athough a completed construction, shows signs of being left without its final embellishments – some limestone blocks on its outer surface remain unsmoothed and the stelae stand devoid of royal inscriptions. At any rate, after the visitors of Dynasty XVIII the chapel rapidly disappeared under the debris; intrusive burials of Dynasty XXII were discovered up to 9 metres above it.

It is worth scrambling up the rubble (the ascent is gentlest from the southeast) to enjoy the panorama from a third of the way up the pyramid. The clear lines of the sides of a square traced in the desert sand mark the course of the now ruined inner enclosure or temenos wall (fig. 13: E). Directly east from the mortuary chapel a causeway, its stone ramps prone to disappearing under drift sand, stretches towards the green cultivation. Irrigation water from the Nile has permeated this area, rendering the archeologists' task difficult. Nevertheless, it can be shown that the valley temple was situated at the eastern terminal of the causeway (fig. 13: VT). As the name implies, this structure was the link between the desert sepulchre and the flood plain of the Nile. From the furthest group of mounds marking the vicinity of the valley temple a mudbrick wall, which enclosed the pyramid complex and its city of priests and officials responsible for the maintenance of the offering cult, could once be traced stretching 300 metres to the south.

From the southern side of the pyramid a glance down to the base will encompass a shapeless depression in the sand and blocks of limestone lying in disarray. These fragments are the sole survivors of a small subsidiary, or satellite, pyramid (fig. 13: s) now razed to the ground. Such pyramids were intended for the burial of queens. In this case the central pit below the original pyramid contained inhumations of post-New Kingdom date, when the assault by stone robbers on the Meidum complex had begun in earnest. I should perhaps mention here that the theory, advocated by Kurt Mendelssohn in his persuasively-argued book, *The Riddle of the Pyramids*, that the outer layers of the Meidum pyramid collapsed at the time of its construction, possibly burying alive labourers under the surrounding debris, has come in for severe criticism from Egyptologists and structural engineers alike. For my part, the eloquent mortuary temple graffiti alone, which could hardly have been inspired by a mound of rubble, invalidate its probability.

Rounding the corner to take in the view to the north, standing above the entrance to the pyramid's interior, you can see the modern road leading to mastaba 16 (fig. 13:16), belonging to Nefermaat and his wife Atet, which is the largest in this fourth-dynasty necropolis. The artistic treasures from these tombs are to be found in the Old Kingdom galleries of Cairo Museum. The painting from the mastaba of Nefermaat and Atet of the row of brightly-feathered geese strutting among or pecking at shrubs, sets, at this early date, the high standard of scenes observed from nature in Egyptian art. Similarly, statuary has a pattern difficult to match in the statues from mastaba 6 (fig. 13:6) of Prince Rahotpe, son of Sneferu, high priest of Heliopolis and commander of the army, and of Nefret his wife, called 'royal acquaintance', the most visited pair in Cairo Museum: his is a stern expression, highlighted by the fact that he is wigless, wears a moustache, and clenches his arm across his chest, while Nefret, in a heavy wig encircled by a diadem of rosettes, has a softer look (*49*). Both stare into eternity with eyes of inlaid rock crystal and with facial features idealized so as to hide any personal traits or blemishes. Hidden from public view in a remote mastaba chapel here at Meidum, they served as substitute bodies for the spirits of Rahotpe and Nefret for over 4,500 millennia, until the excavations of Mariette in the nineteenth century revealed them to the world as masterpieces of Egyptian sculpture.

The monument to our immediate northeast, known colourlessly as mastaba 17 (fig. 13:17) (*39*), was built of mudbrick, forming a niched façade surmounted by a crown of limestone chips gathered from the surplus stone cut for the pyramid itself. Contemporary with the pyramid, it is a splendid combination of mudbrick and limestone, the latter used for extensive flooring on its eastern side, which only an ingenious architect could devise. It is a slight struggle to enter through the narrow gap in the robber's passage forced into the mastaba's southern side, but the effort is rewarded by a huge red granite sarcophagus and stone-lined burial crypt exhibiting the rare feature of a curved wall, reminiscent of the structure mentioned in Djoser's Step Pyramid enclosure. When this mastaba was explored in modern times a male skeleton lay in the sarcophagus. Who was he? King Huni, perhaps, buried here when his pyramid was usurped by his successor? Or a crown prince of Sneferu who died prematurely before gaining the throne of Egypt? Meidum, like so many monuments of the pharaohs, refuses to yield up all its secrets at once.

The Pyramids at Dahshur

North of Meidum, and about 10 kilometres south of Djoser's monument at Saqqara, lies Dahshur (fig. 15). Here we can continue the search for Sneferu's burial place, after all, two pyramids at this location are convincingly ascribed to his reign. These pyramids are by shape and construction the most impressive structures at Dahshur, the sands of which are also marked by lesser pyramid-tombs of Middle Kingdom date (fig. 15:1, 3, 5) (*40*). However, much to our chagrin, the vicissitudes of modern politics impinge upon the monuments of the pharaohs: an important military base at Dahshur has for many years kept this site off limits to archeologists and visitors. At present, tightly controlled excavations are being permitted in the vicinity of Dahshur and the signs are hopeful that the pyramids will eventually become accessible again. Nevertheless, bearing in mind the temporal elasticity inherent in the Arabic word *bukra* (tomorrow), it might be that you will have to be content to survey Dahshur at a distance from the terrace above the southern enclosure wall of Djoser's Step Pyramid complex.

The most visually striking pyramid at Dahshur is the southern

15. Sneferu's Pyramids,
Dynasty IV, Dahshur

1 Pyramid of Senweseret III
(Dynasty XII)
2 Northern Pyramid of
Sneferu
3 Pyramid of Amenemhet II
(Dynasty XII)
4 Bent Pyramid of Senferu
5 Pyramid of Amenemhet III
(Dynasty XII)

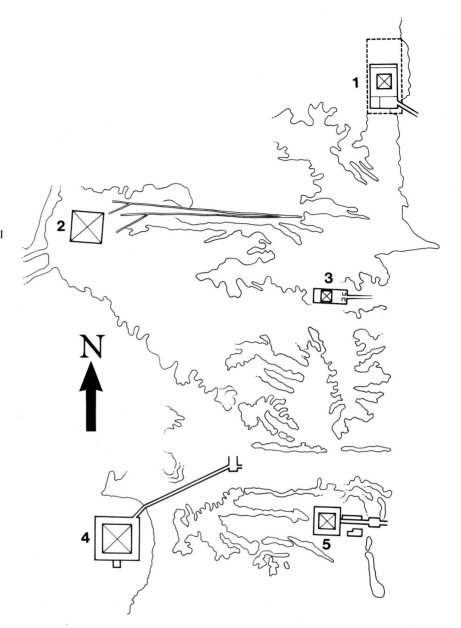

pyramid of Sneferu (fig. 15:4). Its modern name tends to be the Bent Pyramid but in pharaonic Egypt it bore the title 'gleaming pyramid of the south'. Sneferu's name occurs on scribblings by the quarry workers on limestone blocks at the pyramid's corners. Large stretches of its original high-quality Tura limestone casing survive, mainly due to the inwardly inclining individual blocks proving more difficult to strip off for post-pharaonic building projects. However, it is its unique silhouette that has intrigued visitors to Dahshur since the seventeenth century A.D. From desert rock the monument rises at an angle of 54° 31′ up to a height of 49.07 metres; its incline thence is decreased to 43° 21′ until it reaches its present height of 101 metres (fig. 16). What is the explanation for this remarkable change in angle? It is unlikely to stem from an

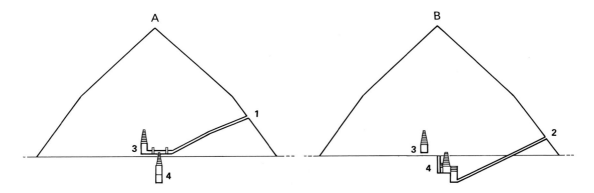

urgency to complete the pyramid with less expense of time and stone, although it must be admitted that the upper part of the structure does display more hurriedly-cut masonry. It is possible that the architects decided to reduce the pyramid's height since they observed (and ordered the repair of) cracks in the internal apartments, and hoped to avoid an excessive weight of limestone crushing down into these chambers. But for my part, I am swayed by a feeling that the southern pyramid of Sneferu was planned with double sloping faces from the very beginning. The monarch has stressed the duality of his kingdom in this pyramid, where the different inclines represent Upper and Lower Egypt. This interpretation is supported by the fact that the pyramid has two original entrances on different sides, and two crypts. An underlying solar symbolism can also be seen expressed in the angle change: the upper portion in true pyramid shape is the mound or *benben* upon which the sun god stood when he emerged out of the primeval water (portrayed by the lower section) to begin the creation of the universe.

From nearly 12 metres above ground on the northern face (fig. 16B:2), a low passageway stretches diagonally downwards for about 80 metres into a horizontal antechamber. At a height of 6 metres the southern wall gives access to the floor of the lower crypt (fig. 16B:4). A glance upwards reveals the well-proportioned corbelled roof designed, as at Meidum, to spread the immense weight of the masonry hanging above the crypt. From the south wall a passage leads into an isolated shaft. From 12 metres higher up on the same wall a bending passage slopes upwards into a horizontal corridor where, beyond the portcullis to the east, the upper chamber is to be found (fig. 16B:3). In it the results of Sneferu's expedition to the Lebanon for cedar wood become a visual reality in the vertical logs that functioned either as scaffolding for the stonemasons or were used to strengthen the lower walls. To the west, the low corridor, deliberately obstructed with limestone slabs, extends beyond a portcullis for nearly 65 metres until emerging about 33 metres above the ground on the western slope (fig. 16A:1) of the pyramid. The existence of this artery was only ascertained in 1951; mysterious gusts of breeze either felt or heard inside the pyramid point towards a yet undiscovered link between its central core and its outer slopes.

To the immediate south of the Bent Pyramid (fig. 17:1) stands a pyramidal mound of stone, identified by stelae on its eastern side as

16. Dahshur: The Bent Pyramid of Sneferu

A Cross section (looking south)

1 Western entrance
3 Upper crypt
4 Lower crypt

B Cross section (looking west)

2 Northern entrance
3 Upper crypt
4 Lower crypt

17. Dahshur: Plan of Bent
Pyramid complex

1 Bent Pyramid
2 Subsidiary pyramid
3 Offering Temple
4 'Valley Temple'

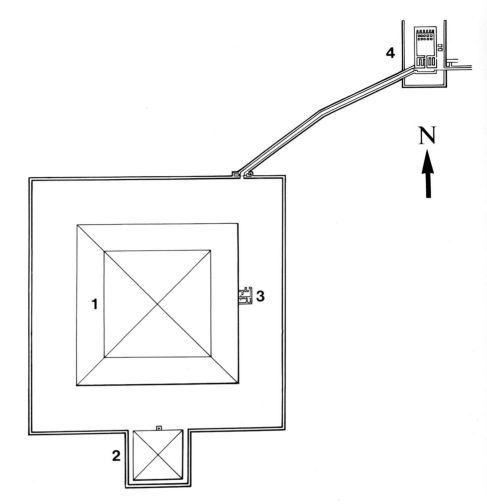

belonging to Sneferu. This subsidiary or satellite pyramid (fig. 17:2) possessed an internal chamber of dimensions too small to have received the sarcophagus and funerary equipment of one of Sneferu's queens, a role which such structures sometimes play. Its purpose here is likely to have been a southern cenotaph for the spirit (*ka*) of Sneferu, proclaiming at Dahshur the symbolic link with the Upper Egyptian ancestral homeland.

Against the eastern face of the Bent Pyramid is the mortuary temple (fig. 17:3), quite uncomplicated in its original design but with subsequent mudbrick additions dating from the end of the Old Kingdom, Middle Kingdom and even as late as the Ptolemaic era. The earliest form of this chapel to the king's *ka* consisted of a shrine with a calcite offering table flanked by two huge stelae. Two millennia after his death, as shown by the archeological evidence of pottery and limestone burners on the altar, priests filled this mortuary temple with the smoke of incense in honour of Sneferu.

The pattern established at Meidum of a causeway leading from the mortuary chapel is varied here; the causeway emanates from the northeastern enclosure wall whence it curves for 700 metres until it

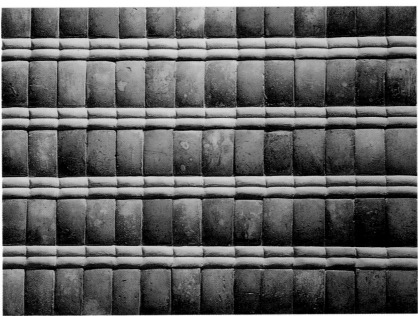

23. (above) The southern face of Djoser's Step Pyramid viewed across the court where two jubilee festival altars originally stood. It was from this side that the Step Pyramid was penetrated in the Saïte period

24. (left) Blue-glazed tiles from the corridors beneath the Step Pyramid of Djoser, Dynasty III, Saqqara, (now in USA)

25. Robing-rooms and pavilion walls leading off to the right of jubilee festival complex in front of the Step Pyramid

26. (opposite above) Parade of jubilee festival pavilions facing the heb-sed *court in the southeast sector of the Step Pyramid complex*

27. (opposite below) Three unfinished sculptures of Djoser propped up today opposite the jubilee festival pavilions of the Step Pyramid

reaches the precinct of a structure which seems to play the role of a valley temple (fig. 17:4), even though it is not situated on the edge of the flood plain. Its importance is immense because, thanks to the excavations of Ahmed Fakhry in 1951, for the first time we are able to see in a fair amount of detail the architectural layout and wall decoration of this element of a pyramid complex. The foundations indicate a rectangular building of 26 by 47 metres following a north-south axis. Outside the southern mudbrick temenos wall were two stelae carved with the name of King Sneferu. In the temple itself the southern hall displayed sculptured friezes of the personified districts (or 'nomes') of Upper Egypt, carrying offerings. Beyond the open courtyard to the north lay a portico of two rows, each of five rectangular pillars behind which were six shrines. Here, I think, the dualism pervading Ancient Egyptian thought can be seen portrayed in the architecture. The farming year of three seasons is represented by a shrine for each, doubled to symbolize the year in Upper and Lower Egypt. The four 30-day months of each season gave 360 days to the year, which the Egyptians increased to 365 by the addition of five days, regarded as gods' birthdays (the gods in question being: Osiris, Isis, Horus, Seth and Nephthys). (This was the earliest approximation to the modern total of days in the year.) Here, the ten pillars are these epagomenal (or 'added-on') days, five for north and five for south Egypt. So Sneferu in his funerary complex maintains a link epitomized in stone with the cycle of the seasons that continues in the Egypt of the living.

Altogether from this temple 1400 sculptured fragments eloquently bear witness to the elaborate measures taken to preserve the funerary cult of Sneferu, centred around eternal provisions for his *ka*. Among the finest is part of a pillar relief showing the king's nose and lips in close proximity to the muzzle of a lion goddess as he breathes in her power. The high quality of the carving in this temple can also be seen in the attention to details of the royal costume such as the fine linen pleats of Sneferu's kilt, or the wavy line and rosette decoration of his bracelets. There was a gateway from the eastern wall of the temenos which probably stretched to the edge of the cultivation where there would have been a canal link to the Nile.

This survey of Sneferu's monuments at Dahshur is completed by considering the northern pyramid (fig. 15:2 and fig. 18). For confirming its attribution to Sneferu – and there is no likely alternative candidate – we can thank his relatives and officials, who chose to be buried in mastaba tombs in a necropolis near this pyramid, and also a decree of King Pepi I (Dynasty VI), discovered just to the east, where the inscription mentions the 'funerary city of the two pyramids of Sneferu'. The first true pyramid, with flat triangular slopes, conceived of as such from the beginning and retaining its shape, now confronts us, a stone edifice which from base to apex symbolizes the *benben* or primaeval mound of the solar-creation legend. Stripped of its fine outer casing to provide palaces and mosques in Cairo, the coarse inner limestone has oxidized into a reddish colour. The base of Sneferu's northern pyramid is 220 metres on each side; only the Great Pyramid of Khufu at Giza is larger in area, being 230 metres square. But here the height stretches

28. *(opposite above) Southern mansion to the side of the Step Pyramid, displaying the khekher frieze above doorway*

29. *(opposite below) Northern mansion, along from the southern mansion: eastern wall with papyriform columns*

merely up to 99 metres at the exceptionally low angle of 43° 40′. Nearly a third of the way up its northern face is the entrance (fig. 18:1) where a 60-metre descent leads into three apartments, (fig. 18:2, 3, 4) each with corbelled roofs and none with any trace of a royal burial. Modern exploration of this pyramid and its immediate surroundings was nipped in the bud, so future generations may well discover elements of this complex which at present lie hidden in the pyramid superstructure or below the encompassing desert sand.

18. Dahshur: Cross section of the Northern Pyramid of Sneferu

1 Entrance
2 Corbelled vestibule
3 Vestibule
4 Sarcophagus chamber

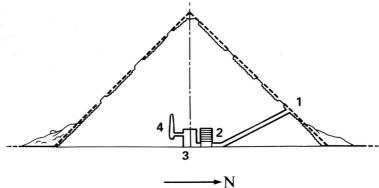

Finally, where was King Sneferu buried? The northern pyramid appears to be the latest in the series of monuments of Sneferu at Meidum and Dahshur. Although this point can only be resolved by further archeological work, the northern pyramid is the prototype, in terms of its base area, for the grandiose scale of subsequent pyramid building by his immediate successors at Giza. Logically, then, this northern monument should be seen as his sepulchre. Irrationally, I am reluctant to accept this, because I cannot escape feeling that the Bent Pyramid, even if built earlier than the northern, is a more sophisticated architectural concept. Why, then, should it not be Sneferu's burial place – a structure proclaiming eternally that its royal occupant was 'Lord of the Two Lands'?

CHAPTER 6

THE AWE OF GIZA

The Great Pyramid of King Khufu

Khufu, who under the Greek approximation of his Egyptian name is probably better known as Cheops, was the son of King Sneferu and Queen Hetpeheres (fig. 20:2) (*41*). It was his decision, taken around 2590 BC, to construct the royal necropolis further north, on the desert plateau of Giza.

The approach to the pyramid site from the centre of Cairo could not be less conducive to recreating the atmosphere of a cemetery of divine monarchs – the traffic-clogged road, concrete water-towers, bushes pitifully shaped to resemble pyramids along the central reservation, pathetically unappealing nightclubs and junk-food restaurants. Once on the road at the desert edge leading to the location of the oldest of the Seven Wonders of the ancient world the visitor will have to transcend mentally the clutter of camels and their tourist-pestering owners, the postcard and trash-souvenir hawkers and, on public holidays, a lovable but inescapable horde of Cairene children. I would advise anyone eager to feel more attuned with pharaonic times either to visit Giza at dawn, or view the pyramid complex from the road leading southwards along the cultivation to Saqqara. Otherwise, you can gain some idea of how the Giza monuments looked for thousands of years after the desert sands had encroached upon them, from views drawn by nineteenth-century artists like Vivant Denon, who accompanied the Napoleonic invasion, or David Roberts, the doyen of painter-travellers in Egypt. Perhaps we all secretly yearn for the last addition in the vicinity of Giza still to be there: the avenue of acacia trees planted in 1868 in honour of Empress Eugénie's visit to Egypt for the opening of the Suez Canal – now we can only look at the oil painting of the Pyramids Road by Edward Lear and lament the decreasing isolation of the Giza necropolis from a relentlessly advancing tawdry and ephemeral urban environment.

There are two places in Egypt that defy word pictures of their size: one is the Great Hypostyle Hall at Karnak and the other is the Great Pyramid confronting us at the northern end of the Giza necropolis (fig. 20:1). All the clever statistics in the world merely hint at the experience of standing at the base of this monument and looking up at its apex (*42*): every block in the mass of its masonry emphasizes our insignificance compared to the part it plays in shaping the edifice of a god-king. Yet despite the adage that the pyramid stands as a threat to Time itself, Time has already won the first round. The monument is nearly 10 metres less in height than when Khufu admired it four and a half millennia ago because over the courses of its light beige stone lay a smooth-sided mantle of white Tura limestone, robbed by the builders of Cairo since medieval times. With a variation of only centimetres, the length of each of its sides at ground level is 230 metres. The slopes reach up to the apex at an angle of 51° 50′ to a present height of 137 metres – an iron pole on the summit marks the original point of the capstone 146 metres above the ground. Climbing the Great Pyramid was popular among earlier generations of tourists and the Baedeker guides of that era give amusingly precise instructions on how it should be tackled with the aid of two locals. Now such an ascent is officially forbidden and any transgressor would be foolhardy to attempt it without help – a serious slip on the upper courses of the pyramid would leave no opportunity to regain a grip or foothold, and you would experience only a couple of collisions with the masonry once the death fall had begun.

The pharaonic name for this monument was 'Khufu's pyramid is the horizon', stressing thereby how it was symbolically the focal point for the crucial phenomena of sunrise and sunset. Under its modern name of 'the Great Pyramid' it is the world's most outstanding sepulchre. At any time of day it never fails to arouse awe: whether at dawn in the subtle colouring of its limestone blocks, in the unremitting glare of the noon sun, or bombarded by artificial light beams during the popular *son et lumière* shows.

What were the steps, then, that transformed the architect's plans into this immense physical reality? Firstly, the royal architects and principal administrators organized the recruitment of a permanent workforce of stonecutters and stonehaulers. In the late nineteenth century Flinders Petrie, who made an archeological survey of the Great Pyramid, studied some rough structures now thought to have been store magazines to the west of Rakhaef's pyramid. He suggested then that these were barracks for the workmen at Giza and estimated that about 4,000 men could have been stationed there. This number would in fact be perfectly adequate for a standing labour force. But if you had been living at Giza in Khufu's reign, every late summer and autumn you would have found the desert plateau teeming with up to 50,000 men. The extra personnel were the peasants performing their seasonal national service during the months when the Nile innundation covered the fields in which they normally worked. No one below the status of scribe was exempt from this manual labour. For their back-breaking efforts these men were provided with ample rations and there must have been a consensus among them that the construction work was worthwhile: such service, acknowledged as beneficial by their god-king for negotiating terms with other powerful deities, could ensure continual prosperity for Egypt. So the Great Pyramid was built with pride by native Egyptian masons and farmers. Since Egypt had no major imperial conquests as yet, we can abandon the notion of thousands of grim slaves endlessly hauling stone under the lashes of overseers' whips – dramatic celluloid images of oppression make splendid Hollywood epics – but abysmal Egyptology.

The next step was to cut level, square borders in the rock and lay some limestone blocks as support for the pyramid's outer casing stones. The whole base area did not have to be smoothed down, and in fact the lower superstructure of the Great Pyramid incorporates within it an expanse of a desert knoll. The internal masonry was quarried from the local limestone of the Western Desert, but a fleet of barges was needed to transport the prized Tura limestone for the outer casing, which was dragged to the eastern bank of the Nile from the quarries of the

Mokattam hills, across the river and along a canal to the edge of the cultivation at Giza. The western terminus of the ancient canal probably lies under the modern village of Nazlet el-Samman built just beyond the mastabas east of Khufu's pyramid. Roughed into shape in the quarry, the masons, employing copper chisels and hardstone pounders, dressed the limestone slabs with precision to fit compactly against such other in the superstructure. The stones of the Great Pyramid (there are over 2,300,000 blocks) were hauled into position by gangs using ropes of papyrus twine along supply ramps composed of mud and rubble thrown up ever higher against each side of the square. Wooden rockers and levers could also have helped move stones onto higher levels.

How long did the workforce toil to complete Khufu's pyramid? A valuable clue lies in the stonemasons' graffiti discovered in one of the cavities above the king's burial chamber. These jottings give the names of the gangs working on the monument; this is the only place in the entire pyramid where the name of Khufu occurs. There also we find a mention of 'year 17'. Thus the construction of the pyramid was well advanced by then, leaving no problem in finishing the tomb by the time of Khufu's death six years later.

The exploration of the interior of the Great Pyramid is fairly strenuous, even though you can smile at the exhortations of the same *'vade mecum'* (*Baedeker's Egypt*, 1908, still I think unsurpassed of its genre) which was so encouraging about the ascent of the pyramid: 'Travellers who are in the slightest degree predisposed to apoplectic or fainting fits, and ladies travelling alone, should not attempt to penetrate into these stifling recesses.' Looking up at the north face of the pyramid the eye is drawn to the huge slabs that form a triangular gable above the entrance about 20 metres from the ground (*43*). But of course this entrance would originally have been concealed by the polished casing-blocks of Tura limestone. No later than five hundred years after Khufu's funeral the casing on this northern side would have been disturbed by robbers forcing their way into the pyramid to steal Khufu's burial treasure. Incidentally, remembrance of this period of lax security around the pyramids at the end of the Old Kingdom comes through in an exaggerated list of woes and turmoil found in literary compositions dating from the Middle Kingdom: from the *Prophecies of Neferty* (papyrus in Leningrad) – 'Men dwell in the necropolis' i.e. for looting; from the *Complaints of Khakheperre-Seneb* (writing board in the British Museum) – 'Possessors of silence [i.e. the dead] are violated'; and most expressively of all from the *Admonitions of Ipuwer* (papyrus in Leiden) – 'See, those buried in tombs are thrown onto high ground, the secrets of the embalmers are cast away ... the king is robbed by the poor ... what the pyramid hid is now empty.'

A steeply descending passage leads from the entrance (fig. 19:1) to the point where it is joined by modern visitors who are forced to use the tunnel cut into the masonry below and west of the true entrance by Khalif Mamun in the ninth century. About 120 metres from the true entrance the descending passage leads into a rectangular chamber approximately 14 by 8 metres and just over 3 metres high (fig. 19:2). In the original plan therefore, it is believed Khufu was to be buried here

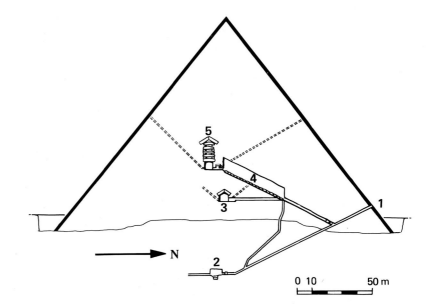

19. Cross section of the Pyramid of Khufu

1 Northern entrance
2 Subterranean crypt
3 Ritual chamber (so-called
  queen's chamber)
4 Grand Gallery
5 Sepulchral chamber with
  weight-relieving apertures
  above roof

more than 30 metres below ground – or in another subterranean
apartment, reached by the 18-metre-long southern corridor now terminating in a cul-de-sac, which never got started because of the orders
received for major modifications.

We can explore this new scheme by following the ascending corridor,
entering it via the robbers' by-pass across the massive granite plugs
positioned to thwart any upward access after Khufu's burial. After about
37 metres we meet the second stage of the pyramid's internal construction. A horizontal passage leads into the central core of the pyramid
terminating in a crypt (fig. 19:3) commonly, though totally erroneously,
called the queen's chamber – royal ladies had their own funerary
monuments as we shall see. Its dimensions (5.2 metres north to south, 5.7
metres east to west) are suitable for it to have been intended to hold the
royal burial before it, too, was abandoned for this purpose. The roof rises
to an apex just over 6 metres high, its colossal blocks overreaching the
chamber walls to rest firmly embedded in the surrounding masonry. The
corbelled niche in the east wall, whence robbers were later to thrust a
shaft to penetrate into the upper chamber, seems originally to have been
destined to contain a royal statue or the chest holding Khufu's embalmed
entrails. From each of the northern and southern walls about a metre
above floor level, an artery leads into the superstructure and would,
before the third change of plan for Khufu's burial chamber, have
provided an outlet on the respective two faces of the pyramid. Now they
lie buried by its casing-stones, so the explanation of shafts like these will
be suspended until you are standing in the royal burial chamber itself.

Back at the northern end of the horizontal corridor a steep shaft winds
downwards for 60 metres to link with the descending passage into the
abandoned underground crypt. There can be few since its discovery in
the eighteenth century who have negotiated its length, but we can all
share in the admiration for the ingenuity of its constructors. This shaft is
not a thieves' tunnel but a lifeline for the last workers remaining in the

pyramid after Khufu's burial. They could escape from the upper reaches of the pyramid to this point, and release the plug stones behind them. However, the lower ascending corridor could only be sealed by its granite slabs from the inside which would trap the workmen. Was it humanity or fear of contamination by lower social orders that led Khufu – assuming he was not kept in the dark about the project – to allow his workmen to spend some time in cutting a rather meandering escape route through the masonry and desert rock into the redundant descent shaft, and thence through a then unblocked corridor to freedom?

The final ascent to the burial chamber is as precise in its engineering as it is majestic in its concept. We are *en route* to the eternal dwelling of a god-king whose spirit demanded a spacious approach road lined with immaculately cut and polished Tura limestone. It has been called the 'Grand Gallery' (fig. 19:4) since the early days of Egyptology: 47 metres long with an 8.5-metre-high corbelled roof of seven courses, it is just over 2 metres wide on its upper walls while at floor level a central sunken channel 60cm deep runs between stones set about 1 metre apart (*44*). Yet in this vast area of masonry you cannot find even less than a millimetre of space between the joins of the limestone blocks. What were the uses of the rectangular holes cut at regular parallel intervals into the tops of the blocks flanking the sunken ramp? Probably they served as receptacles for the wooden struts which originally kept the granite and limestone plug stones upright until they were finally required, though I doubt that there were anywhere near as many stone slabs as the possible facilities for storing them indicate. Dragged in here temporarily from the exterior ramps during the pyramid's construction were the immense granite plugs at the northern end of the low ascending corridor, and those meant to fill the slots for portcullises in the antechamber at the upper end of the Grand Gallery. More than a token number of slabs between these two strategically positioned bastions of granite would have struck the pharaonic foremen as superfluous – especially if only a few had been prepared by the time of Khufu's death.

The king's chamber (fig. 19:5) (5.2 metres north to south, 10.8 metres east to west) is paved, walled and roofed entirely of polished red granite (*45*). The flat ceiling is composed of nine granite monoliths, each weighing 50 tons. We can see low down on the north and south walls of the burial crypt the ends of channels like those mentioned in the queen's chamber. Here the arteries, at an angle of 31° to the north and 45° to the south, penetrate the superstructure reaching the air outside, hence frequently they have been described as ventilation shafts. Certainly this practical side to their purpose would not have been unwelcome to the workers during the final stages of completing the internal structure of the monument. But they are more important symbolically in that the spirit of Khufu would have access via these channels to the hemisphere of the night sky, to join the spirits of the 'imperishable stars' – an astral imagery which complements in a discreet way the overwhelming solar concept of the pyramid's architecture. Above the roof (originally investigated via a small opening off the upper end of the Grand Gallery) five thrust-relieving cavities were constructed to spread the weight of the higher mass of the pyramid from being concentrated immediately upon, and possibly breaking, the monoliths over the burial chamber. All roofed with granite, four are rectangular while the uppermost has an apex, thus forming the device of the relieving triangle, a successful weight distributor – as over a thousand years later and on another continent the architects of the 'tholos' tombs of Mycenae were to realize.

The uninscribed granite casket of Khufu's sarcophagus (inserted contemporaneously with the superstructure's construction since its width exceeds by about 2.5cm the lower aperture of the ascending corridor) is all that remains of his funerary equipment, and with saw and drill marks visible, is not of faultless workmanship. Nevertheless, the golden furniture rescued from the violated tomb of his mother Queen Hetpe-heres provides a tantalizing glimpse of the sort of splendour Khufu must have taken with him into his pyramid (46). But here in the burial chamber the one reality as we gaze upon his lidless sarcophagus is that of a fruitless enterprise. Feelings of awe at the pyramid's magnitude now give way to a sadness for Khufu's thwarted presumption of inviolability by Time or Man. Despite resting in a crypt 42 metres above the desert plateau and enveloped (in the original dimensions) by 2,521,000 cubic metres of stone, it appears Khufu's body was destroyed, thereby leaving his spirit homeless. Ironically, the only image to survive bearing the name of the builder of the Great Pyramid is a miniature ivory statuette depicting Khufu enthroned, which was discovered by Flinders Petrie over 550 kilometres south of Giza in the temple of Khentamentiu at Abydos – it measures 8cm in height.

On the eastern side of Khufu's pyramid stood his mortuary temple, evident today only by its desert-rock foundation and the remains of a basalt flooring. From excavated fragments we get a picture of a temple with limestone walls and red-granite columns. The causeway linking the mortuary temple to the valley temple, now lying below the village of Nazlet el-Samman, was a massive construction, many core-blocks of which can still be viewed along its route. It began to be stripped of its limestone lining under the pharaoh Amenemhat I (Dynasty XII), when the causeway and valley temple became a quarry for his builders working much further south at the royal necropolis of Lisht. There, some reused decorated blocks of Khufu's reign have been discovered (47). The case is thus strong that reliefs were carved on the limestone slabs of Khufu's causeway and its adjoining temples, decorations regarded as later restorations by some scholars, and is also based on the existence of the earlier fragments discovered in Sneferu's complex at Dahshur, and a passage in the Greek historian Herodotus' account of his visit to this site in the fifth century BC. Observing extreme caution it is possible to find amid the information imparted by this chatty prototype of the on-the-spot reporter, a valuable supplement to archeological and inscriptional sources. Herodotus considered that Khufu's causeway was almost as spectacular as the pyramid itself because of its dimensions and its polished stone 'engraved with animals' (48).

The Royal Boat

Khufu's pyramid complex has still more visual surprises. On the eastern side of his pyramid, north and south of the ruined mortuary temple, and west of it parallel to the direction of the causeway, three long naviform

34. Granite figure of a high official, Nedjem-Ankh, Dynasty III, Leiden Museum

35. A typical Old Kingdom female figure: near-life-size tomb statue of the lady Neset in limestone, still enhanced with traces of green paint, Dynasty III, Louvre

cavities were hollowed out of the plateau (fig. 20:3). These pits were for royal vessels, provision for which can be traced back as part of a tradition beginning in Dynasty I with the mudbrick boat-shaped construction in the mastaba complex of King Aha at Saqqara (*see* p. 54). The Giza boats themselves, except for fragments of gilded wood and rope, have long since perished.

20. Plan of Giza Pyramids

1 Great Pyramid of King Khufu
2 Shaft Tomb of Queen Hetpeheres
3 Museum of Khufu's boat
4 Tomb of Meresankh III
5 Pyramid of Rakhaef
6 Temple of the Sphinx
7 Valley Temple of Rakhaef
8 Pyramid of Menkaura
9 Valley Temple of Menkaura

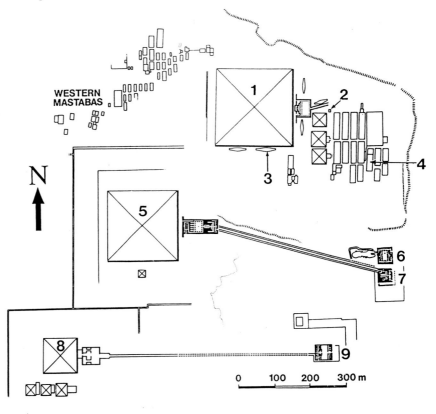

But in 1954 a miraculous discovery was made, below the temenos wall about 18 metres from the south side of the Great Pyramid, by Kamal el-Mallakh – a pit just over 31 metres long, still covered by forty-one limestone blocks cemented together with plaster. What could lie below, preserved in an airtight waterproof cavity? The limestone blocks, each roughly 16 tons and firmly wedged in place by smaller stone fragments, were prised off the ledges on which they rested. Quarry markings on the blocks indicated that the pit had been sealed with its contents after the death of Khufu on the instructions of his immediate successor Radjedef. Perhaps this accounts for the fact that revealed below the slabs was a 43.5-metre-long boat carefully dismantled into 651 pieces of timber to fit the dimensions of a pit still being lengthened at the time of Khufu's death. This Procrustean treatment of the vessel, while a sore test for Khufu's abilities as a shipwright in the next life, was a far more pragmatic approach than cutting out of the rock another 12-metre stretch at a depth of 3.5 metres and width of 2.6 metres – after all Radjedef needed the workforce for his own monument.

From the time of its discovery there were problems of preserving the wood and reconstructing the whole structure. Surprisingly, this modern undertaking received a little help from the era of the Great Pyramid itself. The naval architects and carpenters who had originally constructed Khufu's boat wrote brief reminders in the everyday script called hieratic, actually on many of the timbers to indicate their approximate position in the vessel – such as 'fore' or 'aft', 'port' or 'starboard'. By 1970 the thirteen layers of planks in the pit were assembled into one vessel. Even so, it was not until over ten years later that the oldest boat in the world was displayed to public view against the southern face of the Great Pyramid, in a specially constructed museum which from the outside looks like a Hollywood version of Noah's ark, and is unquestionably the greatest eyesore on the Giza plateau. But once inside what the admission ticket calls the 'Cheops Bark Museum' and sliding along in obligatory canvas overshoes distributed at the entrance, it is possible to absorb the ambience of the most imaginative archeological exhibition in Egypt. The first sections display fragments of reed matting found on the vessel as well as some of the metres of rope used for lashing its timbers together. There is also an excellent archive of photographs illustrating stages in its discovery and justifying its present reconstruction under the able hands of Ahmed Youssef Moustafa.

On the south side the museum envelops the original pit where the vessel was buried, while opposite a staircase leads to the astonishing view of the prow and hull of the 4,500-year-old royal boat (fig. 21). Its bows look towards the west, following its original orientation in the pit, and you can stroll along looking at its southern side, immediately struck by the most noticeable feature: the absence of a keel. The finials fitted over the prow and stern copy ancient craft made of papyrus bundles; in pharaonic times this papyriform structure tends to signify a ceremonial, funerary or solar context. Five pairs of oars ranging up to 8.5 metres in length are lashed across the hull, while another two steering oars lie across the stern. It is unlikely that the vessel was manoeuvred by rowers but was towed along the river with the oars occasionally stabilizing it. Analysis of the water content of the timber and ropes suggests that the boat was once part of the royal flotilla and took part in river processions during religious festivals.

Ascending to the higher platform you can survey the barque of Khufu from above. Altogether 1,224 separate components were fitted or lashed together in its construction. The beams of the hull and deck, predominantly of cedarwood from the Lebanon (perhaps inherited by Khufu from his father Sneferu's massive expedition), are pierced by seam holes through which the ropes pass to bind the planks together. The rectangular royal cabin amidships has its roof beams supported on the inside by three wooden columns whose capitals imitate palm fronds, but its antechamber blocks our view of the interior. The royal quarters are surrounded by a wooden canopy of slender columns with papyrus-bud finials – reminiscent of the gilded canopy, now in Cairo Museum, from the tomb of Queen Hetpeheres, mother of Khufu. On the foredeck ten similar papyriform columns support a baldachin for use either by the skipper or the monarch himself. Later Ancient Egyptian models and illustrations of boats like Khufu's with papyriform finials at the prow and stern often show the hull painted green, but no trace of pigment or adornment has been recorded for the Giza vessel.

What was the purpose of burying this royal boat in the desert? Tourist vernacular looks likely to perpetuate the term of its discoverer, 'solar boat' (or, more quaintly, 'solar barque') for Khufu's vessel, immediately underlying a connection with the sun-god Ra. While not an indisputable designation for the vessel, it is, I think, a useful description not too far removed from the truth. However, in Egyptological circles 'royal boat of Giza' would be more neutral. Nevertheless, the following hypothesis seems – on present evidence – to offer a reasonable explanation. East of Khufu's pyramid are cavities for three boats (excluding the one mentioned below (p. 102), which is clearly assignable to his queen). Two pits were cut along the pyramid's eastern face, one to the north and one to the south of Khufu's mortuary temple. It is tempting to see each of these pits as originally containing a boat orientated for the king's spirit to travel to cult centres either in the Delta or in Upper Egypt. Northern Busiris (or Djedu) and southern Abydos, the major sanctuaries of Osiris, would immediately spring to mind as the likeliest destinations from Dynasty V onwards. But here among fourth-dynasty monuments, which predate the earliest definite attestations of the Osiris cult, we must

21. Funerary boat of King Khufu: the planks are joined together by ropes threaded through holes which would swell in the water, making it leakproof. The royal cabin is preceded by the pilot's canopy, before which the prow finial stretches upwards

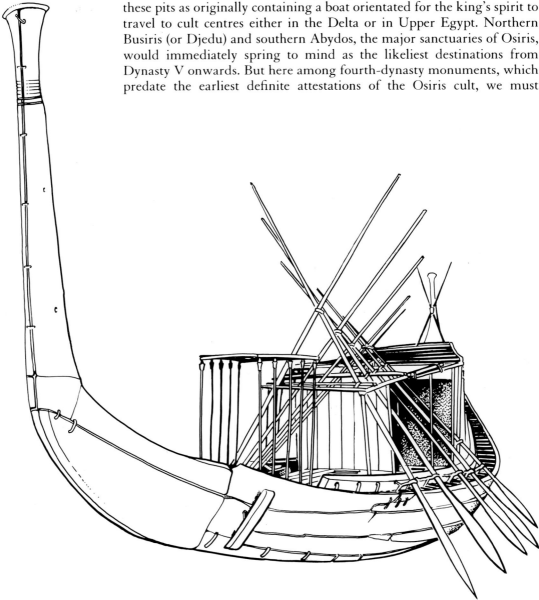

provide alternative possibilities for the boats' journeys. I would suggest voyages to celebrate rituals in the ancient predynastic capitals of Buto in the Delta and Upper Egyptian Hierakonpolis or, using inscriptional evidence from Rakhaef's valley temple, in the sanctuaries of two goddesses: Bastet in the north and Hathor in the south (*see* p. 132). These suppositions do not preclude underlying notions of astral symbolism, prominently featured in the Pyramid Texts which first occur at the end of Dynasty V, whereby the king's spirit has transport to join the stars of the northern and southern hemispheres. The third boat pit on the east is aligned along the direction of the causeway – did this protect the state funerary barge which brought Khufu's body from the Nile to the valley temple?

Back now to the boat discovered south of the pyramid. Not by chance was its prow orientated towards the western horizon. The sun-god Ra was envisaged as journeying westward across the firmament in his day boat called 'Mandjet'. Therefore, employing the complex theology of the Pyramid Texts, Khufu, as son of Ra, joins his father's retinue in this boat buried beside his pyramid, or the pharaoh becomes one with the sun god in the afterlife and the Giza boat, hidden from human sight, actually becomes 'Mandjet', in which the king sails 'like Ra who rises in the eastern sky'. But the god Ra also possessed a special boat called 'Mesektet' for travel in the netherworld after sunset. Directly to the west of the boat museum are forty blocks of limestone which at present are covering a fifth boat pit of Khufu's. Scientific probes reveal that, through air and water seepage into the pit, the state of preservation of this vessel does not match that of the excavated boat. If the cranes eventually raise the slabs away, will the privileged archeological inspector be the first person in 4,500 years to look down upon the timbers of 'Mesektet', the solar *night* boat?

Pyramids of King Khufu's Queens

South of Khufu's causeway at its western terminus are the ruins of three subsidiary pyramids. Here the favoured queens of Khufu were buried. The monuments each represent in varying states of dilapidation the internal nucleus of a pyramid, displaying the vertical faces of the superimposed stages which were eventually hidden by the smooth triangular slopes of the outer casing. No pre-eminence can be allocated from their size – all have a base area of 45 metres square and their sides rose at approximately the same angle of 51°/52°.

The northernmost pyramid survives to a height of only 6 metres. From its northern side a passage penetrates 16.5 metres into the rock, then turns 90° into the burial chamber. On its southern side the queen was provided with a boat pit to house the vessel for her afterlife journeys. No name remains in this pyramid for us to identify the queen but it is likely, being constructed first in the series, to belong to Khufu's chief consort Mertiotes. This is especially probable since the earliest in the rows of the stonebuilt mastaba tombs for the royal children of Khufu, immediately to the east of this pyramid, was for the burial of the Crown Prince Kawab, son of Khufu and Mertiotes. In addition, Prince Hardjedef, another son of Khufu and Mertiotes, had his mastaba in alignment with this pyramid, directly east of Kawab's.

The central pyramid, 9 metres high, has a shorter corridor leading to a similar right-angled antechamber before the crypt, as in the northern tomb. Queenly titles were discovered in the mortuary chapel on the pyramid's east side but its occupant is nameless. A strong possibility is that the queen buried here was the mother of Radjedef, successor of Khufu possibly by a palace intrigue. The southern pyramid, reaching a height of 11 metres is less severely ruined than the others. Its mortuary temple on the east side provides the bonus of giving us the name of the queen – albeit on a stela (now in Cairo Museum) inscribed 2000 years after her death. How? Well, by Dynasty XXI her chapel had been reinterpreted and reconstructed as the temple of Isis Mistress-of-the-Pyramid. During Dynasty XXVI this temple was enlarged. In order to stress the antiquity of the cult of Isis on this site the dedicatory stela claimed that the work was really no more than a 'restoration' of existing structures and statues. It is in this inscription that the name of Queen Henutsen is linked to the southernmost pyramid. Furthermore, we can observe the same cosy family set-up as for Queen Mertiotes in the northern pyramid: to the east of Queen Henutsen's tomb, the mastaba of Prince Khufukhaef lies under the symbolic protection of the pyramids of his father and mother.

Once more at the foot of the Great Pyramid, it is an opportune moment to examine the 'bad press' that Khufu received in later generations. The earliest implied criticism of the king occurs in Papyrus Westcar (in Berlin Musuem), a document for which the prototype can be dated to the Middle Kingdom. The papyrus contains a cycle of stories about famous magicians of the past, told for entertainment at the court of Khufu. Prince Hardjedef (above-mentioned son of the king by Queen Mertiotes) offers to bring to Khufu a living magician called Djedi whose renown had not reached the king's ears. Djedi is the ideal utmost age for an Egyptian – 110 years old – and is in robust health with an incredible appetite for beef, bread and beer. Khufu's interest in meeting him is heightened by the information that Djedi also knows about the secret chambers in the sanctuary of Thoth, god of wisdom. Here perhaps is a hint of an obsession of Khufu's with his funerary monument – possibly to the detriment of other projects – in the mention that the king had been searching for their location over a long period of time in order to copy their layout for his 'horizon' (i.e. his pyramid). Is this search, as related in the papyrus, perhaps a memory of secret high-level discussions between Khufu and his architects that resulted in the scrapping of the two potential burial chambers in the Great Pyramid?

It is when Hardjedef arrives with Djedi at the royal court that a brief conversation between the king and the magician possibly contains the embryo of the tradition of Khufu as a heartless ruler. Khufu, eager to see Djedi's particular magical skill at bringing together a severed head and body into a living entity again, intended to give the order for a prisoner to be beheaded. Djedi interrupts the king saying that he never performs this feat of magic upon the 'honoured cattle', i.e. human beings, regarded as the kine of the sun god. He then successfully exhibits his supernatural expertise by uttering spells (the magical words of which regrettably go unrecorded in the papyrus) over a decapitated goose and an ox. Can we see in this contrast of attitudes a reminiscence of Khufu's arbitrary and harsh treatment of some of his subjects? Certainly by the time Herodotus visits Giza a picture has emerged of Khufu as a merciless tyrant who even had the impiety to close down all the temples so that no resources would be hived off from the construction of his own monuments. This is demonstrably untrue since, at Bubastis near modern Zagazig in the Delta, Khufu's building programme incorporated the temple of Bastet, later cat goddess *par excellence* but conceptualized in the pyramid era as more leonine than feline. The political bias of Herodotus should be borne in mind; driven by a tyrant from his native Halicarnassus (modern Bodrum) on the Anatolian coast, he subsequently became a fervent admirer of ancient Athenian democracy. There is every reason to suppose that, subconsciously at any rate, he interpreted the information gleaned from his priest-guides about Khufu in the least favourable light. Accordingly, he rails at what he sees as Khufu's oppression of the people by forcing 100,000 men to labour as slaves on his monument for a three-month stint then replaced by another 100,000 – a garbled version of the annual 'national service' done by the peasants on the pyramid site during the season of the Nile flood.

CHAPTER 7

IN THE EASTERN SHADOW
OF THE GREAT PYRAMID

Herodotus' 'character assassination' of Khufu is most virulent in his spicy account of the construction of the central subsidiary pyramid belonging to the nameless 'great royal wife'. He writes that Khufu was so short of funds that in his depravity he forced his daughter into a brothel to obtain money. Point by point the allegation collapses. Firstly, Herodotus fails to realize the absolute command of a god-king in the pyramid era over Egypt's resources. Secondly, there is an anachronism in his portrayal of pharaonic wealth in terms of cash. This is, however, pardonable since at the time of his visit to Egypt in the fifth century BC coinage was in circulation among Greek and Carian mercenaries and residents. Thirdly, (leaving aside the mistaken attribution of the pyramid to the daughter, not the queen, of Khufu for which his interpreter must bear the blame) Herodotus is unaware of the jealousy with which a royal heiress was protected and such flagrant contamination of the ruling family would have been unimaginable. To be fair, it is possible to cite scandals from the late pyramid age: the pharaoh Pepi II furtively visiting his general at night or Queen Weretyamtes accused of an undisclosed misdemeanour in a trial held in camera. Also from a risqué series of drawings on a late New Kingdom papyrus in Turin Musuem, we can assume that there were brothels in Ancient Egypt. However, it is the preposterous sequel to Herodotus' libel that makes his story juicy but unbelievable: Khufu's daughter demanded that each of her clients, in addition to the set fee to meet her father's financial difficulties, present her with a stone towards her own funerary monument. Hence, her pyramid arose from the gifts of countless clients.

The physical evidence from the mastaba tombs of members of Khufu's family that cluster round his pyramid (*see* fig. 20) indicate that, in truth, the royal ladies possessed a plain dignity, and were accorded equal respect with the male members of the First Family. Their family tree (*see* fig. 22) is remarkable for the names of both male and female members that are known to us through their monuments. On a day's trip it is usually only possible to see a few of them.

The Rock-cut Tomb of Queen Meresankh III

To obtain an insight into life in the pyramid age, as expressed in the supreme artistry in carving and painting of the time, it is worth looking first at a royal tomb in the necropolis on the eastern edge of the Giza plateau. Allusions have already been made to some of the stone mastabas constructed here for the children of Khufu, such as Prince Kawab. In the southeast quarter of the 'streets' of mastabas in this cemetery lies the tomb of Queen Meresankh III (fig. 20:4), discovered by the American excavator G. A. Reisner during the Harvard University and Museum of Fine Arts, Boston archeological expedition of 1927. The massive core of the mastaba provided, from quarry marks on its casing-stones, the information that the tomb was originally intended for Queen Hetpeheres II, mother of Meresankh III. However, the tomb chapel itself, cut in the rock below the northern end of the mastaba, and the inscription on the sarcophagus in the burial chamber, indicate that the whole structure was eventually assigned to Meresankh III, granddaughter of Khufu, and consort of Rakhaef (*see* fig. 22).

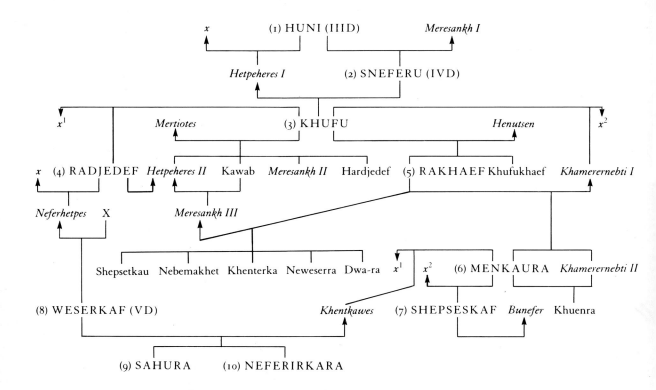

KEY

(1) HUNI = reigning monarch
Meresankh II = queen
Kawab = prince
x = unknown queen
X = unknown prince
↑ = married to
| = child of

To reach the subterranean chapel of Meresankh III you negotiate five sloping steps from the southern approach, bringing you about 2 metres below the stone blocks laid to form the mastaba base. Why did the architects blend the traditional mastaba superstructure with an underground chapel hewn out of the raw rock? Probably the reason was lack of space to expand the mastaba so as to incorporate within its mass a fittingly royal chapel. Anyway, it is possible to rejoice in their decision which allowed this substructure, in subsequent centuries of neglect of the royal necropolis, to become sanded up, thereby affording excellent protection for the vivid colours which Meresankh's tomb now boasts to its visitors. Do not overlook the hieroglyphs incised on the architrave over the entrance doorway. In Egyptian picture-writing the signs face the direction from which the inscription should be read: the birds and horned vipers are here facing right so we know where to begin this list of eternal epithets of Meresankh:

36. (left) The palace-façade design used to decorate Old Kingdom coffins: a detail from one of many found in the Old Kingdom tombs of Saqqara and Giza, Dynasty IV, Cairo Museum

37. (below) Inner core of the pyramid of Meidum, surrounded by the debris of its collapsed outer covering. The ancient entrance is situated well below the hole cut into the superstructure made by treasure-hunters, Dynasty IV

TITLE	KEY HIEROGLYPHS	
'She who sees Horus and Seth'	Hawk, crouching heraldic beast, human eye	IN THE EASTERN SHADOW OF THE GREAT PYRAMID
'Great favourite of Nebty'	Swallow, two baskets	
'Follower of Horus'	Hawk	
'Highly praised'	Tall jar, swallow	
'Beloved of Thoth and Horus'	Sacred ibis on a standard, hawk	
'His friend'	Two vertical signs (= folded linen and a chisel) over horned viper	
'King's daughter of his body'	Pintail duck and sedge plant	
'King's wife'	Sedge plant above a hemispherical symbol (= well)	

38. (opposite above) The two stelae and roof of the offering temple against the eastern slope of the Meidum Pyramid, facing the now sand-covered-over causeway leading down to the Nile, Dynasty IV, Meidum

39. (opposite below) View down from the Meidum Pyramid to the northeast onto Mastaba 17, possibly a royal mudbrick tomb structure, topped by a layer of limestone chips, Dynasty IV, Meidum

The penultimate title is not strictly true since Meresankh's father, though Crown Prince, never reached the throne; the last title refers to her husband Rakhaef, constructer of Giza's second-largest pyramid. The final symbols of a mattock, folded linen and a loop upon a cross followed by a seated lady give the name of Meresankh – anticipating all her hopes for the hereafter in its meaning 'she loves life'. The vertical inscriptions on the façade are immensely interesting in their content, providing detailed dates of her death and burial. On the northern (right) column of hieroglyphs we find the euphemism for Meresankh's death, 'the resting of her *ka* [spirit]', and the information that her body was taken to the embalmers in 'regnal year 1, month 1 of the spring-summer season, day 21'. The reigning monarch was most likely to have been Menkaura. From the southern inscription we learn that Meresankh was not actually buried in her tomb until the following year – 273 days later in 'month 2 of the winter crop-sowing season, day 18'. Mummification would be about a two-month process at the outside, so why did Meresankh's corpse have to wait a further six months before burial? Perhaps her mother Hetpeheres II, who outlived Meresankh into the reign of Shepseskaf, was not satisfied with the state of completion of the tomb which she had given her daughter and held her embalmed body back until the chapel and burial chamber were deemed worthy of their loyal occupant. A clear indication of the close mother-daughter bond can be found in the restored fragments of an unusual limestone dyad statuette discovered in the debris of the main tomb chamber and now in the Museum of Fine Arts, Boston: Queen Hetpeheres II has her arm protectively around Meresankh's shoulders, and holds in her hand her daughter's left breast as a gesture of fondness.

As you enter the tomb chapel, Meresankh can be seen for the first time carved on the thickness of the door jambs on each side of you as she stands facing away from the tomb chapel towards the direction of the rising sun. Above her in each case is a large carving of recumbent Anubis, the jackal god, guardian of the necropolis. In the funerary formulae of the surrounding hieroglyphs it is Anubis and the monarch who are regarded as trustees for the sound condition of the tomb and the constant availability of provisions. On the northern (right) jamb an oryx is being pulled by its horns into the tomb while a hyena is being ushered forward by Rery, a funerary priest (literally the Egyptian *hem-ka* means 'servant of the spirit'). One of the welcome features of Meresankh's tomb is the way her subordinates occasionally step out of the anonymity which normally prevails elsewhere. On the left door thickness, Meresankh, followed by two female retainers carrying a duck and a rotating fan, breathes in the aroma of a lotus blossom. In front of her Khemetnu, the overseer of funerary priests, unrolls a papyrus document for her inspection – an action which reveals that Ancient Egyptian royal ladies were educated at the minimum to a practical level of literacy and account keeping. We shall meet the privileged Khemetnu again inside the tomb chapel. The main chamber of the rock-cut sepulchre is of modest dimensions (approximately 7 by 3.35 metres, and 2.6 metres high), but colourful in decor.

Left of the entrance on the short section of the east wall (fig. 23:1) are five registers of intense activity. At the top are four of Meresankh's travelling boats, one clearly a skiff made of papyrus bundles and one with a prow amusingly shaped as a hedgehog's head looking towards the stern. In this boat the pilot, holding a sounding pole to test the river Nile for sandbars, could be shielding his eyes from the dazzling sunlight on the water surface but I think he is actually scratching his head as he puzzles out how to avoid a collision with the vessel in front. In the register below craftsmen are at work on statues for the tomb of Meresankh: a painter, whose name is now illegible but was read by the excavator Reisner as 'Rehay', applies his brush to colour the standing statue with the mixed pigment contained in the shell palette, while the sculptor 'Inkaf' appears to be chiselling the upper torso of a seated statue. These 'studio' scenes are balanced by two completed statues of Meresankh being dragged to the necropolis to the accompaniment of burning incense. The universal custom of courtiers putting statues of themselves into mastaba tombs has embellished the galleries of many museums. See for example the fine statues of the estate administrator Metjetjy now in Brooklyn Museum (50). The lower registers include stonemasons polishing a granite sarcophagus with a curved lid, metal-workers using blowpipes to heat their furnace – and carpenters making a sedan chair for Meresankh in the style of the gilded one now in Cairo Museum, discovered by Reisner as part of the funerary equipment of her great-grandmother Hetpeheres I. Attracting attention on the south wall (fig. 23:2) are three niches at base level containing altogether six statues of males sitting cross-legged in traditional scribal fashion. (Such a sculptural type for scribes is repeated and brought to a heightened state of realism in this period (51).) Who were these men? No inscriptions help identify them, but it would not be surprising if, as Reisner suggested, they represented Meresankh's trusted retainer Khemetnu and his family, ready to serve the queen as administrators in the afterlife. The theme of the reliefs on the pinkish plaster of the south wall, severely damaged in places, centres around bearers of commodities of which the spirit of Meresankh will magically be able to make use. In the leading position of the second register of predominately food offerings is Rery, the funerary priest met on the northern door jamb and who here has the additional title, 'supervisor of the dining hall'. The most interesting scenes lie just above the westernmost statue niche. The painter identified by hieroglyphs as 'Rehay' is still painting a standing statue of Meresankh, but the hairstyle makes it clear that it is not the same one as on the east wall (fig. 23:1). Then two maidservants prepare the bed of the queen which is surrounded by a canopy again paralleled among the furniture of Hetpeheres I.

The southernmost portion of the west wall (fig. 23:3) consists of an unfinished false door, symbolizing the link between Meresankh and the upkeep of her mortuary cult, flanked by Khemetnu on the left and Meresankh herself on the right looking towards the entrance into the west room. On the west face of the pillar (fig. 23:4) that forms the northern door jamb to the entrance to this room stands Meresankh breathing in the scent of a lotus. Offering a writing board for her inspection is her steward and scribe Khemetnu junior, obviously appointed by Meresankh on the advice of his father who was not necessarily dead but perhaps just a little past sorting out servant problems in a royal household. Glancing at the numerous rectangles containing names of offerings for Meresankh carved on the damaged south wall (fig. 23:5), we cross to the western wall (fig. 23:6) of this room where four standing statues are cut out of the raw rock, divided by a false door in the centre and flanked by low reliefs of the palace-façade motif. All four statues represent royal ladies in wigs and linen dresses. In the southern niche the queen on the left has her arm around the other queen's shoulders while the latter grips her companion's waist; in the

23. Tomb of Meresankh III, Dynasty IV, Giza

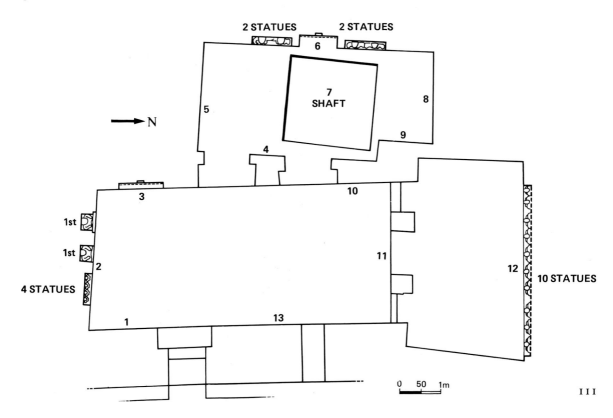

northern niche the two queens hold hands. Bearing in mind the affection between Hetpeheres II and Meresankh III, it seems natural for this emotional and blood tie to be encapsulated in stone for eternity. In front of the statues the tomb shaft (fig. 23:7) was sunk in the rock to a depth of a little over 5 metres. From its northern side the burial chamber stretched for 5.7 metres. The black granite sarcophagus discovered in the crypt has been removed to Cairo Museum together with the bones which it contained. The inscription on it stresses once again the intimate bond between the two queens – Hetpeheres II gave the sarcophagus to the 'king's daughter and royal wife' Meresankh. The body of Meresankh suffered severely at the hands of tomb robbers who hacked away any parts to which gold had been attached – hence her skull was in several bits and most of her hand bones were missing. Nevertheless, the surviving bones were analysed: we can picture Meresankh as a broad-headed lady about 1.5 metres tall, probably over fifty years old at the time of her death.

Great fun goes on in the upper registers of the north wall (fig. 23:8) where performing before Meresankh are two harpists, two flautists and a singer with his hand over his ear to get correct pitch. Some girls clap their hands while others dance a pharaonic 'highland fling'. There is extensive damage to the lower reaches of this wall but it is worth following the bottom register until you come to two kneeling figures kneading dough, one of whom is prodded by the man behind. Above his head the hieroglyphic inscription beginning with the desert-hare symbol has perpetuated his peremptory remark about his oven being ready to bake loaves, approximating to 'hurry up you lot, this is hot!' No other ancient civilization has left such a rich legacy of conversation at all levels of its society. The sketches of a harvesting scene on the plaster on the eastern wall (fig. 23:9) show that the tomb chapel had to be left unfinished, even allowing for the delay to complete it prior to Meresankh's burial.

Exiting from this western room let your eyes feast on the most magnificent depiction in the whole tomb, carved on the west wall (fig. 23:10) of the main chamber. The vertical inscription labels the first figure standing to face left towards the entrance to the inner offering room as 'her mother [hieroglyph of a vulture] ... king's wife, Hetpeheres'. There are two striking features about the queen: her short yellow wig and the linen dress with high-peaked shoulders (fig. 24). From the startling colour of the wig Reisner suggested Libyan ancestry for Hetpeheres II but this ingenious explanation is not really tenable. More likely is the association of the yellow strands with gold, a metal which the Egyptians considered to be the 'flesh' of the sun god. Attendant on Hetpeheres is a kneeling girl holding up a fly whisk or fan. The next tall standing figure is identified by five columns of hieroglyphs as 'her daughter of her body, king's daughter ... great favourite ... king's wife whom he loves, Meresankh'. Over her white linen dress the queen is astoundingly garbed in a leopardskin the tie of which she holds across her right shoulder (*c.f.* 52). This costume, normally worn by a category of mortuary priest, must indicate a religious office held by Meresankh who was a priestess of the goddess Hathor and the god Thoth. She wears her black hair cropped

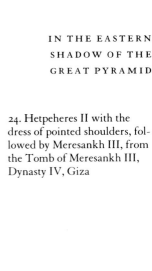

24. Hetpeheres II with the dress of pointed shoulders, followed by Meresankh III, from the Tomb of Meresankh III, Dynasty IV, Giza

short and displays a choker, broad necklace and bracelets. In front of the queen is her very young son Khenterka who grasps a hoopoe by the wings. The last large figure is described as: 'Her son, king's son of his body, superior lector-priest, Nebemakhet.' His high status in society (he was later to hold the office of vizier) is iconographically portrayed by his heavy wig, broad collar, sash across the chest and the folded linen kerchief in his left hand. It can be assumed that the nameless two boys and a girl behind him are his children, still young enough to be represented naked.

If you step back a pace facing north you can take in the view of two rectangular pillars and architrave forming the northern juncture (fig. 23:11) of the main chamber, beyond which you can see a row of standing female statues. You can put off meeting these ladies until you have absorbed the beauty of the representations on the immediate northern façade. On the upper architrave a row of superb hieroglyphs painted in blue, yellow, black and red and starting on the right, despite the reversed image of the jackal god, addresses a funerary invocation to Anubis. Particularly worth noting are the symmetry of, and details on, the hieroglyphic signs of the sarcophagus with its curved lid, the owl (= consonant 'm'), the ox (= provision of cattle), the lady with the staff (= 'old'), the three slender wine jars in a stand (= 'in front of' and forming part of an epithet of Anubis 'foremost of the god's pavilion') and the flag-like symbol which stands for the word 'god'. On each of the two pillars Meresankh stands, wigless but bejewelled, facing the inner entrance to the north room. In front of her in each case a young son has been painted in, almost as an afterthought – on the eastern pillar is Dwa-ra and on the western, sucking his finger and looking back to his mother is Neweserra. In the next dynasty, when the throne was occupied by a king called Neweserra, someone (possibly a funerary priest in a moment of idleness) drew a rather untidy cartouche around the hieroglyphs of this son's name and added the sign of life. On the lintel over the central gap leading to the north room Meresankh's name is written in beautiful hieroglyphs, which are taller than those that give her name elsewhere in the tomb, and preceding it are her titles 'King's daughter [or, rather, granddaughter] of his body and king's wife'. After all, according to Egyptian belief the name is an integral part of a person's afterlife, in as much as it is one of the entities (like the '*ka*' spirit form) to survive bodily death.

It is time to introduce the line of ten proudly-bosomed royal ladies cut out of the rock along the northern wall (fig. 23:12) of the north room (53). The three statues on the east (right) form a definite group with one figure wearing a lappet wig and two in full wigs. Probably these each represent Queen Hetpeheres II. Identical in height, wigs and style the next four to the west are likely to be Queen Meresankh III. The last three statues then gradually decrease in height and perhaps portray Meresankh's daughters – the tallest and eldest being Shepsetkau, whose name is known from the tomb of her brother Nebemakhet.

It remains to contemplate an important stretch of the eastern wall (fig. 23:13) of the main chamber, with its tantalising hints of 'mafia' tactics to gain the throne of Egypt. Striding with his staff of office towards the northern room is a corpulent figure dressed in a linen kilt and wearing a necklace of leopard-claw amulets and a heart pendant. The columns of hieroglyphs above tell all: 'Her father, hereditary prince, king's eldest son of his body, superior lector-priest ... Kawab.' Meresankh's father was, as eldest son of Khufu by Queen Mertiotes, heir to the throne. The marriage to his full sister Hetpeheres II reinforced his legitimate right to rule. But he never made it – although, as we have noticed, Meresankh, child by Hetpeheres, continually maintained his lawful claim to succeed Khufu in her title 'King's daughter'.

A tentative reconstruction can be made of events following on the death of the builder of the Great Pyramid: a 'hit squad' assassinates Crown Prince Kawab and a 'strong man' emerges from the shadows to usurp the throne. Son of an unknown queen of Khufu his name was Radjedef, whom we have already come across in connection with the final rites of his father's boat burial. He consolidates his hold over Kawab's supporters in an astute manoeuvre worthy of Shakespeare's Richard III, and the evidence can be seen on the upper righthand section of this wall. There, a line of thirteen men and women are depicted carrying offerings in baskets on their heads. The figures represent the estates from which the commodities are brought and are identified by a hieroglyphic label. Eleven of these districts are preceded by the cartouche of Khufu, implying that they have been legitimately inherited by Meresankh from her grandfather via her mother Hetpeheres II. But the fifth offering bearer from the left has different signs in the cartouche before her – symbols that render the name of Radjedef. So Meresankh also inherits an estate called 'creation of Radjedef', that belonged to the usurper king. How? Because Radjedef forced through a marriage with Hetpeheres II, widow of the murdered heir-apparent Kawab. This union, attempting to cement together the minor and major branches of

Khufu's family, helped to keep Radjedef in power for about eight years.

Now for a drama of revenge. But to relate it, move back, keeping in the upper register, to the left of the east wall where there is a fine representation of the two royal ladies out boating. Hetpeheres II stands in the prow of a reed skiff and pulls at two stalks of papyrus. The queen is called 'Daughter of the king of Upper and Lower Egypt, Khufu', emphasizing her role as principal royal heiress. But Hetpeheres lost her position as wife of a reigning monarch when for the second time she was widowed through political assassination. Rakhaef (known to the Greeks as Chephren), son of Khufu and Queen Henutsen, led the faction that overthrew Radjedef and became pharaoh. Determined not to be left out in the cold, Hetpeheres' skill in diplomacy bore fruit: her daughter became 'beholder of Horus and Seth' i.e. the consort of the pharaoh Rakhaef. Since Meresankh was not his major queen, her children were never in direct line for the kingship. However, this particular branch of the royal family had probably had enough of high politics and were well out of a power struggle in which the descendants of Radjedef seem to have been a continual source of friction, eventually emerging triumphant at the end of the dynasty (*see* fig. 22 and p. 144). Meresankh holds onto her mother in the papyrus skiff. Her linen dress is covered with a net of beads and she looks splendid in her jewellery and floral diadem, as she too pulls on a papyrus stalk. Her beauty, together with the ritual depicting her and her mother sensuously pulling papyrus for Hathor – love goddess *par excellence* – is charged with sexual overtones. The remaining scenes on this wall focus on the healthy outdoor existence of Egyptian peasants untroubled by palace intrigues. No other nation in antiquity has provided such a rich documentation of working life. To trap birds and geese, fowlers have arranged collapsible nets around a marsh pool. A rope attached to the framework of these nets is held by men some distance away who pull it on receiving a signal from a fowler near the pool discreetly displaying a linen band across his shoulders so as not to frighten the birds. The trapped birds are then collected from the nets and basketed until required for plucking. Also in the marsh area three men can be seen making a papyrus mat. Then following Kawab there is a procession of cranes, geese and cattle. Two men lead oxen described as 'from the fields' or 'from the tethering block'. There is a realistic depiction of a sickly balding peasant leading a 'cow of offering'; another bearded peasant pulls along a calf wearing a matting blanket and which the hieroglyphs interestingly describe as having been 'suckled on the finger'.

Finally, follow the rough and tumble found in the lowest register immediately after Kawab. The stately hieroglyphs above this scene describe marshmen bringing lotus blossoms and field produce to Meresankh. Below, a papyrus skiff laden with lotus flowers and crated birds seems to maintain the dignity of the inscription but in its stern we can see threatening behaviour as one man brandishes a reed bundle and another his punting pole at the smaller paddle boat behind. No doubt a nicety of river traffic precedence is being debated by the two skiffs to the right which are locked in combat, with the boatmen lashing out with paddles. Further to the right on another part of Meresankh's domains law and order is personified by a village headman leaning on his staff watching Barbary sheep being whipped along to tread sown seed into the ploughed fields.

The Tombs of Qar
and Idu

A rung or two down the hierarchical ladder from the Giza 'royals' were priests and officials responsible for the upkeep of cults and buildings in the pyramid towns. Two such men, father and son, living about 300 years after the death of Khufu (*c.*2220 BC), were privileged to have adjacent tombs which abut onto this prestigious fourth-dynasty mastaba field. Located directly east to the northern subsidiary pyramid, the superstructures of their tombs have disappeared – in fact the scant surface indications make it questionable whether these officials ever possessed traditional mastabas. Their mortuary complexes only survive as small courts, chapels and burial shafts cut into the raw rock. Although a case has been made from inscriptional evidence for a reverse relationship between these two courtiers, we will assume that the father is Qar and follow the stairway leading down to his tomb chapel. The descending walls once bore representations of hunting in the papyrus marshes: finely carved painted fragments from this area reside today in the Museum of Fine Arts, Boston. In the courtyard a niche in the east wall contains a rock-cut seated statue of Qar but you can get to know him better by looking at the architrave above the pillar in the south wall (fig. 25A:1). The symmetry of the hieroglyphs and the detail of individual signs make the inscription carved horizontally along this lintel a pleasure to view. The nobleman Qar seated on a lion-footed chair faces inwards at each end of the three lines of hieroglyphs.

Examine his credentials by isolating those titles he bears involving royal names. In the centre of the top line two cartouches, combined with the signs to either side, reveal that the owner of this tomb was a 'tenant of the pyramid Men-nefer Meryre'. Thus it is possible to date Qar's lifetime approximately to the reign of Pepi I (Dynasty VI) and assign some of his duties to that king's pyramid at South Saqqara. In the same position in the line below, the right cartouche and the adjacent nine symbols amplify his career by proclaiming that Qar was an 'overseer of the pyramid town of the pyramid Akhet-Khufu' i.e. the Great Pyramid.

25. The Tombs of Qar, left (A), and of Idu, right (B)

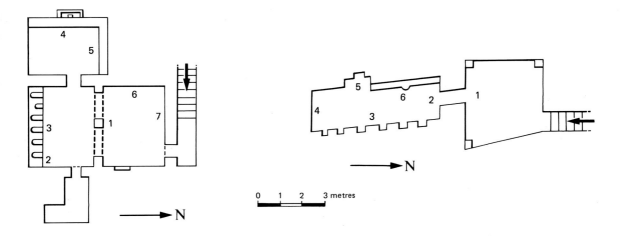

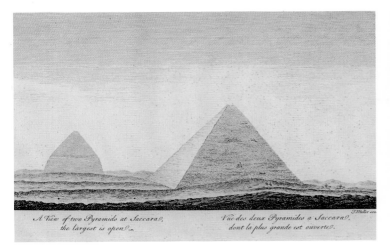
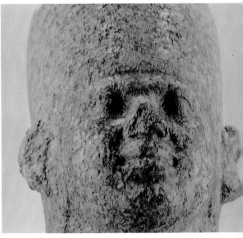

40. *(above left) The Bent and Northern pyramids of King Sneferu, Dynasty IV, Dahshur. This drawing was made by Richard Dalton, who accompanied the Earl of Charlemont to Greece and Egypt in 1749*

41. *(above right) Red granite head (detail), thought by some on stylistic grounds either to be of Sneferu, or of Khufu, Dynasty IV, ?Memphis. 54.3 × 29 cm. The Brooklyn Museum, 46.167. Charles Edwin Wilbour Fund. The only other likeness of Khufu is a small full-figure ivory carving in Cairo Museum which possesses the same thick neck and flat nose*

42. *The Great Pyramid of Khufu, Dynasty IV, Giza*

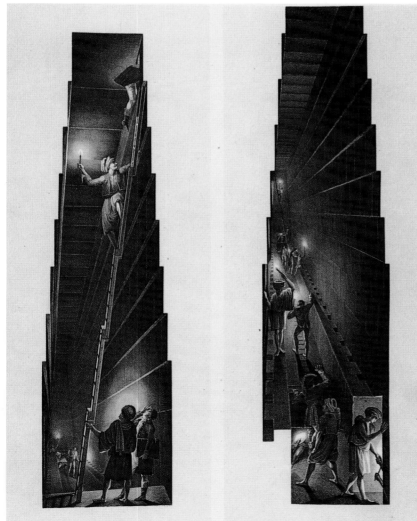

43. (left above) The ancient entrance to the Great Pyramid drawn by Richard Dalton in 1749

44. (left below) Napoleon's savants examine the Grand Gallery of the Great Pyramid in 1799

45. (above) The sepulchral chamber of King Khufu in the Great Pyramid, drawn by Richard Dalton in 1749

46. (opposite above) Detail of the rich covering on a curtain box of Queen Hetpeheres, mother of Khufu, Dynasty IV, Cairo Museum

47. (opposite centre) On a block probably taken from Khufu's valley temple re-used by a later Middle Kingdom pharaoh at Lisht, appear the damaged titles used by every pharaoh, the Horus name being the only one that changes with each individual. The Horus name, 'Khufu', lies in a serekh surmounted by a falcon; the sedge and the bee signify his rule of Upper and Lower Egypt; his allegiance to the vulture and cobra goddesses, Nekhbet and Wadjet, is represented by these animals; then comes the fragmentary Golden Horus name (the falcon over the hieroglyph for 'gold'), and finally on this slab the top of Khufu's own name appears in a cartouche, Dynasty IV, Giza/Lisht, (now in USA)

48. (left) Other re-used blocks from Khufu's causeway, with finely carved long-horn cattle, and the characteristic cartouche containing his name made up of two baby chicks, a viper and a shaded circle spelling out the word 'Kh-w-f-w', Dynasty IV, Giza/Lisht, (now in USA)

The left cartouche introduces the same title in connection with the pyramid of Menkaura while immediately below in the bottom line we learn that Qar was an inspector of priests serving the cult centred upon Rakhaef's pyramid. You can now picture Qar hurtling in his palánquin across the Giza plateau from north to south with an air of self-importance since this inscription also tells (around the symbol of the kneeling man with a basket on his head) that he was a privy councillor with a portfolio for all construction work. The three vertical inscriptions on the façade of pillars below all end with the five hieroglyphs required to write the name of Qar – who also boasts in this monument a 'Sunday-best' name ('his beautiful name' in Egyptian terms) of Meryr-anefer which had the prestige of bearing the 'Sedge and Bee' name of Pepi I (see p. 15). Acknowledge the stately figures of Qar striding as an official on the thickness of the jambs as you enter the statue hall, then turning to the eastern end of the north wall (fig. 25A:2) you will meet Qar's two favoured greyhounds below his chair, and his two sisters Tjetwet and Bendjet.

In the east wall an opening leads into a chamber that was left in its undecorated condition at the time of Qar's burial. To the right of this doorway are very deteriorated reliefs of Qar being carried in a palanquin to receive a document for inspection. Along the length of the south wall (fig. 25A:3) are six rock-cut standing statues. Four are identical representations of Qar in a flared wig. Then a young boy symbolizes the next generation of Qar's family, in an unchildlike formal pose that anticipates succession to his father's position at court. Next Qar appears wigless but wears a full kilt with a Delta flare. Through the door in the west wall, decorated with reliefs of Qar holding sceptres or scrolls, you enter an offering chamber to find that scenes of butchering, purification and offering on the east and south walls are in extremely poor condition. However, the false door in the western wall (fig. 25A:4) shows us where the spirit of Qar entered his tomb chapel to receive provisions – Qar's burial shaft was cut in the rock just outside this chamber to the north, so the journey to his food supply was quite short. On the north wall (fig. 25A:5) you can just make out Qar holding a cylindrical perfume jar to his nose, seated on a divan with his mother Khenut, while his son Idu stands in front of his knees.

Back in the courtyard you can get to grips with the paraphernalia of Egyptian funerary ceremonies for which both these tombs are an important source of evidence. A slab on the western wall (fig. 25A:6) introduces Gefi, Qar's wife, who stands behind her husband seated in front of a table thickly set with long loaves. Before him in the upper register a priestly scribe called Idu approaches holding his arms in front with his little fingers extended in the attitude of anointing. Oils and incense, indispensable in pharaonic ritual, are brought in by the next two men. Then another scribe with the name Idu pours a libation into a bowl containing two incense pellets and held by a kneeling participant. A man carries in two bolts of linen and a lector-priest kneels offering a massive leg of beef. In the lower register Nakhti, an overseer of funerary priests, pours liquid onto a low altar while a scribe (another Idu) offers food provisions to Qar. Three kneeling figures each with one fist upon their

49. (opposite) Limestone statue
of Princess Nefret (detail),
Dynasty IV, Meidum, Cairo
Museum

chest and the other raised are described in the hieroglyphs above them as 'embalmers performing the daily glorification'. This reference sets the tone for the scenes on the northern wall (fig. 25A:7) of a courtyard, depicting the ritual of the funeral procession with immensely helpful hieroglyphic tags. The upper portion is static: Qar contemplates offerings of bread, beef, fowl and vegetables spread before him on mats and tables and a symbolic 'cupboard' of ninety-nine rectangles each containing hieroglyphs labelling a valuable commodity for the afterlife such as unguent, eye paint or beer.

The lower two registers, however, describe a land and river procession at the time of Qar's funeral. Begin on the left where a lady gripping her wrist is called *djeret* or 'kite': women labelled such in funerary rituals represent the chief female mourner. The man in front holding two crossed sticks bears the description 'embalmer' and is preceded by the lector-priest with his scroll 'making glorification' of Qar's spirit. Fourteen pall-bearers carry Qar's sarcophagus with the hieroglyphs above them describing their action as 'transporting in peace to the *ibu*' or purification structure. The *ibu* itself takes the form of a rectangular kiosk with elements of its structure decorated with patterns based on the 'water' motif. Displayed on its roof are tables, jars, a bag and sandals, while on the sides of the *ibu* are signs indicating the meal required in the purification ceremony and two chests containing undisclosed ritual documents and implements of the lector-priest. At the end of the register a 'kite' and an embalmer face each other as they recite an incantation and two calves, whose protruding tongues manifest their bleats of pain through the savage binding of their legs, await their doom as sacrificial victims. Moving below, towards the west the fourteen bearers carry the coffin which differs slightly from the first depiction in lacking the cavetto-cornice-style lid. The next scene takes place on board the funerary barge (called a *shabet*) being towed along the river by twenty men. The coffin (this time with its legs missing) is kept stable on the boat by a trellis, and is steadied also by the hand of the 'overseer of embalmers'. Two 'kites' kneel on either side of the canopy around the coffin: this iconography persists in funerary scenes and the two 'kites' become symbols of the goddesses Isis and her sister Nephthys protecting the body of murdered Osiris. A group of men and women dance and clap in front of the *shendjet* or 'acacia house'. Finally, you view a schematic representation of the vestibule and inner sanctum of this structure now labelled by its more common name of *per-wabet* or 'house of embalmment'. Notice the maze-like arrangement of its walls to preserve the mysteries of the embalmer's craft.

A few steps to the east of Qar's tomb bring us to the rock-cut chapel of his son Idu. The outer court displays puny obelisks in three of its corners, emblems of the solar cult of Heliopolis. Idu, holding sceptre and staff, is carved on the right edge of the architrave (fig. 25B:1) facing seven lines of exquisite hieroglyphs stretching towards the east. From the top lefthand corner you can read an exhortation to the jackal-god Anubis, guardian of the necropolis and to Osiris (the 'eye and throne' symbols in the middle of the line) for a well-preserved burial for Idu. In line four you can see the specification of festivals when Idu wishes to receive an ample supply of offerings: the ox horns refer to the New Year festival, the ibis to the festival of Thoth (god of wisdom), and the hawk on an ornate standard to the feast of Sokar (Memphite necropolis deity). Also, in the fifth line, you are reminded not to forget the monthly and half-monthly festivals indicated by a star beneath the crescent or half crescent of the new moon. The hieroglyphs of the individual lotus stems that you can see in this line and in line six represent the Egyptian word for 'a thousand' and consequently multiply by that amount all the adjacent offerings – including an oryx, geese, linen, calcite perfume jars, bread and beer. A vertical inscription immediately in front of Idu gives his name in the lower four symbols of the flowering reed, hand, child and quail chick. Above his name are two of his most frequently used titles – 'document scribe in the sovereign's presence' and 'overseer of the *meret* serfs', who were agricultural labourers on royal and temple estates. Entering the offering chamber you observe Idu on the thickness of the door jambs. On the eastern one he is wearing a priestly leopardskin garment and is preceded by a figure, carved knee high to himself but clearly a young adult from his titles and costume, named as his son Qar. The western thickness shows a grossly corpulent Idu with a flabby breast and roll of fat hanging over the belt of his long kilt. The vertical line of hieroglyphs before his staff is a warning to all visitors to his tomb chapel: 'As for anybody if he enters this tomb and has not [previously] purified himself in the manner of a purification fit for a god, then punishment will be inflicted on him on account of it – grievously!' Being either ritually clean or plain foolhardy enter the room, turning immediately to look back at the northern interior of the door frame (fig. 25B:2).

The series of vignettes in Idu's funerary rituals are more 'lively' than Qar's. Viewed in the following order the separate stages for the whole burial rite link together into a panorama of extrovert grief and ceremonial. Assume that the building represented by a doorway in the lower right panel is the villa of Idu. Above, six female mourners attempt to outdo each other in displays of lamentation for Idu's death – two are on their knees, one is collapsing and another tugs violently at her hair. The inscription tells that these are Idu's *meret* serfs weeping for him. More distraught women are shown above where their grief is epitomized in the hieroglyphic tag applicable to each mourner 'O my master who was loved!' The iconography conjures up the unearthly high-pitched laments that the vibrating tongues of these women would have screeched out – surely the same flesh-tingling sounds heard at village funerals in modern Egypt. The upper two vignettes illustrate the men's show of grief: lock tugging, brow beating and falling to the ground. The labels here reveal the sense of loss among Idu's retainers: 'O my master, take me to you!' and 'Alas, father who was loved!' Now look down at the lower left panel where the rites continue with Idu's coffin being carried on poles. Above, the river journey is encapsulated into a picture of a boat bearing a shrine below a canopy in which there would have been a statue of Idu for the tomb. At each end stands a 'kite' while an 'embalmer' opens the shrine door. The narrative describes this scene as 'proceeding to the roof of the purification building'; the *ibu* itself takes up the next panel. It is shown as a T-shaped structure with diagonal causeways leading from two entrances to the river or canal. It has been noted that the *ibu* of Idu although humbler in scale, is of a similar design to the roughly contemporary valley temple of Pepi II at south Saqqara. The roof of the *ibu* is crowded with mortuary offerings. In the top panel three men convey, according to the hieroglyphs, the sarcophagus to the *per-wabet* where Idu's corpse is mummified. This structure is represented on the top right corner of the door frame where you can see a pavilion surmounted by a *kheker* frieze, which has a recessed doorway approached by a portico supported by a papyriform column – all architectural elements which we saw as three-dimensional embryos in Djoser's Step Pyramid complex. Following the embalming process the sarcophagus is dragged, under the watchful eye of the lector-priest, from the *per-wabet* by six men and two oxen. One man pours liquid in front of the sledge to smooth its journey to the tomb here at Giza.

Against the east wall (fig. 25B:3) are six rock-cut standing statues. The northernmost, half the height of the others, represents a naked boy. From the four horizontal lines of hieroglyphs above him it is apparent that this is Idu's son Qar, already a holder of minor offices. The five statues of Idu himself show him as a wigged courtier and an interesting detail survives in the form of the bead tassels painted down the front of his kilt. At the southern end of this wall are some panels depicting men transporting a goat, calves, and geese on papyrus skiffs. On to the south wall (fig. 25B:4) to view with Idu the games and dances performed before him. Looking at Idu himself as he sits in a palanquin, his knees drawn up in front, there is the bizarre impression that he has four arms. The ancient senior sculptors have recarved his hands, arms and legs as corrections of their apprentices' work, hoping that the painters would hide the original mistakes: *ars celare artem*. The scenes before him are full of vivacity. At the top boys play the kind of games which Idu himself must have enjoyed when he was young. Four boys are in an enclosure, one of them acting as a prisoner lying on the ground. The other three address a fifth boy, standing outside the boundary, with the words 'Rescue your one from them, my companion', to which he replies 'I will save you'. Obviously a tug-of-war over the 'prisoner' then ensued. Next, two boys in long pigtails wrestle while two others wearing headbands decorated with lotus blossoms oppose each other with short sticks. These latter boys are labelled as Idu's sons Hemi and Qar. Less violently, though just as energetically, the girls in the register below led by his daughter Bendjet raise their arms over their heads in a dance honouring the goddess Hathor. Below them two pairs of men play the game known as *senet* which entails moving counters along squares on a rectangular board with divisions indicating in places an advantage or a hazard. Two people in the centre are playing *mehen* or 'serpent' where a circular board is carved to represent a coiled snake so that the first one to reach its head in the middle is the winner. At the front of the harpists in the register of musicians below are Idu's daughters Iry and Nebet. The damaged lower portion of this wall included life in the kitchens of Idu's villa.

On the west wall, beyond the scene of Idu seated before huge quantities of offerings with his wife Mertiotes kneeling beside him, is the false door (fig. 25B:5), painted to imitate red granite, a more durable stone than the desert rock. Within the niche of the false door is a quite remarkable statue of Idu – from his head to midriff only. He appears to be rising from the ground with his hands outstretched to receive offerings – the sculptural embodiment of the Ancient Egyptian phobia of losing contact with the world of the living. Flanking the false door are representations of jars which contained the seven crucial oils used in the funerary ritual. From top to bottom these unguents are named as:

1 *setjy-hab*   5 *twawet*
2 *heknu*   6 *hatet-net-ash*
3 *sefetj*   7 *hatet-net-Tehenu*
4 *nekhnem*

Beyond the false door at the northern end of the west wall (fig. 25B:6) master sculptors have left the finest representations of the faces of Idu and his wife Mertiotes before a table of loaves and food commodities spread on mats – among which note the expert rendering of the duck with the wrung neck, worthy of inclusion in any 'still life' exhibition. The titles over Idu's head link him with the priesthoods of the pyramids of Khufu and Rakhaef like his father Qar. Leaving his tomb chapel it is possible to feel that here on the west wall was a spot to which Idu would come when supervizing the work on his funerary complex and breathe a sigh of satisfaction as he watched the artists spelling out in hieroglyphs the commodities for his afterlife in the 101 compartments of his 'cupboard'.

CHAPTER 8

PASSING THE ZENITH

The Pyramid of Radj-edef at Abu Roash

Crossing the Giza plateau in a south-westerly direction from Khufu's pyramid (past the restored façade of the tomb of Seshemnefer, a courtier of Dynasty VI, displaying columns and two seated statues) reflect upon the funerary monument of his immediate successor, Radjedef (*54*). After he had completed the burial of Khufu in 2528 BC, the Giza necropolis was deserted by stonemasons and haulage gangs for about eight years. For reasons possibly to do with the proximity of the temple of the sun-god Ra at Heliopolis, diagonally opposite on the eastern apex of the Nile Delta, Radjedef chose to raise the pyramid near the modern village of Abu Roash about 8km north of Giza. The location was on an imposing escarpment of the Western Desert. All pharaonic sites possess an atmosphere often echoing in tones of melancholy to modern ears the grandeur or pride of their ancient builders. At Abu Roash the echoes are faint but intriguing. Radjedef's pyramid is totally dilapidated, making any reconstruction of its original dimensions hypothetical – over 100 metres square and rising at the unusually steep angle of 60° (*55*). A few courses of its granite casing-blocks remain on the eastern side which, since they would be positioned probably only in the later stages of construction, are a strong hint that Radjedef's pyramid was not far off completion at the time of his death. However, the superstructure of the pyramid has been quarried away leaving exposed the burial chamber and its sloping access corridor both robbed of their inner wall linings. The pillaging of the pyramid's limestone blocks continued right into modern times – allegedly in the late nineteenth century AD camels laden with stone left the site at the rate of three hundred every day. What is not entirely sure is if as long ago as Dynasty IV a pharaoh began the deliberate dismantling of this pyramid as an act of revenge for Radjedef's usurpation of the throne. Perhaps it becomes more likely if the same seemingly vengeful pharaonic hand is seen to have smashed around twenty statues of Radjedef set up at Abu Roash and threw the fragments into the 35-metre-long empty boat pit to the east of the pyramid, where they lay until their discovery among the débris in 1900 by the French archeologist Chassinet. In owning the head from one of these shattered statues in red quartzite, the Louvre Museum possesses the finest representation of Radjedef to survive. From under his royal headcloth surmounted by the protective Cobra goddess, the pharaoh wears an unfathomable expression that breaks through the sculptor's idealization of his features: from the long mouth there comes a sense of austerity, from the eyes and brows sadness or regret.

The Pyramid of King Rakhaef

On gaining the throne in 2520 BC Rakhaef chose the traditional site of Giza to build his pyramid. Within the twenty-five years of his reign a monument was raised, the dimensions of which create a worthy runner-up in the magnitude stakes to the Great Pyramid itself. This pyramid (fig. 20:5), called 'Rakhaef is great' in Ancient Egyptian inscriptions, covered an area approximately 215 metres square and, rising at an angle of just over 53°, reached a height of 143 metres (56). The ridges to the north and west of the pyramid are evidence of the strenuous preliminary rock-cutting operation necessary to scrape the eastward-sloping plateau into a surface level enough to support a monument weighing around five million tons. Surviving on the apex of the pyramid are roughly 40 metres of top-grade Tura limestone, its gleaming whiteness now weathered to a beige hue. Below, the pyramid's faces, robbed of their outer layers, are revealed as victims of the stone pillaging begun during the rule of Sultan Hassan in the fourteenth century A.D. The blocks of the superstructure thus exposed are seen to fit together less precisely than those of Khufu's pyramid, with broad gaps between the vertical joints. Nevertheless, such carping fades into insignificance when we look at some of the enormous local limestone blocks 2 metres high which go to make up the pyramid's sturdy inner lining that envelopes its desert-rock core. The lowest course of stone is also an original outer layer consisting of red granite to give a solid support to the limestone mantle – a feature which caught the eye of Herodotus who described this foundation casing as 'mottled stone of Ethiopia'.

The visit to the internal apartments of Rakhaef's pyramid begins on the north side, where you enter by one route to the sarcophagus chamber and exit by another. What, then, was the reason for two entrances? The most probable explanation is that the lower entrance and corridor formed elements of an earlier plan for the pyramid when it would have been sited about 60 metres further north. When this plan was abandoned the subterranean construction work was already well advanced and so the architect incorporated it into the new scheme. This meant that the earlier burial crypt (originally designed to be at the hub of the monument) now became anomolously situated well away from the central core of the structure, while its connecting corridor was shortened and brought up to an opening a few metres north of the pyramid (fig. 26:1) where it was covered over by the paving stones of the courtyard. You can enter the pyramid by this lower access, stooping along a rock-hewn corridor which slopes at an angle of about 22°. Where there once stood a granite portcullis (fig. 26:2) the gradient changes to a horizontal level and you are able to walk upright to the sloping passage off the western wall, which gives access to the original burial chamber (fig. 26:3). Its measurements are roughly 10 metres long, 3 metres wide and a modest 2.6 metres high. No longer destined to house a royal occupant, it had been utilized by workmen as a storeroom for limestone blocks intended to seal off the access corridor after the pharaoh's death. Continuing into an ascending passage which has been coated with limestone mortar you soon emerge into the 60-metre-long corridor leading to Rakhaef's final burial chamber.

The burial crypt is marginally off-centre, being just over 1 metre to the east of the pyramid's north-south axis. Its plastered rock-hewn walls stretch approximately 14 metres east to west but only just under 5 metres from north to south. The roofing consists of limestone slabs slanted to a pointed gable nearly 7 metres above the floor. The architect intended shafts to reach from the burial chamber to the outer surfaces of the pyramid along the lines of those discussed above in the king's chamber of the Great Pyramid. Here, however, the project was shelved when the rectangular penetrations visible at the top of the north and south walls had got no further than about 30cm into the superstructure. The small cavity in the floor against the south wall was cut to receive the casket containing Rakhaef's internal organs removed during mummification. The granite sarcophagus inserted up to its lid level in the floor beside the west wall contained only cattle bones when Giovanni Battista Belzoni, the first European to enter the pyramid, looked inside it in 1818. Rakhaef's body must have been destroyed by the robbers who pulled the sliding lid from the undercut grooves of the sarcophagus in their search for treasure during the disruptive years following the end of the Old Kingdom.

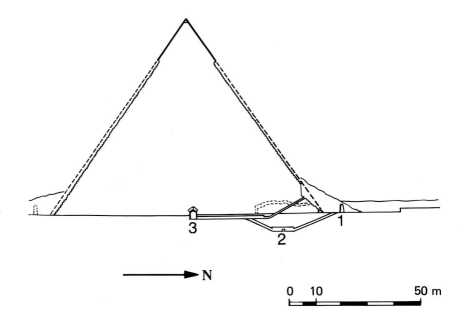

26. Cross section of the Pyramid of Rakhaef

1 Lower entrance
2 Original granite portcullis
3 Burial chamber

N

0   10   50 m

Retracing your steps from the burial crypt along the horizontal corridor you can now follow the route used by Belzoni – in his time the lower passage was concealed, blocked by stone slabs both here where you cross the junction of the corridors, and outside at the courtyard entrance (fig. 26). Glancing up at the limestone ceiling you can observe the breach made by the ancient looters who, as the diagram indicates, preferred to circumvent the granite of the ascending corridor and hack through the softer limestone blocks. The ascent passage is well lined in red granite along its 37-metre length. A granite portcullis, fixed at the lower end, was still in position 20cm from the ground when the indefatigable Belzoni, a giant of a man, met it and raised the slab sufficiently to slide under. The corridor takes us out of the pyramid to descend about 11 metres of its superstructure to ground level.

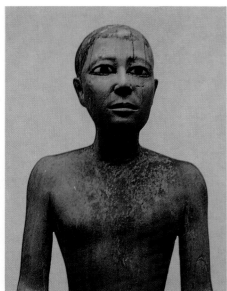

50. *Estate Administrator Metjetjy (detail), Dynasty V/VI, ?Saqqara. Wood, stone, metal, gesso, paint, 61.5 cm high. The Brooklyn Museum, 51.1. Charles Edwin Wilbour Fund*

51. *(below) A painted limestone scribe with rock-crystal eyes sits cross-legged in order to write, Dynasty IV, Cairo Museum*

In front of the eastern slope of Rakhaef's pyramid are the ruins of his massive mortuary temple (112 metres long by 48 metres wide) built upon a desert spur (57). Its foundations exude a sophistication in the design of an edifice for pharaonic funerary rituals beyond that exhibited by any of its forerunners at Meidum and Dahshur, or by Khufu's to the northeast of here. Scramble onto one of the higher blocks of the immense limestone nucleus of this monument to get an idea of its complexity and, referring to its ground plan (fig. 20:5), take an imaginary stroll through it in its pristine condition around 4,500 years ago. From its eastern end you approach a building, the outside walls of which mirror the bitonal scheme of Rakhaef's pyramid in that over an inner core of limestone of the local variety is a casing of bright Tura limestone resting upon a course of red granite at the base. Immediately inside you find a transverse cluster of chambers embued with the symbolism involved in the royal mortuary cult as represented by traditions deriving from two ancient Delta residences. To the south are two alcoves likely to have been for the celebration of the rite of the crowns of Saïs whereas the four niches to the north suited the ritual of Pe (Buto), commemorating the embalmed viscera of the pharaoh. Beyond these four shrines a staircase would have taken you onto the roof of the mortuary temple.

Next you enter a wide hall where fourteen rectangular monoliths of granite supported the roof. You would perhaps ascertain the purpose of the two long rooms leading off the north and south ends of the hall – were they for royal statues or the day and night boats of the sun god? Proceeding westwards you come into a longitudinal hall with five granite columns on each side of the central aisle. From here (in pharaonic times) it all depended on your status whether you had the option of seeing much more of the temple or not. Maintenance staff, such as repair masons working in Rakhaef's pyramid enclosure, and guards, would bear right around the outside of the colonnade, then go up the ramp to exit from the mortuary temple in the northwest corner. The priestly hierarchy conducting processions and rituals could of course cross the spacious open court paved with calcite where twelve statues of Rakhaef abutted onto the granite piers of the surrounding cloister. Five shrines off the western cloister each contained a statue of the pharaoh, probably symbolizing one of the five 'great names' which he had taken upon his coronation. South of these niches you follow a corridor turning at right angles to bring you to five storage alcoves for provisions for the royal cult. A passage south of these magazines can lead you outside by a discreet doorway possibly for use only by the higher echelons of the priesthood responsible for leaving offerings for Rakhaef in front of the granite stela, now shattered but originally dominating the recess in the mortuary temple's rear wall.

52. (opposite above) Princess Nefretiabet in priestess leopard-skin robe, depicted on her funerary slab, Dynasty IV, Giza, Louvre

53. (opposite below) The line-up of royal ladies in the tomb of Meresankh III, Dynasty IV, Giza

Rakhaef's architect incorporated into his plan of the pyramid complex
a natural ridge of desert rock sloping eastwards from the mortuary
temple. This served as the foundation for the ceremonial causeway
leading from the king's temple on the edge of the plateau. The
causeway's superstructure – for certainly there was not just a pavement
open to public view – has been quarried away, and the scene nowadays
reflects more the ridge's use for dragging casing-blocks of Tura
limestone to the pyramid than a processional link between the pharaoh's
funerary monument and the outside world.

Linked to the pyramid by the causeway is the valley temple (fig. 20:7)
of Rakhaef which is best first approached from the east. Its 50-metre
wide façade stands only just clear of the modern tourist assembly point
for the Giza *Son-et-Lumière* show. Visible on an upright red granite
monolith of the northern entrance is a carving of an unguent vase which
serves as the predominant hieroglyph in the name of the Delta goddess
Bastet, a deity more of a lioness in this era than a cat, and symbolic of
pharaonic prowess. The southern gateway was placed under the protection of Hathor, guardian cow-goddess of Upper Egypt. The craggy
higher level of the temple reveals that the inner core of the wall is of local
limestone. Inside, walking through the eastern vestibule of the temple,
you pass a grilled pit, the floor of which usually displays a scattering of
low-denomination coins tossed onto it by wish-making visitors. Its
archeological importance lies in the fact that the majestic diorite statue of
Rakhaef, seated on the throne of Egypt, his head protected by the wings
of Horus the hawk god, which today graces Cairo Museum, was
removed from its original position further west in this temple and
hidden here to prevent its destruction in times of upheaval after the end
of the pyramid era.

On paving stones of alabaster you proceed to the inner reception hall
with six square-shafted columns of granite (58). There used to be in
Rakhaef's time six statues along the western side, of which only the
floor-markings remain. To the south is a murky aperture that leads to
two superimposed tiers of three dead-end corridors, clearly important
since they were lined with alabaster and granite. The main longitudinal
hall has two colonnades each of five granite monoliths. There are clear
emplacements for seven statues on each side of the hall; also for three at
the terminal western end where the diorite statue of Rakhaef found in
the pit, peerless in its assertion of divine kingship, had pride of place in
the centre. Looking at the temple walls you will realize immediately that
this is one of the architectural masterpieces of the Old Kingdom in the
precision of the fitting together of the granite blocks, in an age when only
copper chisels and pounders of hardstone were the masons' tools. The
roof, not accessible and difficult to inspect from ground level, rises in
three stages towards the east and is the only extant example of a valley
temple covering, complete with drainage gutters and cavities likely to
have contained plants or small trees.

The austere architecture of this monument belies the complex
symbolism behind it. It could represent the Purification Pavilion and
House of Embalmment – perhaps in a ritual sense rather than being the
actual location of the mummification procedures. Before burial in the

pyramid Rakhaef's coffin might have rested in the main hall for final ceremonies to be performed over it, while in order to fulfil the ancient Delta rites the four jars containing the royal viscera and the two crowns of Saïs lay in the southern superimposed corridors. Possibly the twenty-three statues of Rakhaef are to be regarded as visual embodiments of ritual 'utterances' carved inside pyramids from the end of Dynasty V onwards. Thus in a passage designed to assist the pharaoh's ascent into the sky, gods and goddesses identified with twenty-six parts of his body are invoked – Wepwawet, a wolf-like deity, is the king's face; Nut the sky goddess is his belly and Apis, sacred bull of Memphis, is the royal phallus. The discrepancy between the twenty-three known statues and the twenty-six bodily parts can be explained because three statues each represented two closely-allied members of the body in the textual list, such as the thighs and the calves of the legs, the hands and the fingers or the soles of the feet and the toes. (For the full tabulation of deities and connected parts of the king's body, see R. O. Faulkner, *The Ancient Egyptian Pyramid Texts*, p. 206, utterance 539.) But I believe that the valley temple of Rakhaef is above all a positive, architectural emblem of the pharaoh's transcendence of death, to remain a life force, and that the structure is full of symbolism beyond embalming or purification rituals, or serving as a vehicle for priestly incantations to identify the royal physique with tutelary deities.

I owe my standpoint here to the Russian Egyptologist, Vikentiev, who put forward the basic argument (in an article in *Le Bulletin de l'Institut d'Egypte*, 1964) for the following interpretation of the monument. The funerary aspect of the temple can be restricted to two features. Firstly, the six southern superimposed corridors off the reception hall reflect the earthly life of the king in terms of the three completed seasons of each year of his reign, doubled to preserve the concept of the two original separate kingdoms of the north and south. Secondly, from the northern end of the reception hall a narrow corridor ascends to the western exit leading to the causeway. Leading off this corridor is a ramp which, turning twice at right angles, eventually emerges into the corridor again, and despite this physical break, crosses it directly by implication to the doorway opposite and ends in a small chamber of red granite and alabaster. Postulated elsewhere as a guard's post or a storage room, this chamber is as plausibly explicable as a symbolic sarcophagus crypt – a reminder of Rakhaef's existence in the pyramid itself. The constructional elements proclaim the indestructibility of the living Rakhaef, free to move at will beyond the confines of his pyramid.

In the reception hall the six statue emplacements divide into northern and southern triads where in each case a central sculpture of Rakhaef as 'Lord of the Two Lands' is flanked by guardian goddesses – Bastet (lioness-cat) and Wadjet (cobra) for Lower Egypt, Hathor (cow) and Nekhbet (vulture) for Upper Egypt. The main hall held seventeen statues which represented the Egyptian year as a continuing phenomenon for Rakhaef, twelve statues for the three seasons of four 30-day months each and five statues for the epagomenal days (*see* p. 87). The centre aisle of the main hall symbolizes the primordial mound emerging from the watery abyss at the beginning of Time, and upon which the sun

god stood to begin the creation of the universe. The flanking ten granite
pillars intensify this underlying cosmogonic theme by representing the
sun-creator under two forms at the head of his pantheon:

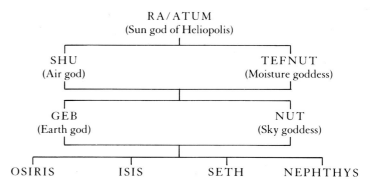

The last four deities are the dramatis personae in the legend concerned
with the transmission of the throne of Egypt to Horus (the son of Isis
and Osiris, embodied in the pharaoh). The sculptural link between the
hawk-god Horus and Rakhaef, stressed in the diorite statue found in the
vestibule (59) leaves no doubt in my mind that the architecture of this
valley temple was designed under precisely the same motivation – to
magnify the pharaoh's inheritance from the primaeval cosmic deities,
and to reinforce his endless jurisdiction over a prosperous Egypt
symbolized by the cycle of its seasons.

The Great Sphinx

From the western exit of the valley temple you emerge onto the ridge
marking Rakhaef's causeway to survey the Great Sphinx, undeniably the
colossal mascot of pharaonic Egypt (60). For over 4,500 years it has gazed
east towards the rising sun, though its view has never before encompas-
sed so much secular clutter – gaudy salesrooms, a myriad of camera
lenses and the camp-followers of Mammon. Yet the Sphinx commands
attention due solely to a weathered majesty on its face: its body today is a
tessellated disaster. The inescapable sight, from the modern road, of the
back of its head suggests a gigantic phallic mushroom. Lacking a mantle
of sand under which to hide its time-ravaged torso, the Sphinx is robbed
of that enigma and mystique that irrefutably emanates from paintings or
photographs of it from up to 1925, when it still lay buried in the desert
as high as its neck.

It is necessary to return to Old Kingdom Egypt to discover the origins
of the world's most famous hybrid. In the reign of Rakhaef a crag of
limestone too friable to be cut into building blocks was left isolated in the
quarry here on the eastern escarpment. It must have formed an irregular
obscuring silhouette against the causeway and valley temple. Gone
forever is the name of the person who had the imagination to change this
mass of jutting rock into an architectural enrichment of the pharaoh's
pyramid complex. Clearly the length of the crag was not too unlike the
recumbent body of a lion. In the royal iconographical repertoire there
existed (at least from the time of Radjedef) a symbol consisting of
leonine and human features intended to stress the bond between pharaoh

and sun god, and to proclaim kingly might. The lion was a creature manifesting Ra the sun god of Heliopolis and, if we go by the inscriptional evidence of Dynasty V onwards, the living pharaoh was the 'son of Ra'. Furthermore, in the afterlife the king could even 'claim the horizon' as if he were the sun god himself. Hence the royal head could be superimposed onto the leonine body to assert this link with startling visual impact. The combination also stands for the invincibility of the monarch through symbolism that goes back to the late predynastic era. Battle scenes carved on slate palettes show the ruler of Upper Egypt conquering his enemies as a lion or a wild bull. Thus no hostile force could approach Rakhaef's pyramid without being torn to pieces by the Sphinx guarding the approach.

The Sphinx (a Greek word, incidentally, which might well derive from an Ancient Egyptian phrase meaning 'living image') is approximately 57 metres long and 20 metres high. It stood taller in antiquity when it sported a plumed crown that fitted into a socket (now filled in) on the top of the striped royal headcloth. Wadjet the protective cobra goddess, or Uraeus, survives in part on the king's forehead, but the nose is missing from the battered visage, destroyed early in the fifteenth century AD by a member of a Sufi sect as a protest against idolatry (61). Fragments of the Sphinx's granite plaited beard were found in the earliest excavations made below the chin of this monument, where they had fallen in pharaonic times (62). Stelae from the New Kingdom show the beard on the Sphinx as well as a striding statue of a king against its chest which has now worn to an amorphous knoll. The soft limestone rock carved into the paws, flanks and tail-end of the Sphinx began to crumble before the eroding winds of the Giza plateau. So not later than the Ptolemaic era repairs took the form of constructing a leo-morphic 'body-stocking' of stone blocks, thereby severely crippling the original awesome image of the Sphinx at one with the raw rock.

In the centuries following the pyramid era the desert sands drifted across the torso of the Sphinx, leaving only its head visible. Also, in a theological development, the Sphinx became interpreted unequivocally as the sun god under his form of 'Horemakhet', meaning 'Horus in the horizon'. So with eyes fixed on the red granite 'Dream stela' between the front paws of the Sphinx the story can be taken up at about 1400 BC. Prince Djehutymes (also known by the 'Graecized' version as Tuthmosis; he was not *known* to the Greeks) rested after a morning's hunting in the shade proffered by the head of the Sphinx. In his sleep he dreamt that the god Horemakhet complained of being almost smothered by sand and promised Djehutymes a coronation as the next pharaoh if the prince freed him from the grip of the desert. (Is it possible, in passing, to assume by this promise a dispute over the succession to the throne?) So the prince, on waking, vowed to carry out Horemakhet's wish, and his word was sufficient surety for the Sphinx. Thus the first recorded clearance of the Sphinx from the sand can be dated to the years following the accession of this prince to the throne as Menkheperura Djehutymes IV (1401–1391 BC). On the top of the stela commemorating this early archeological 'rescue-dig' the pharaoh is depicted twice in the act of offering to Horemakhet as a Sphinx.

To the east of the Sphinx beyond the stairway constructed in the Roman epoch lie the ruins of the Temple of Horemakhet (fig. 20:6), possibly originally a sun temple built in the reign of Rakhaef. At its northwest corner New Kingdom pharaohs raised a second temple to Horemakhet combined with a Canaanite deity, Haurun. In its inner hall the father of Djehutymes IV, Amenhotpe II (1427–1401 BC) set up a colossal limestone stela, of which only the ugly modern protective casing of wood is open to view. However, from the twenty-seven lines of its inscription extolling his prowess as an archer and horse-rider we again get a picture of the Giza plateau as an attractive location for princes. Amenhotpe II rode here before becoming king and explored the regions around the pyramids of Khufu and Rakhaef and the Sphinx. When crowned pharaoh he remembered these pleasures of Giza and erected this stela on which he describes himself as 'Akheperura, beloved of Horemakhet'.

The Pyramid of King Menkaura

Southwest of the Great Sphinx lies the funerary complex of King Menkaura (63) whose pyramid (fig. 20:8) stands dwarfed by its two northerly predecessors called 'god-worthy' in Ancient Egyptian inscriptions. The reduced dimensions of this pyramid are about 108 metres square and rise at an angle of just over 51° to an original height of nearly 66 metres. The eighteen years of Menkaura's reign from his accession to the throne in 2490 BC were evidently not sufficient for him to complete his pyramid or its ancillary monuments. This is surprising when it is remembered that the workforce of Khufu was above his sarcophagus chamber in the much greater superstructure of that pyramid by year 17 of his reign. Also, why did Menkaura's original plan envisage a pyramid of even smaller measurements than the monument at which you look today? Possibly this is the period of the protracted dynastic intrigue between Menkaura and the descendants of Radjedef, or else perhaps building operations were curtailed for a time through economic distress as a result of poor harvests. Certainly this pygmy pyramid puzzled some early Greek visitors to Giza, since it was so out of keeping with the scale of its neighbours. They felt constrained to attribute its construction to the wealthy and illustrious courtesan Rhodopis who lived inside the Greek city of Naukratis in the Nile Delta. Herodotus rightly refutes this tale on chronological grounds. Rhodopis, originally a slave-girl in Egypt who had charmed Kharaxos, brother of the poetess Sappho of Lesbos, into purchasing her freedom, won her renown nearly two thousand years after the death of Menkaura.

Approaching the pyramid (64), consider for a moment Herodotus' narrative of the misfortunes of Menkaura's reign. Apparently his humanity was his downfall. In contrast to the alleged cruelty of Khufu, the rule of Menkaura saw a reopening of temples and a restitution of rights to religious devotion and to the law. But the benign kingship of Menkaura flouted an edict of the gods that had insisted on Egypt suffering unmitigated woes for 150 years. Khufu and Rakhaef had complied with the divine command but Menkaura was guilty of disobedience. Consequently, from the oracle at Buto he learned the merciless decision of the gods that he would die after a reign of a mere six years. This brief span of power probably satisfied Herodotus concerning the lesser dimension of his pyramid. Even more so since Menkaura, on learning his fate, became totally obsessed with living life to the full and spending his days in pleasurable excursions – with no mention of any pressing concern for his pyramid – and staying up all night by lamplight carousing so that his allotted six years would double into twelve.

The northern face of the pyramid has been severely ravaged by the mania to penetrate into the superstructure in hope of finding a 'treasure chamber'. As the diagram indicates (fig. 27:1), from the gouged-out stretch a tunnel was forced through the pyramid, only to reach the fruitless desert bedrock. Contemplating the exterior of the pyramid there is tangible evidence that granite casing-blocks reached at least sixteen courses higher – Herodotus writes that half the pyramid was encased in 'Ethiopian stone', i.e. granite from the quarries at Aswan. The majority of these blocks are in the rough state they arrived in from the quarry, but those around the entrance on the north side have been smoothed – a process which Menkaura's successor deemed too time-consuming to complete. The upper reaches of the pyramid superstructure would have been in dressed Tura limestone. Thus, although Menkaura's monument did not dominate the Giza plateau in terms of size, it would have presented an attractive appearance with the contrasting colour of the white limestone and red granite. One is struck once again, as in the case of the Bent Pyramid of Dahshur, by the pervading dualism of Egyptian symbols. For in Menkaura's pyramid more than in any other, the line of the colour change would be higher and more emphatic, stressing his role as 'Lord of the Two Lands' by the very casing-blocks of his funerary monument.

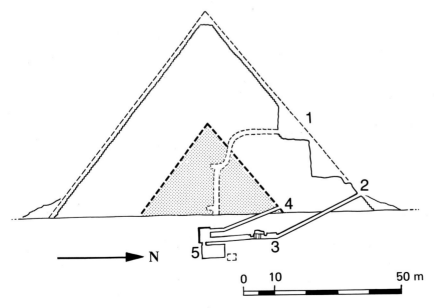

27. Cross section of the Pyramid of Menkaura

1 Gouge into superstructure
2 Northern entrance
3 Vestibule
4 Original entrance from pyramid stage 1

54. (opposite above) Head of
Radjedef in red quartzite,
Dynasty IV, Abu Roash, Louvre

55. (opposite below) The
approach to Radjedef's pyramid
at Abu Roash shows little but
the stump of natural rock used as
its base, with remains of nobles'
tombs in front. On the other side
the view is down to a deep chasm
which formed the inner passage,
now exposed to the open,
Dynasty IV

About four metres above ground level on the northern face is the entrance to the pyramid (fig. 27:2). The descending passage is roofed with granite slabs up to the point at which it meets the desert plateau, whence it continues to slope until levelling into a vestibule (fig. 27:3) with panelled walls. Ahead, in antiquity, three portcullises sealed off the approach into the original burial chamber. It was here that the remains of an intrusive burial dating from the Saïte period (or earlier) were discovered, including the wooden fragments of a coffin, inscribed with the cartouche of the long-dead Menkaura – an ancient forgery now in the possession of the British Museum. From this chamber a tunnel reached up into the outer casing of the pyramid of the first architectural plan to form the entrance-passage (fig. 27:4). This route now ends buried in the mass of superstructure masonry just above bedrock level. As can be seen, the stage I pyramid was positively miniscule in conception. The change in plan for the monument turned this chamber into a reception hall, from the western end of which a passage leads into the final sepulchre of Menkaura, splendidly walled and roofed in red granite (fig. 27:5). The vaulted ceiling of this chamber has been carved from rectangular roofing-slabs which were arranged in the first instance to form an apex. A finely-cut basalt lidless sarcophagus, uninscribed, but with its sides carved with the palace-façade motif was recorded in this chamber and drawn at the time of its discovery. Now these drawings are the only solace, for in 1838, while being transported to England, Menkaura's sarcophagus sank with the merchant ship it was in to the bottom of the Mediterranean sea. Re-entering the passage you can explore the chamber reached via a flight of steps off to the left. Carved out of the desert bedrock, there are four deep cells along its east side and two niches on the north. Without a doubt you are in the room designed to hold the valued regalia of Menkaura – the crowns of Upper and Lower Egypt – and the four cult symbols of his embalmed viscera. These six cavities, devoid of their riches, are poignantly eloquent reminders of the hopelessness of all attempts by the monarchs buried at Giza to travel with their earthly accoutrements into eternity.

The ruins of Menkaura's mortuary temple indicate the king planned a monument in limestone and granite. His successor, Shepseskaf, completed it in mudbrick, thereby fulfilling the letter of the Ancient Egyptian concept of filial piety, if not the spirit. But perhaps the political climate did not permit him to be too lavish with Menkaura's funerary complex. Possibly power and resources were already beginning to be diverted to Radjedef's line, future founders of a new dynasty. Anyway, Shepseskaf's intentions appear dutiful from the fragments of a decree found in the mortuary temple protecting the upkeep of Menkaura's pyramid. To the south of the main pyramid are three subsidiary ones – all roughly 10 metres high and 36 metres square, and all with mudbrick chapels on their eastern sides. It seems logical on the analogy of those east of Khufu's pyramid to presume that these satellite pyramids were for the queens of Menkaura, even though there are some problems of attribution. The most impressive subsidiary pyramid is the one on the east, partly cased in granite and containing a granite sarcophagus. Menkaura's chief queen was Khamerernebti II, eldest daughter of Rakhaef. The

56. (left) The pyramid of Rakhaef, Dynasty IV, Giza

57. (below) Ruins of the mortuary temple against the east face of the pyramid of Rakhaef, Dynasty IV, Giza

58. (opposite) Inner reception hall of the valley temple of Rakhaef's pyramid complex, Dynasty IV, Giza

complicating factor in assigning this pyramid to her is the existence of her rock-cut tomb discovered south of Rakhaef's causeway more or less opposite the rear-end of the Sphinx. That tomb's two halls do not form a striking monument for a king's wife and it seems likely that it was carved early in the reign of Menkaura in the years of uncertainty when, as has been seen, even his own pyramid was being conceived on a lesser scale. With the revival of royal fortunes Khamerernebti II surely abandoned her rock-cut sepulchre in favour of the eastern subsidiary pyramid. A look at the genealogical tree (fig. 22) shows two important but anonymous queens of Menkaura, mothers of Shepseskaf and Khentkawes. Regrettably no definite archeological proof can be offered for the neat assignation of the two other small pyramids to them. The central satellite pyramid contained a smaller granite sarcophagus, and the human remains suggest a fairly young queen was buried here, while no trace of a burial was discovered in the western one.

It is possible to survey the contours of the desert eastward from the mortuary temple of Menkaura. Excavation has shown that his causeway was a 660-metre-long stone embankment with mudbrick walls and a roof of palm logs. It joined a corridor leading into Menkaura's valley temple (fig. 20:9) now returned under the sand. There were pavements and columns of stone, but again on the death of Menkaura his successor finished the superstructure in mudbrick. A decree of Pepi II found in the ruins proves that at the end of the pyramid age there was still a small town in the vicinity of the valley temple dedicated to the cult of Menkaura. From the western end of this temple come some of the finest royal statues to survive from Ancient Egypt, now on display in Boston and Cairo Museums. Four slate triads in Cairo Museum each depict Menkaura and the goddess Hathor 'mistress of the sycamore' together with a deity representing one of the forty-two nomes (administrative districts) of Egypt (65). Also from here is the slate dyad statue in the Museum of Fine Arts, Boston, still unfinished and uninscribed at the king's death, but nevertheless outstanding in the portrayal of idealized royal features: Menkaura, wearing the *nemes* headcloth strides forward grasping the sceptre shafts in each hand while his queen holds him protectively, perhaps symbolizing her role as royal heiress and 'power behind the throne'. However, the throne of Egypt did not pass to Prince Khuenra, the eldest son of Menkaura and his chief queen Khamerernebti II, doubtless because of his early death. The prince was given a rock-cut tomb in a now sanded-over cemetery just south of Menkaura's causeway. A limestone statue from it in the Museum of Fine Arts, Boston represents Prince Khuenra as a scribe seated cross-legged (one of the earliest examples of this important style of private statuary) and his facial features seem to mingle the slightly bulging eyes of Menkaura with the plump cheeks of Khamerernebti II.

Thus the throne of Egypt was inherited by Shepseskaf, son of Menkaura by an unnamed queen. He chose a new location for his burial and radically changed the style of a pharaoh's funerary monument. But before saying goodbye to Giza, glance at the region just to the northwest of Menkaura's valley temple. Here on a square outcrop of desert rock is a

King Shepseskaf, last of the Dynasty

59. (opposite) Green diorite statue of Rakhaef from the valley temple attached to his pyramid. He is protected by Horus, and the design on the side of his throne symbolizes the unity of Upper and Lower Egypt, Dynasty IV, Giza, Cairo Museum

tomb built of limestone blocks to resemble a royal sarcophagus (67). This unusual funerary structure belonged to Khentkawes, daughter of Menkaura. Her marriage to King Weserkaf, first ruler of Dynasty V, provides the link between the direct descendants of Khufu and the Radjedef branch of the royal family who eventually won control of the throne. Khentkawes bore the title, 'mother of the Two Kings of Upper and Lower Egypt' – referring to Sahura and Neferirkara, whose monuments lie at Abusir. However, for the final throes of Dynasty IV it is necessary briefly to follow Shepseskaf to South Saqqara. In the five years of his reign from 2472 BC Shepseskaf presided over the dwindling fortunes of the main line of the ruling family. This decline is marked by a funerary edifice which is a mere echo of the Giza pyramids in magnitude but similar in style to the monument of Queen Khentkawes. Shepseskaf's tomb (known since its discovery as Mastaba el-Faraoun) represents a huge rectangular sarcophagus on a low base (68). Its dimensions are 100 metres by 72 metres and its height reached 18 metres. Granite was used to line the burial chamber but local limestone constitutes the core of the building. Why did Shepseskaf construct at South Saqqara a modest, atypical funerary complex so far from his predecessor's pyramids at Giza? There has already been a hint of pressure from the ambitious scions of Radjedef's line, perhaps already consolidating resources from the state treasury. One has the feeling Shepseskaf must have known that the impetus behind the raising of the colossal pyramids of his ancestors was now a spent force. It must also have been evident that no son of his would ever wield the royal sceptre, but would in fact be destined to live as a nonentity. So possibly Shepseskaf was content to spend eternity away from court in his sarcophagus tomb, the view to the north dominated by the Step Pyramid of Djoser and bounded at Dahshur on the south by the two monuments of Sneferu, founder of his dynasty. The last line of T. S. Eliot's *The Hollow Men* conjures up just the right atmosphere of petered-out grandeur clinging to the last of Sneferu's descendants: 'Not with a bang but a whimper'.

CHAPTER 9

NOONTIDE: The Ascendancy of Ra

The coronation of Weserkaf as first pharaoh of Dynasty V around 2465 BC inaugurated an era of architectural experiments designed to extol the cult of the sun god. Monuments of this era, whether at Saqqara or at Abusir and Abu Ghurob, resound with the leitmotif of the pre-eminence of Ra of Heliopolis. In terms of rivalling the grandeur of Djoser's funerary complex at Saqqara or the pyramids on the Giza plateau, the current dilapidated superstructures of this dynasty are woefully wanting. Yet the imaginative traveller to these ruins will be rewarded, particularly at the tourist-deserted sites of Abusir and Abu Ghurob. Resources from the royal treasury were now lavished on two categories of building: edifices for the pharaoh's funerary cult, and temples for the god Ra, both on the desert escarpment west of Memphis and on the other bank of the Nile from the sun god's principal sanctuary at Heliopolis. On present archeological and epigraphic evidence most Western Desert solar temples were an innovation of Weserkaf (*see* p. 147), which is one reason why trouble should be taken to visit his burial place, the heap of stones flattered by the term 'pyramid', about 200 metres northeast of the step pyramid at Saqqara.

Crossing the sand mounds to reach the northern side of Weserkaf's pyramid, recall the plausible family link between this king, via Neferhetpes his mother, and Radjedef, son of Khufu (*see* genealogical tree, fig. 22). Ancient Egyptian sources proclaim 'new blood' in a mythological origin for the first three rulers of Dynasty V, making in the process Weserkaf the brother of his two successors rather than their father. This account involves Ra's intervention in Egypt's line of succession and for it we must return to Papyrus Westcar in Berlin Museum, written roughly 800 years after Weserkaf's reign. It can be recalled how in it Prince Hardjedef, son of Khufu, brings the magician called Djedi to his father's court to perform feats of supernatural skill (*see* above p. 103). But it is Djedi's prophecy about future kings which is of most interest at this point. To Khufu's question concerning the number of the secret chambers of the Sanctuary of the god Thoth, Djedi replies that while he does not know the answer he can locate the place where the figure can be found – in a flint-chest in the sun god's temple at Heliopolis. He refuses to bring it to Khufu, saying it will be conveyed by the eldest of the three children yet unborn in the womb of Reweddjedet, wife of a priest of Ra. From his further assertion that they will each be pharaohs and that the eldest will be High Priest of Heliopolis before his accession, we can only believe that the sun god himself is their father. Certainly historically, from Dynasty V onwards, royal protocol names kings of Egypt as 'Sons of Ra'. Khufu, naturally upset, is then assured by Djedi that his own son and grandson will reign (Shepseskaf is ignored as insignificant) before the new rulers take over. The Papyrus goes on to describe how Ra sends the goddesses Isis, Nephthys, Meskhenet and Heket disguised as dancing-girls together with the god Khnum as their porter, to assist Reweddjedet in her labour pangs. They deliver her of three sturdy future kings with limbs covered in gold and headdresses of lapis lazuli: Weserkaf, Sahura and Neferirkara.

*The Pyramid of
King Weserkaf at
Saqqara*

Approaching Weserkaf's pyramid from the north, its ruinous super-structure confronts the eye with the internal core of limestone blocks originally covered with high-quality stone long since laid bare through looting (69). The pyramid's pristine gleaming white mantle would have added some justification to its pharaonic name 'Pure of places'. It has been calculated that, rising at an angle of 53° 7′, the pyramid reached a height of 49 metres with the length of its base-sides stretching over 73 metres. Now the sides are about 63 metres long and the height reduced to 32 metres. Thus Weserkaf's funerary monument, partly built on this location to bask in the repute and grandeur of Djoser's Step Pyramid beyond it, stands dwarfed and humiliated. The other reason for choosing this spot on the Saqqara plateau, where the rise of the eastern escarpment would seem to argue against providing a suitable site for a royal funerary complex, lies in the orientation of the mortuary temple, unusually located to the south of the pyramid.

But first, here on the northern slope, examine the ancient way into Weserkaf's sepulchre. The architect's entrance situated at ground level just beyond the end of the original casing gave onto a corridor cut diagonally through the bedrock for nearly 24 metres before becoming horizontal. The passage-way lined with granite has one L-shaped chamber off its eastern side before reaching the two-roomed sepulchral quarters where a basalt sarcophagus presumably once held the body of Weserkaf. The robbers who violated the burial chamber, destroying the king's corpse and escaping with his jewellery and valuable funerary equipment, gouged their way into the pyramid through the gaping tear in its side now before you. They cut their way through the limestone and past a massive plug of granite in the corridor to reach the sarcophagus chamber. However, since access to the interior apartments of Weserkaf's pyramid is physically barred to tourists you can only scramble round to the eastern side. Excavation revealed a small limestone offering chapel here but not a full-scale mortuary temple like those against the eastern slopes of the pyramids of Giza.

A practical consideration, as mentioned above, would have been the levelling of the steep terrain to the east. But if Weserkaf had really wished to keep the traditional pattern of the Giza complexes then the problem would have been tackled. So go round to the southern side so as to try to understand the religious symbolism that dictated the lay-out of Weserkaf's mortuary temple. Understanding, incidentally, has not been helped by courtiers of the Saïte era, two thousand years after Weserkaf's reign, who sank 20-metre-deep shaft graves into the already severely quarried temple complex. The visitor's eye surveying the levelled vestiges makes out with certainty only the original basalt flooring of the temple and elements of the square granite monoliths that formed its portico. Cairo Museum now houses the impressive pink granite head of

Weserkaf found in the temple court and originally facing the pyramid
(70): three-times life size, and to date the only example of colossal
statuary (excluding Rakhaef's Sphinx at Giza) to survive from the Old
Kingdom. Also in the museum are fragments of reliefs from the temple
walls showing Weserkaf hunting in the papyrus swamps and superb
representations of bird life like the hoopoe displaying its crest or two
birds locking their heads together.

The plan of the mortuary temple reveals access was from the southeast
corner (at the end of a causeway from the yet unexcavated valley temple)
through the temenos wall into two oblong antechambers. The orientation of the main court, and its colossal statue, together with niches for
smaller cult statues and regalia storerooms, all point northward to the
pyramid itself. At Giza in the comparable temples, architectural features
and statue enclosures faced away from the pyramids east towards the
rising sun and the capital city of Memphis where the Pharaohs had lived
so much of their reigns. Here at Saqqara in Weserkaf's complex,
developing on a different side facing away from the pyramid would have
meant the monument and statues of the king facing the lifeless desert
plateau. Consequently Weserkaf preferred his architect to plan the
temple to focus on the pyramid 'Pure of places' in which he would lay
buried. The choice of the southern side of the pyramid for the mortuary
temple that led to this inverse arrangement seems to be based on the
phenomenon that it would never lie in shadow. The sun would always
be shining from east to west in the southern sky; Weserkaf's monument
would always be bathed in the rays of his father the sun god. That said,
one must admit it is a 'one-off' among the royal mortuary temples of this
dynasty; pharaohs preserve, modify or abandon the architectural formats
of their predecessors at will. Finally, in this area southwest of Weserkaf's
pyramid, within the enclosure and next to the mortuary temple, are the
ruins of the small 'satellite' or 'ritual' pyramid – probably a structure
where the king's spirit (ka) could unite with the sun god. Its corridor and
rectangular chamber were sufficient to admit the royal ka to fulfil the
ceremony of coalescing with Ra, but the internal dimensions of this
pyramid are too reduced for it ever to have contained a sarcophagus. A
little further south outside the temenos wall was a pyramid which once
protected the body of a principal queen of Weserkaf.

*The Sun Temple of
King Weserkaf at Abusir*

The pyramids of Abusir (*see* p. 149) were not in existence when
Weserkaf chose a lonely desert site for his innovative sun temple just to
the northwest of where they were to be raised. Its ruins of mudbrick and
limestone, rendered incomprehensible by the drifting sand, are worth
pausing among if only because of its seniority in the list of six solar
sanctuaries built in this dynasty. Sadly only one other of these, namely
that of Neweserra, is extant. Architecturally, Weserkaf's temple proclaimed the supremacy of Ra; a graffito of a Theban tourist showed it was
still worth a visit a thousand years after its construction. During the
seven years of Weserkaf's rule, his architect established the podium of
the temple but the symbolic primaeval mound (*benben*) in the form of a
squat granite obelisk which stood on it came as a gift of King
Neferirkara two reigns later. The temple was connected by a causeway

leading northeasterly to a valley pavilion where the daily offerings to the sun god, consisting of a minimum of two oxen and two geese, were received by the priests, no doubt eager for the moment when the commodities would revert to them as supper. Here, on the edge of the Nile flood plain, subsoil water prevented full-scale excavation of the pavilion, though one prize for Cairo Museum was the fine schist head of Weserkaf wearing the red crown of the Delta.

The Sun Temple of King Neweserra at Abu Ghurob

On a site known as Abu Ghurob a short distance northwest of Weserkaf's monument are the most prominent remains of the sun temple of King Neweserra (fig. 28). Torn down, quarried and scattered, Neweserra's temple still asserts impressively the obsession with the solar cult by the pharaohs of Dynasty V. A limestone-faced terrace supported the Upper Temple whose dimensions were approximately 80 metres by 110 metres – much more, then, than a token edifice to the sun god.

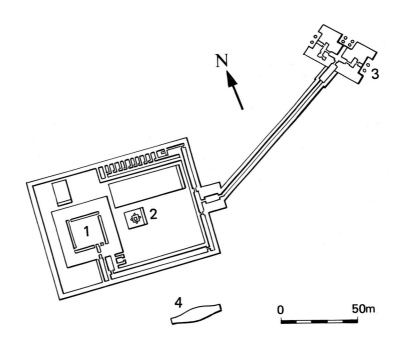

28. Sun Temple of Neweserra, Dynasty V, Abu Ghurob

1 Obelisk podium
2 Sun Altar
3 Valley Temple
4 Boat of Ra

Beyond the east entrance a courtyard had as its focal point an altar of alabaster (fig. 29:2), six metres in diameter, the sides of which were each shaped to represent the hieroglyph of a conical loaf on a papyrus offering-mat. Standing beside it and looking at the solar disc in its centre one realizes the quintessence of the sun cult in Ancient Egypt: gifts laid on a altar open to the sky to be absorbed by the rays of the sun god. Turning your attention westwards to the amorphous stone hillock patched with blown sand, convert it in your mind into the symbol of Ra of Heliopolis (fig. 28:1). It is an architectural rendering of the 'High Sand' or primaeval mound upon which the sun god emerged from watery chaos to create the universe. This motif has, of course, been met in the superstructures of the pyramids. From excavations carried out around 1900 by the Deutsche Orient-Gesellschaft, it is possible to imagine the ruins before us as a sloping-sided base nearly 20 metres high, mantled in polished granite and limestone, terminating in a platform. On this stood a thick-set obelisk built to a probable height of 35 metres of irregular blocks of masonry – a colossal image in stone lauding the procreative omnipotence of Ra and sharply contrasting with the arid desert plateau above which it soared.

Imagination again is required to construct from the extant vestiges a covered corridor connected to the obelisk ramp round the sides of which it penetrates, stretching along the southern side of the temple and turning at a right angle to meet the eastern gateway. From this ambulatory come many fragments of magnificently painted reliefs originally decorating the walls. Illumination of them for the priests on duty was by the occasional rectangular skylight, and by oil lamps too vulnerable to be left at Abu Ghurob. Today the majority of these fragments are to be found in the museums of Berlin and Cairo. Two themes predominate in these masterpieces of Old Kingdom carving: the jubilee festival of Neweserra and the universality of the sun god's creative force. So some reliefs show Neweserra carried in his palanquin or enthroned in a pavilion, with priests and banners in his jubilee procession. However, more interesting reliefs come from where the corridor in its northern approach to the obelisk ramp opened into what is called the 'Room of the Seasons'. A female figure wearing an insignia of a lotus-pool represents the Nile Inundation season while a male with ripened barley on his head personifies Harvest Time. Other figures personify the Nile river, Delta lakes and provinces of Upper and Lower Egypt to indicate the breadth of Ra's domain. The diversity of nature is proclaimed in a panorama of undomesticated animals like gazelles and panthers giving birth. This wildlife documentary also delights us with depictions of pelicans, turtles and hedgehogs.

The northern precinct of this temple contained food storehouses and abattoirs. Large basins of calcite south of the butchering quarters were probably for collecting the blood from the slaughtered oxen. From the eastern gate through the temenos wall a causeway led to a valley pavilion (fig. 28:3) which had three reception porticoes for the processions, or provisions arriving by boat along the link canal to the Nile. You can walk by the oblong ruins south of the temple enclosure which originally were in the shape of a mudbrick boat about 30 metres long (fig. 28:4). It is impossible to escape the sun god, for here was symbolized one of his vessels for sky or underworld sailing.

You need to negotiate the soft inclines of desert sand for about a mile south-easterly to reach the pyramids of Abusir seen silhouetted against the skyline. (Alternatively, it can be more practical to approach the Abusir pyramids travelling by vehicle south from Giza along the road on the western edge of the cultivation and crossing the canal in the vicinity of Sahura's valley temple.)

The Abusir pyramids exude a melancholy that draws you to them to reflect on the vain ambition harboured by the pharaohs who built them for eternal survival in pristine splendour (71). Yet the aggressive ravages

The Pyramids at Abusir of Kings Sahura, Neferirkara, Neferefra and Neweserra

of time and stone-looters, while mocking the monarchs' hopes, excite one to reconstruct mentally the original complexes while scrambling over fragmentary architectural elements. It seems that the predilections and time schedules of most tourists to Cairo permit only excursions north of Abusir to Giza or south to Saqqara, so there are no distractions to concentration in refurbishing the ruins with their pillaged walls and columns. Even so, as long as your feet are on the sands of Abusir it is impossible to avoid the pervading atmosphere of solitary pride and regret, mingled with a dignity that has endured the continual ravages of Man and Time.

29. Pyramids of Abusir, Dynasty V

A
1 Pyramid complex of Sahura
2 Mastaba of Ptahshepses (see B)
3 Pyramid complex of Neweserra
4 Pyramid complex of Nefer-irkara
5 Pyramid of Neferefra

B
1 Entrance
2 Portico with lotiform columns
3 Statue niches
4 Pillared court
5 Entrance to burial chambers with sarcophagi for Ptahshepses and his wife Khamerernebti
6 Naviform-rooms for solar or funerary boats (either actual or symbolic)

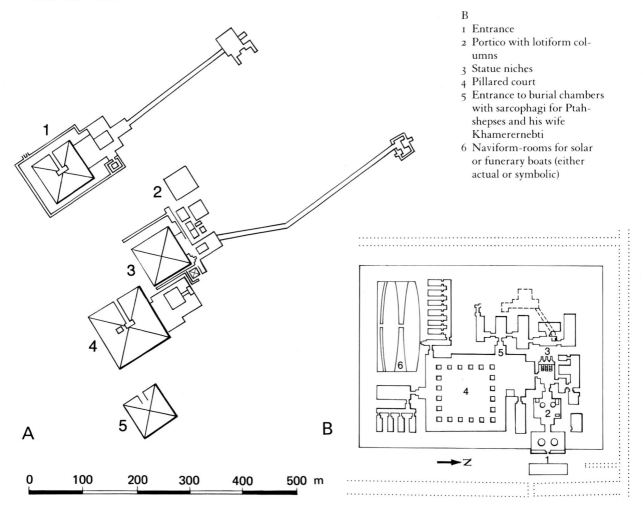

Once King Sahura had completed the funerary niceties for Weserkaf at Saqqara, he decided on a new location for his own pyramid and so began the necropolis in the Western Desert at Abusir (fig. 29A:1). It is his complex you should therefore study at this site first of all (fig. 30). Having shaken off the local persistent children living by the canal that flows along the desert margin, note the mounds of sand patched here and there with reeds that now mark Sahura's reception hall or valley temple

60. The Great Sphinx looks east, guarding the causeway to the pyramid of Rakhaef, Dynasty IV, Giza

(fig. 30:5). Here visiting Egyptian officials were made aware that the king's retainers in the pyramid town were exempt from demands the bureaucracy might wish to make on their time. Fragments of a decree protecting the town were excavated here. The plan of this valley temple reminds us of the now disappeared phenomenon of the Nile Flood; it was constructed on a ramp with porticoed accesses from the east and south. This was to allow for the rising waters presumably, and to avoid the approach to Sahura's upper temple and pyramid becoming waterlogged. The upwardly inclining path to follow from this eastern pavilion is on the line of the 200-metre ancient causeway (fig. 30:4) from which a few fallen wall reliefs survived to show it was once decorated.

61. (opposite) Although battered, the Sphinx's face still shows the majesty of kingship, Dynasty IV, Giza

62. (inset) A fragment of the Great Sphinx's granite beard, possibly a later addition, found in the sand between its paws, British Museum

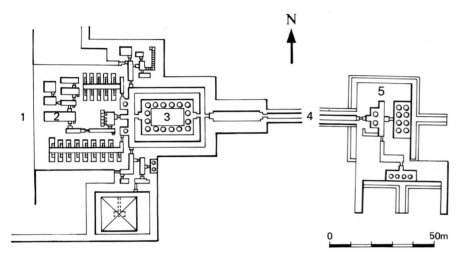

N

0   50m

30. Pyramid Temples of Sahura, Dynasty V, Abusir

1 Pyramid
2 Sanctuary
3 Columned Hall
4 Causeway
5 Valley Temple

Eventually, you stand on the basalt paving stones of the columned hall (fig. 30:3) of the upper temple where the priests gathered to celebrate the royal-offering ceremonies nearly 4,500 years ago (72). Our eyes light upon a fragment of the capital of a red granite column. In this hall columns with capitals imitating palm leaves make their first appearance in Egyptian architecture. Also, now fallen from the upper heights of the temple is a massive ceiling-slab carved with the stars of the sky. Probably the best way to 'absorb' this monument is to climb on an elevation in the western section of the temple. Beyond the columned hall was a transverse vestibule, from where a granite column with a papyriform capital was taken to grace the entrance hall of Cairo Museum. The vestibule led off into an offering area with five niches which, based on a papyrus dating to the next king's reign, we can call 'caverns', each housing a royal statue. We can see some of the fine calcite flooring of the principal sanctuary (fig. 30:2) against the eastern face of the pyramid (fig. 30:1) and to the south flights of steps originally giving access to storehouses, the roofs of which were supported by columns with capitals styled like a cluster of closed papyrus plants. Ten Treasury strong-rooms for temple valuables lay to the north of the hall of niches. The rain which occasionally beat down on the roof of Sahura's temple was channelled into lion-headed gargoyles. Redundant ritual liquids, however, were gathered into copper-lined basins, then poured into an underground copper pipe which took them the length of the causeway before discharging them at the eastern end of the complex.

Looking across the ruins of the temple one could be forgiven for cursing the insatiability of the lime-kilns of post-pharaonic Egypt into which so much of Sahura's stone was fed. Not only has the flesh been stripped from the architecture of the monument but also its adornment of 10,000 square metres of outstanding low raised reliefs has been reduced to about 150 square metres now mainly scattered across museums in Germany and Cairo (73, 74 & 75). So in Dynasty V in the columned hall and surrounding passages you would have feasted your eyes on scenes of Sahura massacring his Libyan enemies, hunting desert game or spearing fish from his canoe, on his ships, keelless and curved by hogging-trusses returning from profitable trading missions to the Lebanon, and with exotic cargoes of bears from Syria. Had one been in the southern area of Sahura's temple much later in Dynasty XVIII – when probably the maintenance for most of the structure was already severely neglected – then one would have found it taken over for a flourishing sanctuary for the lioness deity, Sakhmet. Take a brief look at what remains of the monument called in Ancient Egypt the 'Rising of the *ba* spirit', i.e. Sahura's pyramid. (The *ba* is a soul-force surviving physical death.) A thick enclosure wall surrounded the pyramid and also in its southeastern corner encircled the satellite or ritual pyramid, now an amorphous mound. What remains of Sahura's pyramid is the internal superstructure of indifferent stone and such poor engineering that its six large support steps failed to hold the outer mantle of Tura limestone in position. Supply, then, in your mind's eye an original gleaming white pyramid whose smoothed sides stretched 75 metres along their bases and rose at an angle of just over 50° to a height of 47 metres. Investigations into the heart of the pyramid from its northern entrance – where exceptionally keen visitors can make a short scramble on all fours to get inside – revealed a rectangular burial chamber of which the roof is shaped as an inverted letter V and consists of three layers of masonry, each increasing in dimension over the one below.

If you have time, you can investigate the pyramid complexes of the later kings of Dynasty V, from north to south, Neweserra (fig. 29A:3), Neferirkara (fig. 29A:4) and Neferefra (fig. 29A:5). These are even more ruined and confusing, especially since Neweserra usurped Neferirkara's causeway and valley temple (76). Also worth a visit is the adjacent stone mastaba (fig. 29A:2 & fig. 29B) of the noble, Ptahshepses, despite the fact that entry may have to be by ladder over the enclosure wall (77). Ptahshepses was the chief justice and vizier of King Neweserra who made a good marriage with a princess called Khamerernebti. His massive tomb complex, one of the largest private mastabas extant, admirably excavated and restored by the Czechoslovak Institute of Egyptology, provides the earliest example of lotus columns in pharaonic architecture, as well as a naviform double chamber for solar or funerary boats.

CHAPTER 10

'THE BOAST OF HERALDRY, THE POMP OF POW'R': Tombs of the Saqqara Courtiers of Dynasties V and VI

Returning to Saqqara, it is time to wander around the tombs of government officials who served during the Old Kingdom. Like all civil servants, many lived through more than one regime. They and their positions in society, are, of course, of interest but it will be the work of their tomb craftsmen which excites the eye. These artisans unfurl not just scenes of daily life in Old Kingdom Egypt, fascinating and invaluable as that is, but also capture on the walls psychological feelings and emotions. Through their art we react to the dignified (possibly even smug) composure of an official under a sunshade watching his retainers swelter in the heat and we respond to the ebullience of boatmen squabbling on the Nile. So let us now inspect the most important tombs of the courtiers of both Dynasty V and Dynasty VI, strolling from the south at the causeway of King Wenis' pyramid, crossing north-westwards in the direction of the underground burial vaults for the sacred Apis bulls, known as the Serapeum, and returning directly east to the vicinity of the pyramid of King Teti.

Begin just south of the short roofed section of the Wenis causeway. Before Wenis constructed his funerary complex this area of the Saqqara plateau formed an east-west depression serving as a readily accessible source of limestone for the pyramid of King Djoser. With the neglect of the Saqqara necropolis during Dynasty IV when, as we have seen, officials' tombs clustered round the pyramids at Giza, this quarry fell into disuse. However, in Dynasty V certain courtiers of mediocre rank were awarded tombs cut in the limestone ridge that had previously been the quarry. On the accession of Wenis their modest sepulchres were sacrificed to the plans of the royal architects responsible for the causeway: the tombs, surreptitiously looted by the causeway labourers, became buried below sand and rubble to make way for the extensive link road between the valley and mortuary temples of King Wenis (*see* chapter 11). Of course this was hard luck for the courtiers who hoped that their tombs would be kept in reasonable condition and supplied with offerings by the mortuary priests commissioned for their care, but in another respect it was fortunate since obliteration of the tombs' location meant that for over 4,000 years tomb robbers and iconoclasts were foiled.

Nefer and Kaha:
Choral directors

The small dimensions of this tomb preclude its inclusion on the itineraries of large groups of tourists, but it is interesting to begin your visit with the memorial of a courtier who lived probably about the time that King Neweserra ruled Egypt, in roughly 2400 BC. You pass the vestiges of the mudbrick wall that formed a small courtyard, before it was destroyed by the workmen of King Wenis, and enter a small chapel cut into the rock, an L-shape, with the longer corridor lying on a north-south axis (fig. 31). It was originally designed as a double tomb by Nefer for himself and for his father Kaha, but other members of his family have made their presence felt, so that you are in a tomb in which three generations of court musicians were buried. The family relationships are set out in a genealogical table (fig. 32). Before making a detailed examination of this gem of a tomb, glance at the walls and note the brightly-coloured raised reliefs, varying in depth – different craftsmen have been at work, some at a leisurely pace, others in a more urgent fashion. Nefer stands facing the vivid scenes of the top three registers on the northern end of the east wall (fig. 31:1). His authority is proclaimed by his staff and his kerchief folded in his right hand, his wig, his wide necklace and the shoulder-knot normally tying the priestly leopardskin in position – here it had not been painted on his body by the time death curtailed his personal supervision of the tomb decoration. His hunting dog is beside him. Less than the height of his waist, his daughter, whose bust is portrayed well developed for her age (indicated as youthful by virtue of her nakedness and her hair plaited into the sidelock), stands before him holding a lapwing, and flaring her nostrils to breathe in the scent of a lotus blossom (fig. 33). She wears a wide collar whose outer ring consists of drop beads, below which is a rosette pendant. Sadly, this delightful young favourite of her father is doomed to remain anonymous. Since it was Nefer's wealth that earned him the privilege of a tomb in the Saqqara necropolis, unpretentious in size but exhibiting technical mastery in its wall-carvings, one ought to pause here and consider his status.

Nefer took over his father's social standing by acquiring two titles in particular: 'Inspector of the Great House' (i.e. the Royal Palace) and 'Inspector of the Craftsmen's Workshop'. Through this latter position he could see to it that some of the most skilled artisans at Memphis were employed on his tomb. These titles, which made him the most important man in his family, were supplemented by the office which his father Kaha also held, namely 'Director of Singers', although not so much is made about the actual quality of his voice as shall be found extolled on the false door of his father.

The vertical line of incised hieroglyphs in front of Nefer tell that he is 'viewing the fishermen, bird-trappers and scribes of his estates of Upper and Lower Egypt': the extent of his domains is thereby left discreetly vague. About to report on the agricultural activities is Nefer's agent, the major-domo also called Nefer, who as a mortuary priest is also the man responsible for the upkeep of the tomb. Walk up and down the length of this wall – from Nefer standing in the top register – to cover the upper three rows of scenes – no hardship in a tomb this size. Possibly I am not alone in finding the first vignette of daily life distressing: a goat is tied up by its hind legs to the branches of a tree while a man kneels in front disembowelling it. Beyond the tree a nanny-goat kneels down to chew at the branches as a kid sucks milk from her udder. One of the features of Nefer's tomb is the attempt to give the peasants identities instead of leaving them nameless. So, through a few rough strokes of a scribe's brush two goatherds are introduced, who wear bags of provisions tied around their necks, pulling branches of a tree down to enable their goats

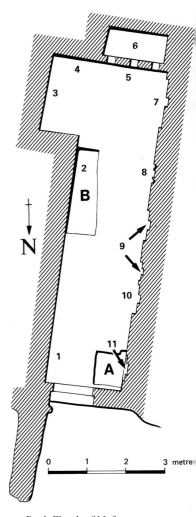

31. Rock Tomb of Nefer at Saqqara, Dynasty V, Saqqara

A Burial shaft (?of Nefer's brother), with corpse
B Burial shaft with mummy of Waty

156

to chew them – an ecologist's nightmare. Next, rising from the register below is a clump of papyrus plants: an idea of depth to this thicket is achieved by carving the umbels of the stalks at different heights and causing some of them to overlap. Perched on the papyrus plants are herons, shrikes and a kingfisher, while in flight over the clump is another kingfisher and a lapwing whose crest pierces the definitive border of the row. Two butterflies grossly out of proportion to the birds complete this witness to the ancient craftman's observation of wildlife.

32. The Family of Nefer, Controller of Singers

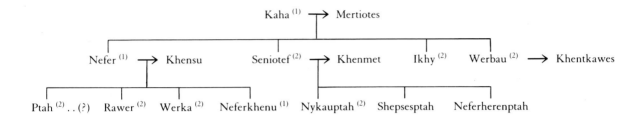

Two other peasants both called Tjenty each stoop under the weight of a bundle of five papyrus stalks. One of them is in the act of lowering the bundle from his back onto the ground – not, it can be assumed, onto the foot of his companion as the relief depicts, although of course humour is one of the delights of daily-life scenes on tomb walls. His arm is impossibly elongated to encompass the stalks but this is a convention of Egyptian artists in their attempts to portray energy and movement. The fate of the papyrus bundles becomes clear in the next scene where a skiff made out of these reeds is all but ready for the Nile. Once again a few traces of painted hieroglyphs enable us to rescue these peasants from anonymity. After all, why should it just be the courtiers of Ancient Egypt who are saved from namelessness in the next life? Why should their personalities be the only survivors on 'that night of the counting of the years' evoked in Spell 25 of the New Kingdom recension of magical utterances, old and more recent, popularly known today as *The Book of the Dead?* So here Khuptah puts his knee against the hull to knot the last rope around the papyrus stems. Kneeling at the other end of the boat Iydjefa ties the twine held for him by Shemsu.

In mastabas and rock tombs the courtier's authority is often stressed by a scene where he passes judgement on lesser mortals guilty of minor misdemeanours, or failure in meeting the tax quotas. So a reckoning is being made here with headmen from Nefer's estate, while two other headmen standby, perhaps smugly awaiting commendation, and two others look as if they would rather be somewhere else. Writing up the official record of the proceedings are two scribes using green reed brushes for the black ink that predominates in the hieratic script; yellow brushes behind their ears are for red-ink headings or totals. Actually, they are probably making rough notes on a board which can then be edited into a presentable document written out on the two scrolls of

KEY

→ married to
| son of
(1) controller of singers
(2) inspector of singers

157

papyrus we can see alongside the palette on the writing-chest in front of them. Next, one such document is held open by Khet, 'inspector of ten men of the Great House' to read to Nefer, who is now introduced by a vertical line informing us that he is 'viewing the scribal records of the estate and the catches of the bird-trappers and reckoning with the headmen'.

33. Tomb of Nefer: Nefer and his daughter

Beginning at this end of the west wall (fig. 31:2) follow the second register back northwards. Cattle are being presented to Nefer's scrutiny, led by a herdsman carrying a bundle of their green fodder. One beast is wearing a 'coat' of yellow reed-matting. Another herdsman faces an ox which he is trying to pull from the vicinity of a small papyrus marsh. Beyond sits a man preparing food, his shoulder jutting forward from his neck at an angle impossible to western eyes but satisfactorily conveying the idea of vigorous activity to an Ancient Egyptian. In the collective consciousness of the human race foremen and supervisors – even if they lead by example – seem to be categorized as watchers rather than workers. I shall never forget a local magnate from Hagg Qandil (a village just south of the central city of King Akhenaten at El-Amarna) standing dressed in a spotless white *galabiya* below an umbrella, in pompous scrutiny of only two fieldworkers on their haunches before him tilling the ground newly reclaimed from the desert. The feeling of the continuity of life in the Nile valley from the time of the pharaohs came across very strongly as I recalled the scene now met in Nefer's tomb. Leaning on his staff, his right leg slightly relaxed, wearing a linen scarf draped over his shoulder and a fringed kilt, Nenkheftka supervises a small herd of cattle being tended. A herdsman leads the cattle, carrying on a pole across his shoulder a waterjar and a folded reed mat – no need to ignore physical comfort just because you are officially a peasant. The second herdsman, called Tjenty, pushes the head of a tethered beast down to a bowl of water.

Beyond the papyrus clump there is a lively vignette of fishermen stretching over the second and third registers. Two groups of men pull on ropes attached to a seine-net, their legs straining, and variety is achieved by depicting their bodies at differing angles. The two fishermen at either end wear sashes around their chests tied with a large bow – possibly a buoyant life-saving apparatus with a loop for grabbing onto, especially since these two are closest to the water (*cf. 78*). The triangular floats on the upper edge of the net are quite clear, as are some of the oval weights that keep it below water-level. Within the length of the next, ichthyologists can feast their eyes on mullet, perch, carp and pike. The fringe-kilted foreman presents a gutted fish to Nefer. The remainder of the third register begins midway along the wall under the papyrus clump. Egyptian peasants in modern times have a reputation as phenomenal bread-eaters, and of course it was a staple item of diet for their ancient counterparts – though none perhaps could equal the magician Djedi living in the reign of King Khufu who, as noted in the Papyrus Westcar, at the great age of 110 years still consumed 500 loaves of bread washed down by 100 jugs of beer (not to mention the half-ox) every day. Well, here on Nefer's estate peasants are making bread in the open fields: one man kneels holding a pottery jar in which he kneads the dough while the baker, seated on a low stool, uses sticks to position the loaves in a crackling fire. The scene then changes to a fowler carrying two wild geese by their wings.

Now you draw near to a pool in the marshes, passing *en route* two fowlers lifting bird-crates on a pole and carrying the pegs and coil of rope required for setting up a clap-net. Beyond the pool a look-out has

63. *(opposite top left) Small seat-ed statue of Menkaura (detail), showing his name cartouche, Dynasty IV. Green diorite. Cairo Museum*

64. *(opposite below) The pyra-mid of Menkaura at Giza seen from the west, with three satel-lite pyramids probably for his queens, Dynasty IV, Giza*

65. *(opposite top right) Menk-aura flanked by Hathor and a district goddess, carved in schist, found in the valley temple of his pyramid complex, Dynasty IV, Giza, Cairo Museum*

66. *(overleaf above) Mudbricks are still a staple building ma-terial in Egypt; a local kiln at the village of Gurna, and part of a dwelling made of them*

67. *(overleaf below) The funer-ary monument of Queen Khent-kawes in the southern sector of the necropolis, Dynasty IV, Giza. An Islamic cemetery lies beyond*

leapt up on seeing enough birds have landed on the water within the confines of the net, and given a signal by means of a white scarf stretched along his shoulders, to four men holding a rope attached to the net on the pool. The first one, whose loincloth is tied up in its own waistband, reveals the one disputable, but possible, instance that peasants too were circumcised, as he feeds the rope vigorously through his hands to his companions. They run pulling the rope to cause the nets on the pool to collapse and so trap a dozen wild fowl, losing only two pintail ducks shown escaping in flight. At the end of the register strangled geese are presented to Nefer.

The two lower rows of reliefs on this eastern wall begin at the northern end (fig. 31:1) below the figures of Nefer and his daughter. Framing both registers is Tjenty, perhaps a relative of Nefer, but no evidence for this comes from his titles given in front of him here as he stands holding his folded kerchief and a papyrus roll: 'Participator (literally 'brother') in the funerary endowment, King's Acquaintance, Foreman of the Palace, Overseer of the commissions of the palace'. All one can say is that Nefer regarded him highly enough to award him a share of the provisions left by the mortuary priests. Tjenty's other titles merely tell that he was probably a bureaucrat in a minor government department. The first scene is, in my view, one of the most amusing in the whole Saqqara necropolis. Begin by looking at the four men treading grapes. They cling onto a trellis and hold each other's waists to avoid slipping over into the juice which has been indicated by the paint across their feet. In front of the treaders two men beat time for them by clapping two sticks together. The row starts, however, with the method of squeezing grapes or the pulp from treading in a sack, a process well attested in other tombs. Four men twist poles to crush the grapes so that the juice (represented here by vertical zigzag lines) can be caught in the large pottery bowl below. Normally a fifth man is shown exerting pressure, stretching his body between the poles to keep the sack of grapes taut and extract the last drops of juice. Hilariously, however, in Nefer's tomb a large baboon throws himself energetically into the task of stretching the sack. So Nefer had a sense of the ridiculous in the visual humour we are looking at. He also enjoyed, it seems, a good pun: the Egyptian word for 'to turn' or 'to twist' (i.e. the sack) is not too dissimilar from the word for 'baboon' (fig. 34).

In Egyptian society a person suffering from a physical abnormality was not isolated but integrated into the working population. Dwarfs can be found in scenes on mastaba walls and in statuary represented in a dignified manner – an iconography that seems to be a translation onto the visual plane of the sentiment found in the *Wisdom Book of Amenemope* (c.1000 BC): 'Do not ridicule a blind man nor mock a dwarf.' In Nefer's tomb three dwarfs and a man with deformed legs have been trained as jewellers and can be seen stringing two bead collars. The scene now shifts to festivities. An unidentified but eminent lady sits in a pavilion supported by wooden columns styled in the shape of blossoming lotus flowers. A young girl stands before her turning round to rest her arm on the lady's knee. In the pavilion is arrayed a spread of meat and wine-jars for the banquet. Although men are depicted at the beginning

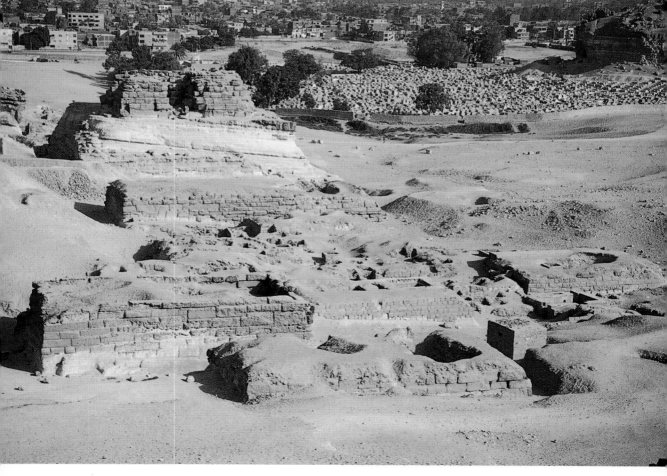

68. (above) Mastaba el-
Faraoun, which from its structure looks like the first stage of a
pyramid, Dynasty V, South Saqqara

69. (left) Pyramid of King
Weserkaf, northeast of the Step
Pyramid, Dynasty V, Saqqara

70. Granite head of King Weserkaf from the remains of his pyramid complex, Dynasty V, Cairo
Museum

71. *(opposite above)* The pyramids of Abusir to the right – Neweserra, Neferirkara and Sahura – with, to the north, the pyramids of Giza in the distance beyond

72. *(opposite below)* The pyramid of King Sahura, Dynasty V, Abusir

73. *(right above)* Relief from the courtyard of the pyramid of Sahura showing an early example of the god Seth, opponent of Horus in the battle over Osiris, who was Seth's brother and Horus' father. Despite being cast as the villain, Old Kingdom pharaohs sometimes paid open respect to Seth, but none with more certainty than had Peribsen in Dynasty II, Dynasty V, Abusir, Berlin Museum

74. *(right centre)* The fineness of the carving lost from the pyramid courtyard of Sahura is seen in this fragment of a boat in sail that survived, Dynasty V, Abusir, Berlin Museum

75. *(right below)* District gods bring offerings – these would have run all the way round the lower border of the courtyard at the pyramid of Sahura, Dynasty V, Abusir, Cairo Museum

76. *(overleaf inset)* Bust of a king, Dynasty V (possibly from the reign of Neweserra). Red granite, 34 cm high. The Brooklyn Museum, 72.58. Charles Edwin Wilbour Fund

77. *(overleaf)* Vast mastaba tomb of the courtier, Ptahshepses, a relative of King Neweserra, that nestles against his pyramid complex. The earliest known lotiform columns form the front portico of the tomb, Dynasty V, Abusir

of this scene carrying bouquets of flowers and strangled geese, it does seem to be a women's festival. Before the kiosk three girls in long linen dresses clap their hands in rhythm to the 'Highland Fling' being performed by the four girls in short skirts. They each kick one leg behind them, place one hand on their hips and raise the other in the air over their heads. Who is this mysterious lady and what is the lively celebration of the women all about? A marriage? A birth? A festival of the goddess Hathor? From Nefer's tomb these details will never be learnt.

78. (opposite) Egypt today: fishermen on the Nile. Compare with similar scenes in the tomb of Nefer

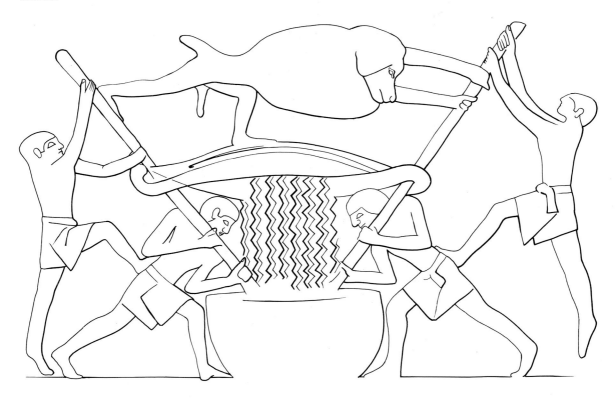

34. Tomb of Nefer: Squeezing grapes with the help of a baboon

Return to the beginning of the fifth and last register on this wall. The first section shows the farmers working on Nefer's estate. Two of them scatter seed from sacks onto the silt while another beats forward a flock of Barbary sheep to tread the seed into the ground. A team of oxen then draw the plough. The pastoral tranquillity of this agricultural scene sharply gives way to a mood of horse-play and high spirits as we meet seventeen boatmen jostling with one another on four papyrus skiffs. The aim of the game seems to be to transfer the cargo of papyrus stalks, lotus flowers and figs from one boat into another. The boatmen have punting poles which are put to violent use in the dispute (fig. 35): one opponent has been knocked into the water by means of two poles while others receive hefty blows in the chest or groin.

The last scenes cover both the fourth and fifth registers. Here you will follow the two men carrying a steering-oar on their shoulders, from which a coil of rope is suspended, and visit two large sailing boats. In the first boat two men stand in a cabin and the stern, operating the

35. Tomb of Nefer: The fishermen's game

steering-oars while another pulls on ropes connected to the sailbeam and the mast. With the sail billowing the boat is obviously making use of winds blowing from the north to travel against the current of the Nile to Upper Egypt. From the deck a sailor leans overboard, dipping a bucket in the water or possibly – if the scene is closely correlating with the two men on land carrying the coil of rope – dropping an anchor for these crew members to join the boat. Nefer rests on his staff of office in a cabin in the centre of the boat while seven sailors sit in the galley. The prow of the boat is curved back in an unmistakable hedgehog head. The second vessel gives the impression of more sailing activity going on: a man kneels on the cabin pulling at ropes, and fourteen oars rest idle as the sailors – one climbing up the rigging itself with all the agility of a modern felucca boy at Aswan – cluster round the mast in an effort to get the boat ready for travel. One feels their exertion thanks to the artist's skill in overlapping the sailors against the ropes, mainsail and each other.

You now reach a small recess (fig. 31:3) in the east wall. Again the colour on the low-cut reliefs is unbelievably preserved and you do not even have to move to study the five registers of daily-life scenes. A foreman watches herdsmen assisting goats to graze in the tree branches while another prominent official shielded by a sun-shade stands in a small dockyard supervising the launch of a boat. The wooden hull of the vessel is being warped by men stretching papyrus (on which a baboon is doing a balancing act) across a forked stanchion – a rare depiction in tombs. The boat itself has the prow shaped as an inward-facing hedgehog's head. Nefer's fondness for mimicry comes across again when we look at the stern of the boat: normally one would expect a foreman giving orders to the shipwrights, and there is an inspector on this boat holding a papyrus roll (fig. 36). However he looks at a loss: the

undisputed boss is a baboon brandishing his sceptre of authority. The
two baboons already met in Nefer's tomb defy you to keep a straight face
in the light of their anthropomorphising antics. Surely they are the
precursors of the genre of illustrated satirical papyri where, for example,
in a topsy-turvy Egypt a hippopotamus stands on its hind legs to make
beer, or a lion and an antelope sit peacefully together playing the
board-game *senet*. Below the stern a man pulls away the wedge acting as
a brake-block and the boat can then be dragged to the river, its path
smoothed by a docker pouring water before it.

Moving down, lumberjacks are found felling trees and carpenters
smoothing the trunk of one with their adzes. Studies of technology in
Ancient Egypt are enhanced by scenes of craftsmen at work in their
shops. A carpenter pushes a large saw through a plank tied to a post and
two others place the bevelled lid on a rectangular sarcophagus on the
narrow end of which is the 'palace-façade' motif. A bed with legs styled
into bulls' hoofs is being polished as another carpenter works on a door
bolt exaggerated in size for clarity. A wooden column with its capital
fashioned into an open lotus blossom rests on a frame as carpenters plane
off any roughness. The lowest register consists of cattle-tending and the
inspection of strangled geese.

The rest of Nefer's tomb is really concerned with the perpetuation of
provisions for himself and for those members of his family privileged to
share in the funerary endowment. So, beginning on the upper eastern
side of the south wall (fig. 31:4) Nefer, seated on a stool to which an
awning has been attached, holds his fly whisk of fox-tails in one hand
and stretches out the other to receive an open papyrus scroll from which

36. Tomb of Nefer: Boat construction

a retainer has just read. Khensu, his wife, kneels at his feet wearing a
linen gown and a petite green chaplet on her wig. The couple face three
short registers of low painted reliefs. Two scribes armed with papyrus
scrolls squat on the ground, their palette and writing case behind them.
Then a collection of six papyri scrolls is being arranged by a dwarf who
himself holds a writing palette. A parade of geese, one clearly honking,
waddles towards Nefer and Khensu. Below, with the relaxation of the
idealizing artistic convention in the case of peasants, a herdsman with a
crippled leg leads a long-horned ox. In the next register, between an oryx
and a Dorcas gazelle a man is pulling an ibex along by the horns and
beard. This section finishes with scenes of livestock being slaughtered
and a procession of bearers bringing produce from Nefer's domains.

Now view the larger expanse of the south wall (fig. 31:5). The three
rectangular apertures were to admit the aroma of the incense into the
serdab, the small niche where the *ka* statues of Nefer originally stood (fig.
31:6). It was only after the introduction of the statues that the south wall
was finally completed – hence the contrast between the hastily-finished
scenes above the slits in paint applied onto the plastered wall surface, and
the low raised reliefs below. In the upper east corner Nefer is shown
before a table of bread savouring the incense being burned before him.
The rest of the area above the incense-niches need not detain you since
only the green-coloured hieroglyphs of the ninety items listed as
requisites for the eternal 'cupboard' survive. Below, a proudly corpulent
Nefer, leaning on his staff, measures the length of the five registers of the
serdab wall under the niches. Three relatives stand behind him but it is of
course Nefer, depicted in his own short-cropped hair, wearing an
immaculately-pleated linen kilt and high-looped sandals, that demands
attention. That is until you catch sight of the diminutive kneeling figure
of his wife, not even reaching the height of the hem of his kilt. She
breathes in the scent of a lotus, is bedecked in jewellery, the most
magnificent piece of which is the coronet. Notice also in front of her the
maidservant washing her hands so as to deal hygienically with the food
for her mistress which is on the low table between them. Nefer himself
looks towards three rows of offerings presented to him. Below, following
the retainer presenting him with a fox-tail whisk, spend a minute
looking at the music-makers. Two singers raise their right hands to their
ears to gauge the pitch of the song, accompanied by two flautists. The
harpists in the lowest register squat, each holding a large harp in the
same position but, with an eye for detail, the artist shows them each
plucking a different chord.

Now survey the 'family gathering' of false doors along the west wall,
beginning naturally with that of Nefer himself (fig. 31:7). In the upper
southern section of the wall sits Nefer in his leopardskin wearing a
collar of green beads facing a variety of provisions, in addition to the
table of yellow and brown leaves. We cannot see his spirit starving, when
the magical power of these carvings is constantly supplying him with
wine-jars, bread, grapes, figs, onions, cucumbers and cakes to supplement the slaughtered ox, ibex and antelope. Named offering-bearers
ensure that servants will always be present to prepare the food and drink.
Below the table of loaves a priest ritually washes his hands in front of

three seated figures who from left to right are Nefer's brothers (all 'Inspectors of Singers') – Seniotef, Ikhy and Werbau.

The horizontal band of sunken hieroglyphs, read from right to left, is a funerary invocation to the god Anubis – arranged over the sign of a loaf on a mat towards the beginning of the line. Below, Nefer sits opposite Khensu, both stretching their hands to the loaves of bread. The recesses either side display the palace-façade motif that is familiar. The lower section shows three representations of Nefer, each accompanied by a different young son. Their names are painted in ink, not incised. From right to left are Rawer holding a lapwing, a son who has a name compounded with that of the god Ptah, but the rest of it is blurred, and Werka. Although depicted as children here on Nefer's false door they all had the title 'Inspector of Singers' by the time the tomb was closed. Completing this section is a tall relief of Nefer – the hieroglyphs of the heart and windpipe, the desert viper and the mouth spelling out his name immediately before his face. The head of Nefer in his long straight wig with a short beard is a masterpiece of carving. He is decked out in jewellery and wears the leopardskin. Reaching the height of his sceptre stands the elegant Khensu with a duck grasped by its wings, her other hand clenching the lower shaft of Nefer's sceptre.

Moving northwards along this wall (fig. 31:8) is a 'palace façade' with the green and yellow colours of the pattern surviving well. Here the mortuary priest would leave offerings to Nefer – and subsequently to another Director of Singers called Khenu who is buried in the shaft before this door. In the next decorated stretch (fig. 31:9) we meet Nefer's parents. In the upper section sits a splendidly garbed Kaha – the head of the leopardskin exquisitely carved on his flank. He held the office of 'Director of Singers' as well as the title 'Priest of Meret' (a minor goddess of melody). His own singing seems to have been held in high esteem since he is described on an offering basin found in this tomb as 'Director of the beautiful voice' and 'Beautiful voice for his lord'. Sadly, Kaha must remain ever mute and you pass by the three officiating mortuary priests to look upon Mertiotes his wife. Her representations on Kaha's false door and her own combined actually outnumber by one those of her husband. Dare one deduce female persuasiveness or outright dominance from the inescapable presence of this priestess of the goddesses Hathor and Neith?

In the two short registers behind Mertiotes are presumably her four children, excluding the illustrious Nefer. Clad in leopardskins the three sons are Seniotef, Ikhy and Werbau again. All hold their title, 'Inspector of Singers' written in three hieroglyphs: a folded cloth, a mace and a seated figure of a singer with arm outstretched in a way suggestive of the flow of melody. The first son, Seniotef, is also a palace scribe. Regrettably, the daughter Sentiotes is merely a name, but with a forceful mother like Mertiotes and an influential brother like Nefer, one can suppose that family interests (hopefully coinciding with Sentiotes' own preferences) secured her an enjoyable life among minor court ladies. The lower portion of this section consists of a doorway on the left for Kaha and on the right for Mertiotes. The panel between shows Kaha and Mertiotes facing one another, her arm around his shoulder: one cannot deny an affectionate gesture from a wife to her husband – until you look at Mertiotes' feet. Like him she is wearing looped sandals, and so the interpretation I would place on this scene is more along the lines of Mertiotes' insistent participation in Kaha's outdoor activities.

Next, along the western wall (fig. 31:10) is the false door of the Inspector of the Singers, Werbau, brother of Nefer. There is certainly no falling off in quality of the raised relief. Werbau is shown on the upper wall, seated at table opposite his wife Khentkawes. Worth admiring are the skilfully fashioned stools with bull-shaped legs. Under the table of loaves separating the couple are minute depictions of three of their children – a girl in front of Werbau and two boys in front of Khentkawes. Eight more relatives, their names scratched or painted in, are kneeling behind Khentkawes, probably her children, although this is not specified. Below her is a female figure kneeling before a small table whose name is more carefully incised; she is 'King's Acquaintance, Mertiotes'. Now, together with the lower left jamb of the actual doorway it is possible to make a positive identification of this lady. There stands a lady described as 'King's Acquaintance, possessor of veneration before the Great God, Mertiotes'. Such a prominent position on Werbau's door suggests that this Mertiotes is his mother. Consequently, you meet again the irrepressible wife of Kaha from the false door just to the south. On the other jamb, facing the representation of Werbau in the centre, stands his wife with two sons clinging onto the hem of her dress. The tree in the hieroglyphs above her head writes out part of her title, 'Priestess of Hathor, Lady of the Sycamore'. To the right a fine relief shows Khentkawes, her braided wig dividing over her shoulder and wearing an alluring choker necklace. Her right arm rests on her husband and we are now not perturbed by the fact that the hand of her left arm is reversed, the artist seeing no need to break the convention of 'rightward' orientation for parts of the human body – the concept of the hand overriding the physical reality. Werbau in his leopardskin holds, for similar reasons, his sceptre in a way that makes it disappear behind his thighs and emerge before him. His young son holds out the long staff of office, his hair plaited into the sidelock and his hand grasping a lotus bud.

The last false door (fig. 31:11) belongs to Nefer's brother Seniotef. Lack of paint seems to indicate that this element of the wall decoration remained incomplete at the time of the tomb's closure. It does give a more cramped impression in its layout as if all formulae and representations were thrown together in a hurry. At the top Seniotef faces his wife Khenmet. Below on the left is his eldest son Nykauptah and on the other side of Seniotef at the offering table kneel two figures: the priest Neferherenptah performing the ceremony known as 'spiritualization' of the deceased, aimed really at vivifying the inanimate decor for sustenance for the *ka* of Seniotef. Another son of Seniotef called Shepsesptah assists at this funerary ritual. Seniotef's status is proclaimed in the vertical inscription on the left outer door jamb. Find the sedge plant at the top corresponding to the level of his son Nykauptah's head and follow his titles downwards:

TITLE	IDENTIFYING HIEROGLYPH
'King's Acquaintance'	sedge plant
'Overseer of the ten men of the royal priests of the palace'	owl and man being purified below pouring water
'Sole one among the Great'	three swallows
'Priest of Meret of Upper and Lower Egypt'	heraldic plants
'Overseer of the six men of the boat'	papyriform boat
'Scribe of the palace'	writing palette
'Inspector of Singers'	man with outstretched arm
'Seniotef'	arrow and horned viper

The two inner door jambs show Seniotef, once in a wig and with sceptre and once with his own short hair; the centre niche depicts the lady Khenmet with her son Nykauptah. You are now at the north wall where the entrance to the tomb of Nefer is cut. A few sketches in paint on the Tura limestone blocks reveal the outlines of Nefer's family together with the preliminary grid lines used by the artists to proportion the human figure.

Looking back from the entrance into the tomb of Nefer we can share in the pride of this family of singers over three generations. Meret, patron goddess of music and song, certainly favoured them and ensured they received the benefits of middle-rank courtiers.

This tomb has demanded your time, but has provided a treasured insight into fifth-dynasty Egypt and prepares you for making sense of other tomb reliefs. This tomb is of personal interest because it was here that I had my first experience of meeting one of the ancient occupants of a pharaonic tomb. It can be seen that the floor has clear indications of the original burial shafts. Alas, only two (fig. 31:A & B) of the eleven burial pits constructed survived the ransacking that occurred as King Wenis's workmen were building his causeway. One against the western wall near the north entrance (A) contained a male body orientated east-west lying on the rock floor of the shaft. Its situation in front of the false door of Nefer's brother Seniotef is the only clue to the possible identity of this corpse. On the eastern side of the tomb is the spot (B) where I witnessed Dr Ali el-Khouly, then Inspector of Antiquities at Saqqara, open the floor like a genie revealing a cave of wealth. A shaft not three metres in depth contained a wooden sarcophagus in which lay a middle-aged man wrapped in linen bandages moulded over with plaster to reveal all the contours of the body – bulging eyes, sharp nose, upper lip with a moustache painted on, chin sporting a ceremonial beard made of stiffened linen and sexual organs bandaged separately with unashamed precision. Gazing starkly into his face produced the closest link I have ever felt with Ancient Egypt. In the debris of this shaft the fragments of a wooden box were discovered bearing some cursive hieroglyphs in now-faded ink. A date is given as 'Regnal Year 6, Month 4 of Winter-

Sowing Season, Day 22'. The royal cattle census was traditionally held every two years so the date could be in Year 11 of the reign of a late fifth-dynasty monarch: Djedkara Izezi, predecessor of King Wenis, is a likely candidate. Probably this burial against the eastern wall, not, we note, in front of one of the false doors, since space there against the western wall was already occupied, was one of the later, if not the last, in Nefer's tomb. From the inscription on the box we are given a name and title – which can be assigned to the body – though not without reservation, since the box could be an heirloom, a gift or scattered plunderers' loot. However, there is no harm in asserting that he is named as Waty, who held an administrative post involving the linen supply for weavers, and was a contemporary of Nefer's sons.

Yet perhaps you should leave the tomb with the name of its constructor last in mind, in gratitude for the panorama of vignettes of the human condition which he has provided. In pharaonic phraseology, let us wish a minimum of 'a 1000 of bread' and 'a 1000 of beer' to the Palace Inspector, Inspector of the artisans' workshop, Director of Singers, and Possessor of Veneration before the Great God, Nefer.

Niankhkhnum and Khnumhotpe: Royal manicurists

Just northeast of the tomb of Nefer, on the opposite side of the Wenis causeway, lies the more complicated funerary monument of two priests who served in the pyramid complex and sun-temple of King Neweserra of Dynasty V. In addition to these duties, Niankhkhnum and Khnumhotpe were 'Overseers of the palace manicurists'. Their expertise in nail-paring is reflected in the reward of a tomb extensively carved in low raised relief with surviving hues of yellow, green, blue and various shades of reddish-brown. Wander beyond the pillars of the northern portico, and step back into their environment of around 4,500 years ago. Flanked by scenes depicting the transport of funerary shrines you can gaze at the upper registers of the portico's south wall (fig. 37:1). Khnumhotpe and Niankhkhnum are seated facing each other on the eastern and western ends of the wall respectively. Below are hieroglyphs giving the funerary formula to the god Anubis and the courtiers' titles. In the third line, divided in the centre by the signs meaning 'palace', the ideograms for 'claw', below 'eye', form the word 'manicurist'. Framing the doorway are two papyrus skiffs: Khnumhotpe is spearing fish in a pool in the marshes while Niankhkhnum is about to hurl his throwstick at wild fowl. Everyone in the two families shown here will be introduced by name. Breathing in the scent of the lotus and holding Khnumhotpe's leg, her height reaching just above his knee, stands 'His wife whom he loves, Royal Acquaintance, Possessor of honour, Priestess of Hathor, Lady of the Sycamore, Khenut'. At the prow of the skiff is his son, the 'Royal priest Ptahshepses', while towards the stern sits his daughter 'Rewedjkawes. Opposite, Niankhkhnum's wife Khentkawes grasps her husband's knee more tightly to steady herself; she is described as a 'Priestess of Hathor'. His son, the 'Royal priest, Hemra', sucks his forefinger and holds a hoopoe by the wings. Niankhkhnum's daughter, Hemetra, kneeling by him is called a 'Priestess of Neith'.

The doorway thicknesses (fig. 37:2) display some interesting reliefs of rituals being performed on statues of the deceased so that they might act

79. Ptahhotpe breathes in perfume and stretches his hand towards a table of bread. Scene from the mastaba of Akhtihotpe and Ptahhotpe, Dynasty V, Saqqara

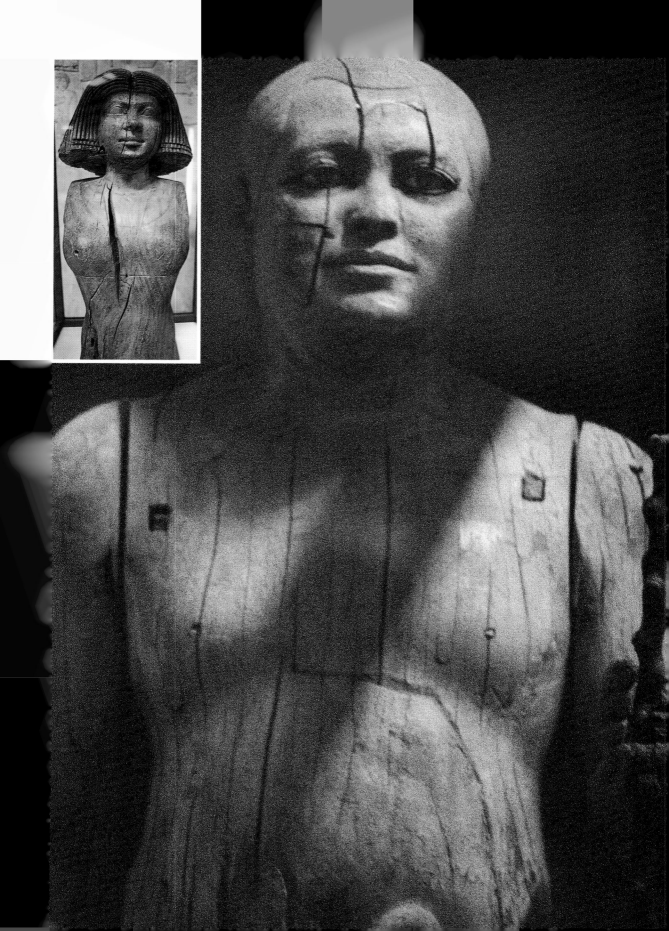

as substitute bodies in the afterlife. The mortuary priest burns incense and presents flowers to the statues as they are dragged to the tomb. One shrine contains a double statue of the courtier, a genre of which three-dimensional examples from the Old Kingdom survive in the museums. Two shrines are surmounted by ostrich feathers suggestive of the plumes on the *Atef* crown of Osiris. The lowest register illustrates the difficulty of overthrowing refractory bulls for sacrifice. In one instance no less than eight men are involved: one sits astride the bull's neck twisting its horns in the direction of the attached rope being pulled by another, separated by the hieroglyphs meaning 'lasso the long-horn'; other men with ropes are hobbling the front legs of the bull, while one man gives an energetic tug at its tail to help ground the beast.

Further on in the entrance, six registers of reliefs portray the major procedures of baking bread and brewing. From cylindrical storage bins men collect grain and send it to be pounded with long pestles. One of the numerous rewards of studying Egyptian daily-life scenes comes in the snippets of conversation between the workers preserved in the hiero-glyphs, the elegance of which often disguises colloquial or everyday phrases. Here a squatting woman holds a bowl out to her companion with the words more or less equivalent to 'Hurry up, sunshine, I want to sift the flour!' The other woman is leaning over the millstone in the act of grinding the barley and the gist of her reply is 'I'm doing it, so come on let's have just one kind word from you!' She is also being plagued by a young boy tugging at her shoulders and demanding attention by shouting, 'Look at me! Look at me!' Below, next to the baker piling up loaves in pottery moulds in the oven, kneels a woman with her arm raised to shield her face from the heat. Alternatively, although this is a well-attested posture for baking-women, one could interpret here a gesture of weariness resulting from the vicious clasp which the child she is suckling gives to her breast. In the lower scenes brewers are shown crushing barley loaves through a sieve and then treading them into a mash to produce the beer popular at all levels of Egyptian society.

Turning immediately east, once in the outer vestibule the wall-reliefs (fig. 37:3) unfurl a tapestry of mundane activities of the sort that makes you feel at one with the Ancient Egyptian. In the damaged top register you meet the profession in which Niankhkhnum and Khnumhotpe were senior personnel. An overseer seated cross-legged receives a manicure while another man performs a pedicure on a scribe. Barbers armed with razors are also busy shaving hair from a client's head, chin or groin. Below is an Egyptian market, a place of free mobility but not without its hazards for petty criminals. A baboon on a leash bites determinedly into the thigh of a running thief, its teeth every bit as effective as a modern guard-dog trained by a security firm. Its handler shouts 'Seize! Seize!' Leave this scoundrel to his punishment and move through to legitimate market transactions. A woman with a child in tow hands a bowl across a large basket of sycamore figs to the seller. This is the basis of economic life in Ancient Egypt – she is exchanging a manufactured item, the dish, for what the tradesman describes as 'exceedingly sweet sycamore fruit'. (Coinage did not enter the Egyptian market place until two thousand years later.) The wet fishmonger seems prepared to sell from his catch in

80. *(opposite inset) Sycamore figure of the so-called 'Wife of the Sheikh al-Balad', Dynasty V, Saqqara, Cairo Museum*

81. *(opposite) Sycamore figure of Ka-aper, nicknamed by Mariette's workmen the 'Sheikh al-Balad', Dynasty V, Saqqara, Cairo Museum*

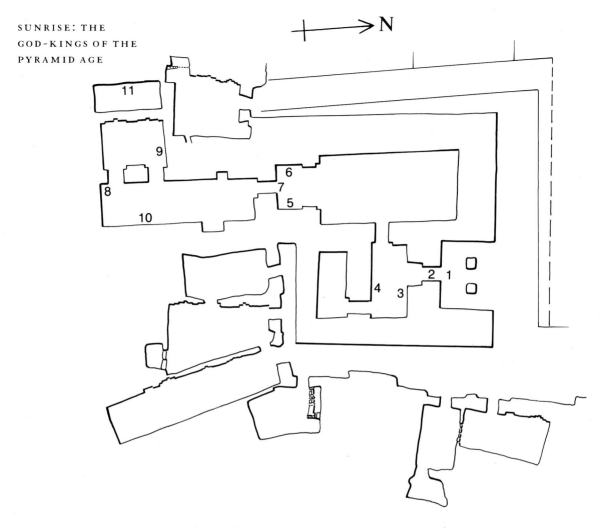

37. Mastaba of Niankhkhnum and Khnumhotpe, Dynasty V, Saqqara

the basket for a loaf of bread. Next, the greengrocer leaves us in no doubt what he is shouting to the man with a baboon on a leash helping itself to the vegetables and fruit in his basket. Below, at the baker's, where round loaves are on sale, a customer sucks or chews something that is most likely to be the lower stem of a papyrus plant; villagers in Upper Egypt today have merely substituted sugar cane for the same pastime. We can pass by the trader selling beakers since he is busy with a customer, and by the coppersmith with a fistful of grappling-hooks. Possibly it is your nose which guides you towards the basket piled high with gutted and dried fish. The fishmonger is chatting to another 'stall-holder', a seal-carver by trade. He offers the engraver the contents of his fish-basket in exchange for an amulet called 'Joyful Heart'. The curt reply amounts to 'Tough! I'm carving a cylinder-seal!' Negotiating in the market place can be thirsty work so one can fully appreciate the feelings of the man who has stopped off at the local 'bar'. A woman in charge of a large pottery jar stood upright between some stones pours a drink for him into a bowl. He encourages her saying: 'Fill it up, I've done the rounds! Barley is beautiful as an art!' His latter words mean of course that grain is so much better when transformed into beer. Immediately below you can look in on the draper's where, as a bolt of linen cloth is being inspected, a seated 'high-pressure' salesman asserts that 'I'm telling the honest truth: this "Gods' linen" is of superb workmanship'. He looks trustworthy but doubtless the maxim *'caveat emptor'* applied every bit as much in an Ancient Egyptian market as it does today in the streets of modern Luxor where the 'saffron' sellers never fail to find the gullible.

At the top of the south wall (fig. 37:4) of this vestibule, Khnumhotpe and his son Ptahshepses face Niankhkhnum and his son Hemra, separated by horizontal registers of reliefs predominantly concerned with marsh activities and fishing. Of particular note are the men with balls of thread and spindles manufacturing or mending the nets used in bird-trapping. Fishermen below are working with dragnets and others are either angling with lines or setting basket-traps made of reeds into which the fish can swim, only to be confronted by unpassable sharp stems when they try to get out. The variety of Nile fish depicted in these scenes reveals the accurate eye of the artist towards nature. Ichthyologists can rejoice to find, among other types, the *Lates niloticus*, the *Tilapia nilotica*, the *Mormyrus kannume* (the Oxyrhyncus fish, swallower of Osiris' phallus), the *Synodontis*, the *Mugil cephalus*, the catfish and the common eel. Ready to snap up any fish eluding the human predators are two pelicans and a crocodile. The fate of the catch, as can be seen, is to be gutted and dried or cooked in the fish-kettle. As you proceed through the west door from this vestibule Niankhkhnum and Khnumhotpe can be seen on the thicknesses, travelling in palanquins set on the backs of donkeys.

Through the court turn south to a vestibule decorated with reliefs of the two tomb-owners. In the other hall, passing agricultural scenes, let us pause on the east wall (fig. 37:5) to inspect the activities of the craftsmen on the estate. Sculptors, whose energy is visually rendered by the different angles at which they approach their task, carve standing statues for the deceased. Painters – or 'scribes of the drawings' as the hieroglyphs call them – are shown at work colouring the statues and a shrine-casket. Below, four men sit around a blazing furnace, reaching inside with their blow-pipes to increase the temperature. Sheet metal is being hammered and smoothed into shape by two craftsmen, while another is knocking the underside of a metal vase or cup into shape. In a crucible a goldsmith is blowing down a pipe, an action elucidated by the inscription as 'heating the gold for tomb equipment'. As with further items destined to the same end in the burial chamber, other goldsmiths are overlaying with gold a sceptre, a kilt-clasp, a walking-stick and a diadem. Wide funerary collars are being threaded, tied at their terminals and held under pouring water while nearby the carpenters shape a bed, headrests, chair, chests and 'Djed-pillar' amulet.

Cross to the opposite wall (fig. 37:6) where next to Niankhkhnum hurling his throwstick and Khnumhotpe spearing with nonchalance two fish at the same time, their retainers are hard at work. Men cut up the papyrus plants to make matting, and others bake bread. But who is this bearded man seated on the ground in a comfortable corner doing nothing arduous? He can only be the supervisor. A worker has come up to him in a deferential manner, holding a bowl and a dried fish and is saying, 'This is pleasant – you will be satisfied with it'. In the next register a herdsman assists at the birth of a calf which he holds by the head and front legs as it emerges from the cow. Others tend young cattle and one milks a cow of which the hind legs are tied and held by his companion. Behind a herdsman butchering a goat sits 'Khuwy, controller of the cattle pastures', a cheerless individual despite the food and drink at his disposal. Below, cattle are driven across an expanse of shallow water and boatmen ferry papyrus bundles and cages of trapped birds. In one papyrus boat stands the 'Supervisor of funerary priests and controller of the herdsmen, Ankhredwinisut' leaning on his staff and scratching his nose with his thumb. The lower register depicts five papyrus skiffs full of squabbling boatmen and lots of horse-play. However, it is surely not a chance encounter but a 'friendly match' of men well known to the two courtiers, since the hieroglyphs reveal names and titles inappropriate to humble boatmen, such as Giyu 'funerary priest and barber', Redjy 'funerary priest and manicurist' and Djaay 'funerary priest and butler'.

On the central door jamb (fig. 37:6) you are confronted by a dramatic visual statement of the close relationship between the two courtiers. On the right Khnumhotpe stands with his hand on the shoulder of Niankhkhnum whose left hand grips the other's wrist; with their noses all but touching, the tenderness of their emotions towards one another is poignantly obvious. Their children are represented with them. Passing through the doorway (decorated with offering-bearers also leading cattle, antelopes and geese) you enter the offering or inner hall of the tomb. The southern wall (fig. 37:8) shows us Niankhkhnum, with a forceful rendering of his facial features, stretching his hand to the table of loaves. Before him are arrayed his 'cupboard' of the everlasting necessities of a courtier's life, offering-bearers and men slaughtering cattle in his honour. The north wall (fig. 37:9) shows in a similar vein the perpetual commodities before Khnumhotpe. However, the most striking feature of his chamber is brought home to you if you stand in the centre and glance at the immediately central portions of the east and west walls (fig. 37:10, 11). Here in the innermost recess of the whole tomb, where wives and children seem not unintentionally excluded from the reliefs, your eyes rest on the embracing figures of Niankhkhnum and Khnumhotpe: it is time to leave them together – alone as they desired to be for eternity.

Akhtihotpe and Ptahhotpe: Inspectors of pyramid-priests

Close to the desert slope that rises towards the western face of the step pyramid is situated the mastaba of two high officials, Akhtihotpe and his son Ptahhotpe, who lived under the later kings of Dynasty V (fig. 38). Keeping important ministerial positions hereditary was, unsurprisingly, one of the prime objectives of families moving in the upper echelons of Egyptian society. Firstly, it is interesting to see what glimpses one can catch into Akhtihotpe's Egypt. The carvings in the oblong corridor (fig. 38:1) beyond the mastaba's northern entrance were never completed, and remain as an uneven cocktail of red, yellow and black inks mixed with occasional sculptured figures. The west wall is the most rewarding area of this chamber to study. Akhtihotpe, the pharaoh's chief executive or vizier, has a number of cartouches in the titles over his head. These represent the kings for whose monuments he had maintenance responsibilities in his function as Overseer of pyramid towns, and Inspector of priests attached to the pyramids of Neweserra, Menkauhor and Djedkara Izezi. His eldest son Ptahhotpe, represented in his father's tomb, boasts as main title here 'Overseer of the pyramid town of Izezi'.

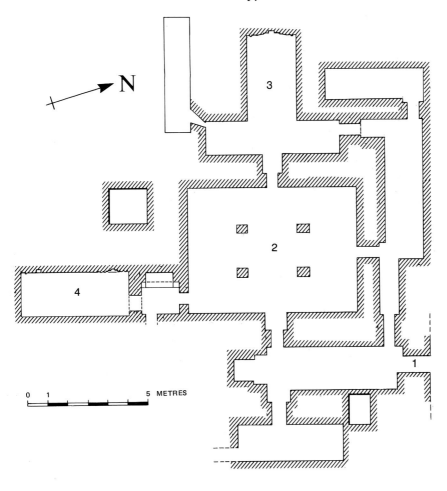

This mastaba, then, was made towards, and into, the reign of the last ruler of Dynasty V, King Wenis. Among the harvest scenes which Akhtihotpe and his son survey is one showing men reaping barley. Perhaps the worker, with one hand to his mouth, was dropping a hint to the foreman about a break for food or drink. Stubborn donkeys are tugged at to be laden with paniers while one ass on the threshing-floor is about to be beaten on its hindquarters for nibbling at the corn. In the central pillared hall (fig. 38:2) it is best to proceed due west to the T-shaped offering chapel of Akhtihotpe (fig. 38:3), leaving the finest room in the mastaba, belonging to his son, till last (fig. 38:4).

Once through the doorway of the chapel look back at the designs on the east wall. On your right Akhtihotpe, seated on his lion-footed style chair, watches Nile boatmen with lotus flowers tied in their hair and round their necks going for rivals in another skiff with their poles. In the

scene where cattle are being guided across a canal, a mother-cow licks
the tail of its calf carried securely on the shoulders of a herdsman. Above
the door the relief displays the vertical stalks of bird-haunted papyrus-
clumps but unfortunately the wild fowl here are severely damaged. To
the left Akhtihotpe surveys boat-builders constructing papyrus-skiffs.
Balancing the fisherman using a dip-net on the opposite side of the door,
a man seated here in a canoe has caught a catfish on a line. The base
register of this wall exhibits the personified family estates laden with
produce, and leading animals into the tomb for Akhtihotpe's afterlife.

If we turn to the south wall there are '*ka*-servants' (*see* p. 192) dragging
six shrines with feathers on top into the tomb. Through this wall robbers
made a forced entry into the *serdab* in the hope of loot. The lower
register depicts vividly realistic butchering reliefs. The comments of the
slaughter-house men as they slice off the forelegs of oxen survive in the
hieroglyphs: 'Tug hard!' 'I'm doing just as you say!' One butcher
plunges his hand into the carcass of an ox to pull out its heart while the
knife-sharpener pushes a blunt flint blade across the whetstone hanging
from his kilt. In the opposite wall is a doorway leading to an undecorated
series of rooms. There are still the red guidelines that the ancient artist
used for the rows of offering-bearers and cattle. Bid '*bon appétit*' to the
man in the top right who is tucking into a handful of palm-stalks. The
offering room to the west boasts a beautiful array of named produce
carriers approaching Akhtihotpe. In here is the false door, on the lower
façade of which six well-carved figures of the courtier stand, captioned
by splendid hieroglyphs.

Retrace your way through the central hall to the offering chamber of
Ptahhotpe, son of Akhtihotpe, of which the entrance lies off the
southeast corner (fig. 38:4). The technical construction of this section of
the mastaba is impressive: the west wall is formed from two enormous
blocks of limestone covering an area of about 60 square metres. Two
immense roofing stones approximately 5 metres by 2 metres have been
grooved to imitate palm logs with trimmed edges. The oblong gaps in
the east walls are due to repair originally by slip stones, which have been
taken away for alien building projects. In contrast to this vandalism you
can see deliberate ventilation shafts just below ceiling level in the east
and south walls. Sadly, however, the walls of this chapel have suffered
severe injury from two distinct human assaults: firstly the picks of the
ancient tomb robbers smashed against the decorated walls in the hope
that they would reveal secret treasure cavities behind. Then the fashion
of nineteenth-century AD visitors in making wet squeezes, or taking
plaster casts, of the superb reliefs denuded the images of much of their
original colour.

Immediately you are through the entrance to this chapel look back at
the northern wall where Ptahhotpe sits on his chair. A retainer beside
him holds his greyhounds and pet monkey. Others approach him with
bolts of linen while some attendants see to his pedicure and hair.
Everything in fact is meant to recreate the dignity of Ptahhotpe, the
grandee (79). It is likely that his highest status, that of vizier like his
father, came to him only late in his active career, since that title does not
occur in the hieroglyphs in this chapel, but was awarded to him later by

the time his sarcophagus was being carved and was included in his honours listed there. Follow down the scenes of the harpist and singer, dwarfs manufacturing jewellery and official squatting ready to submit accounts until you come to the butchers. Here the accompanying hieroglyphs are of interest in our understanding of the ritual slaughter and offering of oxen. Irenakht, who is called by the Egyptian term meaning 'physician', smells the ox-blood on the fingers of a butcher. He then states 'It is pure' – accordingly a fit and unpolluted beast for Ptahhotpe.

Superior craftsmanship can be found on the east wall while we approach from the northern side. Ptahhotpe, as the vertical line of hieroglyphs reveals, is 'viewing every beautiful pastime going on in the entire land' i.e. a 'blanket' coverage for every pleasure he might fancy in the next world, not only the ones depicted here. His major titles are given, including 'Inspector of the priests of the Pyramids of Neweserra, Menkauhor and Izezi'. His son, also called Ptahhotpe, is shown as a child holding the lower end of his father's staff and grasping a hoopoe by the wings. Feast your eyes with those of Ptahhotpe on the numerous activities occurring on his estates.

At the top the papyrus-harvest is underway to gather the reeds for writing material, boat-building, rope sandals and baskets. A boatman holds the front leg of a calf crossing the canal to keep it safe from a lurking crocodile. Then there is a register of boys playing games, some of which are clearly mimicking the jobs of the vineyard scene below. Once more there is a point of connection between ourselves and people of Ptahhotpe's Egypt, 4,500 years ago – especially if one is prepared to admit to remembering 'rough and tumble' games in the school playground. Firstly, two boys throw pointed sticks at a target stuck in the ground. Irreverently they are aiming at a crude symbol of Shezmu, god of the wine-press – it is dangerous too since he could have a malevolent side to him where he was sometimes thought to squeeze the heads of sinners in the Underworld just like bunches of grapes. Then another boy is kneeling while two children hold each other seated across his back – a parody of the donkey carrying two panniers. Next, giving vent to their pent-up aggression, two boys struggle to get each other in a neck-lock. Beyond, there is a vignette of a form of 'high jump' still popular in Egyptian villages – but the artist has compressed the full activity to save wall-space. So, the two boys facing in the same direction, seated on the ground with their legs stretched out so that the heel of one foot rests on the toes of the other and their hands reaching forward to rest above their feet, are in reality sitting opposite each other. They form the barrier over which the boy in the headscarf running towards them will have to leap. Elsewhere a boy kneels on the shoulders of three companions to give the image of a vine trellis. Six boys form a ring and fall back at full stretch to revolve round on their heels – four times as the inscription says. Then one unfortunate boy is being attacked on all sides by four companions with exclamations approximating to 'Watch it! you're kicking me!' 'Ouch! my ribs!' and 'Get a taste of that!'

In the vineyard men water the vines and trample the grapes holding onto the trellis. Grapes are squeezed and twisted in the sack with one

82. (opposite) The wife of
Mereruka, daughter of King
Teti, carved in Mereruka's mastaba as a tiny figure standing on
his foot, Dynasty VI, Saqqara

worker exerting the pressure by keeping the poles held by Intef and Tjeni well apart. Next, the desert hunt in this tomb really repays close attention (fig. 39). The Nubian greyhound attacks a hyena, biting its ears and another grounds an oryx. A gazelle raises its rear leg to suckle a fawn. Perhaps one should not intrude too long on the mating leopards and jackals and go down to the next register where the huntsman Iry, in a striped garment, kneels pointing out to his greyhounds the wild bull caught by its muzzle in the lion's mouth. Greyhounds are bringing down a gazelle and an oryx – one gazelle is hiding by a bush. There is an ichneumon on the prowl and a jerboa bolting towards its hole in a hillock while a hedgehog seems to be only just winning against the grasshopper in its mouth. Below are scenes showing the making of papyrus-canoes and ropes, men gutting fish to dry in the sun, trapping wild fowl with clap-nets and the lively turmoil between Nile boatmen. With a brilliant device Niankhptah, the sculptor of these magnificent reliefs, steps out very discreetly from perpetual anonymity. You can see him in the boat on the left sitting drinking with figs piled before him, subtly carving a prosperous niche for himself in the vizier's afterlife. He deserves a round of applause for his cunning and craftsmanship.

39. Mastaba of Akhtihotpe and Ptahhotpe: Desert hunting scene in the Chapel of Ptah-hotpe

The southern section of this east wall presents Ptahhotpe reviewing the gifts and tax-returns of the villages on his estates. He is accompanied by another son who bears his grandfather's name of Akhtihotpe. A few more games recreate the leisure-hours of children. Now the skill already witnessed in carving animals and birds emerges again in the depiction of the trophies of the hunt. Two strong wooden cages dragged along sledges confine a lion and a leopard. Men with yokes carry antelope and ibex skins and cages with hares and hedgehogs. Here the striped robed

83. (opposite) Statue of Mereruka in the chapel of his mastaba, Dynasty VI, Saqqara

84. Egypt today: modern Egyptian children would have no difficulty playing the games shown on the walls of Mereruka's chapel

85. *Kagemni's mastaba: a man places drops of milk in the mouth of a suckling pig, Dynasty VI, Saqqara*

huntsman brings in his hounds and some hyenas – the latter probably for attempted domestication as shown in the mastaba of Mereruka. A faithfully carved row of cervids enables us to see some of the hunted species of desert fauna – oryx, ibex, addax, Bubalis and Soemmering's gazelle. Then herdsmen tend cattle destined for sacrifice at the festival of Thoth – hence the ibis, his sacred bird, in the hieroglyphs over the oxen – which took place in July at the time of the New Year, heralded by the rising Nile. The birds now documented with incredible totals in the figures beside them illustrate the eye for detail of the Egyptian artist. Three groups of geese add up in the account book to 253,510 birds. Look at the swan, much rarer of course, but still totalling 1225. Additional insurance against Ptahhotpe's peckishness in the next world consists of 120,000 pintailed ducks, 121,022 widgeons, 111,200 pigeons, an unspecified number of goslings and a flock of cranes herded together by an overseer. On the west wall the colours of yellow, red, blue and green still survive over large areas of the relief of Ptahhotpe holding an alabaster perfume jar to his nose and stretching his hand towards the table of loaves. His retainers approach doing amazing balancing acts with trays of produce. Now leave Ptahhotpe, perhaps hoping that the Egypt portrayed in the reliefs gave him, as he inspected work in progress, the peace of mind with which to face the inevitable sojourn in the burial crypt.

Mastabas in various states of preservation are scattered all over the Saqqara plateau: from around this period from another large brick mastaba near the ruined pyramid of Weserkaf come the statues of Dynasty V carved in sycamore, popularly nicknamed 'The Wife of Sheikh al-Balad' and 'The Skeikh al-Balad' (*80 & 81*). He looks the picture of a present-day Egyptian mayor, with the corpulence which in Ancient Egypt signified worldly success.

Ty: Overseer of Pyramids and Sun Temples

North of the Avenue of Sphinxes and the route to the Serapeum, the Saqqara sand drifts into mounds hiding the ancient necropolis below. But one mastaba rescued from its grip boasts an unrivalled combination of artistic skill and masterly selection of themes of daily life (fig. 40). It belongs to the courtier Ty who lived sometime during the later reigns of Dynasty V, and although now seemingly subterranean because of the enveloping sand, originally commanded a view of the monuments at Abusir to the north, built by the kings whom he served.

You meet Ty on the two pillars of the portico (fig. 40:1) – his name is written in hieroglyphs by a tethering-rope and two flowering reeds above the back of the head of the standing figure of him holding his sceptre and staff. Passing through the entrance notice that on the left thickness Ty is making a speech – in front of his head are the hieroglyphs of 'cobra', 'hand' and the 'horned viper' which put together mean 'he says'. His address ends with the request for bread and beer to be supplied endlessly from his estates.

The court where you now stand (fig. 40:2) has had much of its decoration eroded. Some representations of Ty can still be seen on four of the twelve pillars that enclose a central area from which a descending passage leads into the crypt (fig. 40:3) containing the empty sarcophagus

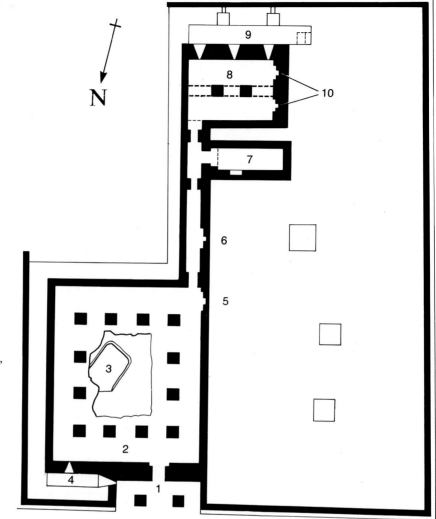

N

40. Mastaba of Ty, Dynasty V,
Saqqara

1 Portico
2 Court
3 Entrance to Crypt
4 *Serdab*
5 Demedj False Door
6 Neferhetpes False Door
7 Storeroom
8 Inner Hall
9 *Serdab*
10 False Doors of Ty

of Ty. Following the surviving scenes by turning left from the entrance,
the meat-courses for banquets in the next-world are being provided for
with men throwing oxen over for slaughter. There is a gap in this
northern wall connecting the court with the statue-chamber or *serdab*
(fig. 40:4) where Ty's substitute bodies in stone could receive his
life-force (*ka*). Along the east wall, below the remains of Ty carried in a
palanquin, is a dwarf in charge of a monkey. Once again and not for the
last time one is struck by the compassion in Ancient Egypt for persons
with special needs in terms of work. Retainers carry furniture but turn
your attention to the three kneeling figures. Facing Ka-aper, the
Overseer of '*ka*-servants' i.e. those personnel responsible for the routine
of the funerary cult, are Ty's two sons. The one on the left is his eldest
son, called Demedj, who has the 'Mikadoesque' title of 'Overseer of the
duck-pond'. His younger brother, called Ty, is described as an 'Inspector
of manicurists in the palace'. Crossing back towards the entrance to the
northern corner of the west wall of the portico, Ty and his wife watch

scenes of bird rearing and feeding. He had married Neferhetpes and in typical style ensures that she will be with him forever by depicting her frequently in the scenes which doubtless he chose personally from the draughtsman's established repertoire. She belonged to two guilds of priestesses like other respectable courtiers' wives – one of the goddess Neith 'north of the wall' (referring to her sanctuary at Memphis) and the other of the goddess Hathor. Their older son Demedj faces them with arms full of papyrus-rolls; their younger son, Ty, is represented as a child – naked, sucking his finger, wearing the sidelock of youth and clinging onto his father's staff. Clearly the boy's title, here in the accompanying hieroglyphs, of 'Inspector of manicurists' is either anticipatory or added later when he had begun his career. In an instance such as this Ty the tomb-owner is remembering years of idyllic happiness with his wife and sons recreated in these reliefs in the hope of repeating them in the afterlife. As a kind father he would not, however, want Ty the younger to be without status in the next-world hierarchy.

Ka-aper, responsible for the upkeep of the mortuary cult of Ty, approaches armed with documents concerning the estate livestock. You can follow some of the activities – of men cooking and preparing the pellets of food which others are forcing down the beaks of ducks and cranes, or further south along this wall of Ty receiving accounts in his office. You can sense the bustle going on in the nearby fenced-off poultry yard which has a pool in the centre: ducks are milling round to get at the grain pellets scattered by the men with sacks.

Beyond the niche displaying the false door of Demedj (fig. 40:5) we enter the narrow corridor that will take us eventually into the tomb chapel. The reliefs in this tomb deserve lingering over as a prize legacy of the draughtsmen, sculptors and painters who lived under the pharaohs. There are three reliefs of Ty as a high dignitary on both sides of the corridor. His sceptres, kerchief or baton, mark him as a man of authority, as do his long-flowing or tightly-curled wigs. In the inscriptions cartouches give us the names of the pharaohs Neferirkara and Neweserra of whose pyramids he was overseer. The squat-obelisk-on-the-podium hieroglyphs refer to the sun temples in which he served as an administrator – in all he was involved with four of these architectural statements of royal piety to the sun-god Ra from the reigns of Sahura, Neferirkara, Neferefra and Neweserra. A procession of offering-bearers guides you to the niche in the west wall containing the false door of Neferhetpes (fig. 40:6): her name with the honorific title of 'Royal Acquaintance' blazoned above the central recess over the doorway, and she herself stands elegantly in her choker necklace and wide bead collar. At the top a central panel shows her seated at a table of loaves breathing in burning incense and being presented with bales of linen from two 'ka-servants'. More offering-bearers bring you through the narrowing of the passageway which marks the door into the second corridor. A glance back above the doorway reveals Ty in a skiff pulling two stalks of papyrus while Neferhetpes breathes in the scent of a lotus blossom. On the east wall above, butchers slaughtering oxen introduce the important ritual of dragging statues of Ty in kiosks on sledge-runners into the tomb for use by his ka. Above the kiosk shaped like a shrine with a cavetto cornice, the inscription tells that the standing statue of Ty below is made of acacia; above the shrine with the curved roof, the hieroglyphs describe the statue below as carved from ebony – the high-quality wood brought up from Africa for the pharaoh and upper echelons of society. In each case one man smooths the shrine's path by pouring water before the sledge-runners and seven men perform the dragging, chanting the phrase 'splendid parade' as they proceed to the tomb.

A store chamber (fig. 40:7) leads off the western wall opposite these reliefs. On the right entrance-thickness the rowing and sailing boats of Ty's flotilla are executed in fine detail. Among the six rowing boats is one with a terminal carved with the now familiar reversed hedgehog head. Ty stands in a vessel under sail while in the two following boats men kneel on the cabin roof near the boom and shout to their companions pulling on the rigging: 'Tie the knot.' Inside the storeroom around the doorway are carved cylindrical and rotund vases giving a glimpse of the variety of styles available in the Old Kingdom. On the southern wall the draughtsman has left a small mistake uncorrected – if it were ever noticed: in front of his father stands young Ty with a bird in his hand but by confusion the hieroglyphs give him the titles of his elder brother Demedj. Among such daunting artistry it is occasionally welcome to come across odd errors. The west wall introduces the bakery where women knead the dough and bake the loaves in ovens. The grain for bread comes from three cylindrical silos. Moving into the pottery, men are shaping vessels, one using a hand-operated turntable. It is likely that this room stored utility items such as pots, some perhaps containing the aromatics needed in the celebration of the mortuary cult of Ty by the 'ka-servants'. Real valuables like gilded metal vases or jewellery would have been buried below the tomb chapel with Ty's body.

Once more in the corridor you pass through the doorway, above which carvings recreate music for Ty to listen to while his eyes can feast on the dancers. Now you are in the inner hall (fig. 40:8) from where so many scenes, often surviving in colour, have been reproduced in works on Egyptian life or art. Yet no amount of familiarity seems to detract from the infinite variety of these reliefs. The two pillars in the centre of this hall give Ty another opportunity to display himself as a dignitary and boast his titles. Time is frequently at a premium on a visit to Egypt but if you cut out any of the reliefs in this area you will lose out on an intimate feeling of involvement in life under the pharaohs.

Taking the east wall northern section first of all, Ty and Neferhetpes are in a 'summer-house' watching harvest scenes. In the horizontal line of hieroglyphs near them you can see, for example, a man cutting barley, a donkey laden for the granary and three circles with grain dotted in them to represent threshing-floors. Ty wears an amulet of a stylized fist grasping a dagger. Covering the registers of reliefs from the top downwards, men pull up stalks of flax for the linen industry, whereas below they use sickles to reap the barley. One man is playing a long flute and a field worker has put his sickle under his arm, stretching one hand in front of him and lifting the other to his ear – this does not mean excruciating pain through grating unmusical flute-playing but is the conventional way of representing a person giving a song, as with present-day Indian singers. In the sixth register two men are pulling on ropes to tie up sheaves of corn. Donkeys are being cudgelled into the field and donkey boys are enjoying a rhythmic race with one man beating time with sticks and another, with his hand to his face, chanting. Below, a donkey refuses to cooperate so one man pulls its ears and a foreleg while another beats its rump. Bales are loaded onto the donkeys – except in the case of a foal running in front oblivious to the fact that its gamboling days are numbered. The sheaves are piled into stacks to be taken to the threshing-floors and the hooves of the cattle and donkeys. Women wearing headscarves assist at winnowing the grain.

The southern area of this east wall shows severe damage to its upper registers. However, still surviving is the lion leaning over an enclosure fence to seize a gazelle, a visual encapsulation of the fear expressed so vividly a thousand years later in the hymn to the Aten of the lion leaving its den and stalking its prey at night. Below, carpenters are at work in a dockyard – in one boat Ty stands watching them constructing the hull with their adzes, axes, saws and mallets. One carpenter saws down a plank set upright with a binding and weight at the top to help him keep a true line.

Three apertures in the south wall link a second *serdab* (fig. 40:9) to the inner hall. Peering through the slit you can see a cast of the statue of Ty now displayed in Cairo Museum. It represents an idealization of Ty as a courtier in the prime of life, unmarred by any physical blemish, and with a confident expression destined to last for eternity.

You can begin your survey of the reliefs on this southern wall to the left of the eastern aperture, where Ty is seated with his greyhound below his chair. On either side of the viewing-slit to the *serdab* a '*ka*-servant' burns incense, recreating the ritual whereby a priest would ensure that the fumigations reached the nostrils of the statue.

The registers to the right of the *serdab* represent a number of artisans working at their crafts, scenes of great value to anyone interested in the history of technology. Metal-workers use blow pipes to heat the furnace and pour metal out for casting and hammering. The sculptors' studio reveals craftsmen chiselling, carving and polishing two statues of Ty shown naked in the way that the Egyptians sometimes chose to indicate themselves athletically fit and in the full command of physical faculties (fig. 41). Two other sculptors use drills to work on seated statues of Ty and vase-makers are shown drilling into the necks of cylindrical stone vessels. Among the busy sawing and adzing carpenters, some are making a bed and headrest. One kneels operating the bow-drill by pressing with a pebble on the upper drill-shaft and gaining friction by sawing movements with a bow of wood and papyrus twine. Straightening poles for tent-supports involves one man sitting on the wooden cane which is attached at its other end to a pivot (fig. 42). A leatherworker stretches an ox-hide over a three-legged frame and nearby sits a man cutting into a cylinder seal. These objects were incised with the names and titles of officials which could be rolled over a clay stopper to indicate ownership of, or authority over, a commodity stored, for instance, in a jar. The cylinders were perforated and strung on papyrus such as seen in the hand of the person observing the seal cutter at work.

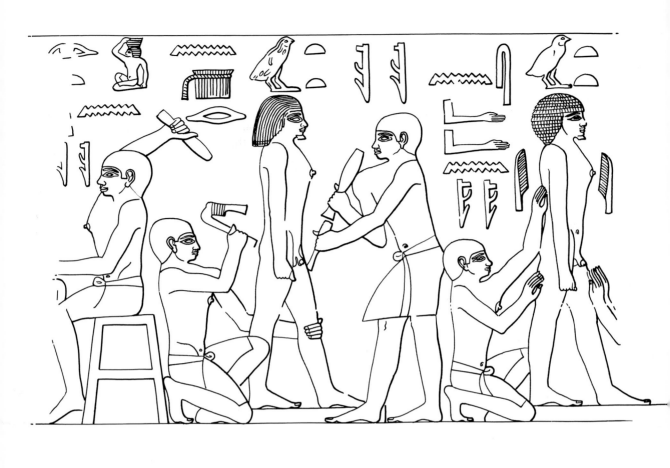

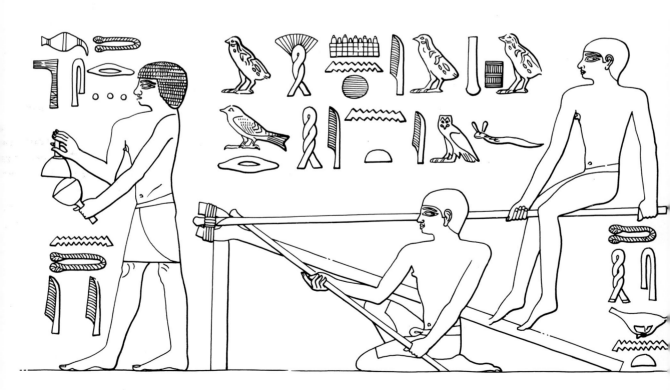

41. (above) Mastaba of Ty:
Sculptors carving statues of
the tomb owners

42. (below) Mastaba of Ty:
Straightening poles for tent
supports

Next, the market place scenes explain the method of purchasing in an economy devoid of coinage. Go into the market with the man carrying a cylindrical jar of oil. If he was after a pair of leather sandals then he is too late, since a man is already exchanging a linen bag for them. Further on you find a man offering a walking stick to a prospective customer in exchange for barley – he might just do a deal since the bearded shopper says 'I like its head' referring to the cane's smoothly bevelled terminal.

To the upper right of the centre *serdab* slit, stand Ty and Neferhetpes reviewing accounts from the scribes concerning the livestock on the estate. In the top four registers Ty's attendants pull along antelopes and oryx for inspection, the young animals carried in baskets or on men's backs. A wild deer is proving a struggle for the men to control. Below herdsmen are presenting cattle, some decorated with collars, and Ty's scribes push village headmen forward on their knees for a tax-reckoning concerning the cattle. In fact, the office accounts-section are furiously documenting the figures, using bundles of papyri. There is an exquisite group of feathery cranes being herded together by fowlers with sticks. In the vicinity of the aperture into the western *serdab* the draughtsmen have perpetuated in relief the lavish offerings that would have been left for Ty at the time of burial – including onions, figs, cakes, ducks and calf heads. Perhaps you will choose not to dwell on the vigour with which the nearby butchers sever the forelegs off antelopes, oryx, gazelle and oxen. Turning the corner to the west wall there are the recessed panels of the elaborate false doors of Ty (fig. 40:10). Below ground slightly to the west of this symbolic portal for the *ka* of Ty, his corpse once rested in the sarcophagus.

The north wall, however, provides more exciting scenes of estate activity. But you cannot start on them until you have noted the dignified realism with which the dwarf with the monkey and the hunchback leading two Saluki hounds have been rendered. The convention of impeccable and idealized physiques was not observed in the case of Ty's retainers. The top registers on the western end of this wall concern bird-trapping. Men organize the clap-net around the marsh-pond; the wildfowl then land in its catchment area. Ty, behind a clump of papyrus to avoid scaring the fowl, gives the signal at which the men farther off fall back as they pull on the rope attached to the clap-net. The nets collapse over the water birds. Manufacturing these clap-nets and ropes was the work of the men in the next register down, using spindles. Nearby is a shed where ducks have their necks wrung and their feathers plucked. Fishermen (notice the elderly man with a distended abdomen) have drawn in an extremely rich catch of fish – two men cut open the fish to dry in the sun and remove roes. Below herdsmen are tending cattle. A man holds the forelegs of a calf to hold it back from the udder of the mother-cow which is being milked. In a humorous touch the artists have depicted calves poking their tongues out all over the place. A herdsman assists a calf which has become tangled up in a bush by its tethering-rope; another pulls the head and forelegs of a calf from its mother's body as she strains to give it birth. In the lower row, fibres are being tugged and brushed to form matting. Then two canoes on a canal can be seen escorting cattle across the water. The boatmen utter spells and gesticulate

with arm-sweeping across the surface of the canal in the hope of
counteracting the danger of the 'smiling' crocodiles lurking near each
canoe.

43. Mastaba of Ty: Hippopotamus at bay and the death of a
crocodile

The masterpiece of the whole tomb lies in the centre of this northern
wall. There is a background of vertical papyrus stalks so the scene takes
place in the thickets of the marshes. Ty stands unruffled and pompous as
he is punted along in his papyrus canoe. In the skiff in front three men
lasso and spear hippopotami with barbed harpoons – one beast at bay
roars defiantly, exhibiting a splendid pair of tusks. Another hippopotamus which has been lassoed seems more engrossed in despatching the
crocodile which it has raised up in its jaws (fig. 43). Oblivious of all this
intense excitement a man in a papyrus coracle is pulling from the water a
cat-fish which he has caught on a line (fig. 44). But now look over Ty's
head at the agitation going on in the marshes. You can almost hear the
two parent birds screeching at an ichneumon (or mongoose) crawling
towards the nest where their fledgelings sit squawking. No ornithologist
can fail to go away impressed by the detail of plumage or the variety of
birds shown, like the cormorant, heron and lapwings. To the eastern side
near the doorway Ty surveys men carrying bundles of papyrus-stalks on
their backs and tying them together to make canoes. Scenes like this
multiplied by several thousand years make it all too understandable why
the papyrus plant eventually vanished from the Egyptian environment.

86. (left) Ruins of the valley temple of the pyramid of King Wenis, next to the bend in the road that takes tourists up to the Saqqara pyramids

87. (below) Causeway of King Wenis, Dynasty V, Saqqara

88. *(right) Emaciated figure from the fragmentary reliefs on the causeway of King Wenis at Saqqara, Dynasty V, Saqqara, Louvre*

89. *(below) Ruins of the mortuary temple and the pyramid of King Wenis, Dynasty V, Saqqara*

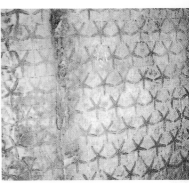

90. *(top left) Pyramid texts written on the walls of the burial chamber of King Wenis's pyramid, Dynasty V, Saqqara*

91. *(top right) The palace-façade design, painted on the walls surrounding the sarcophagus of Wenis inside his burial chamber, Dynasty V, Saqqara*

92. *(left) Detail of the palace-façade design showing the paired bound lotuses, exactly as carved on earlier Old Kingdom sarcophagi (see 36)*

93. *(above) Star decoration on the ceiling of King Wenis' burial chamber, Dynasty V, Saqqara*

94. (left) Model votive sistrum (sacred rattle) of King Teti as 'Beloved of Hathor' in alabaster, Dynasty VI, Saqqara, (now in USA)

95. (above) The Pyramid of Teti, Dynasty VI, Saqqara

Then we find a register of jousting boatmen – is the man displaying acrobatic agility as he clings round the prow to grab at his opponents' pole, or is he falling in the water? Elsewhere men catch fish with baskets and empty out their catch. Below, cows are milked and the ground broken up by mattocks to assist the ploughing. The Barbary sheep as usual are both enticed and whipped to drive them along over the newly sown seed which they can then firmly embed in the mud with their hooves. The three horizontal lines of hieroglyphs over the sheep form the 'libretto' of a shepherd's song about sheep in a riverine landscape. Its tune, forever lost, must have been one that haunted Ty and one that he would want to hear, carried by the breeze across the fields in the next life. Below, is a fine relief of herdsmen guiding cattle across a canal – their feet and hooves hinted at by the artist, below the ripples of the water. The gem of this vignette is the calf carried on the back of a herdsman for safety, which turns and bleats pitifully at its mother anxiously watching it from the herd fording the canal. There is a stark contrast with the lower register of reliefs consisting of superbly carved but austere personifications of Ty's domains as women carrying produce into the tomb. It is time to follow the corridor out and leave Ty's *ka* to enjoy the offerings brought by these elegant ladies.

44. Mastaba of Ty: Fisherman pulling out a catfish

203

In 1893 a huge mastaba was discovered just northwest of the temenos wall around the pyramid of King Teti, first king of Dynasty VI (fig. 45). It housed the three tombs of Mereruka, his wife Waetetkhethor and his son Meryteti – all aristocrats moving in the court circles of Dynasty VI. Architecturally this mastaba is the grandest in the tradition of Old Kingdom courtiers' tombs and even if the carvings lack the *finesse* of the graceful representations in the tomb of Ty it remains a monument full of force, and intensely rich in the scenes of daily life. Occasionally, some walls reveal sculptors at work, endowed with less expertise than their colleagues in other parts of the tomb, but overall the reliefs comprise a legacy to be treasured and admired. Throughout the mastaba the figure of Mereruka himself consistently epitomizes the dignity of the chief executive of the state in the pyramid age.

At the foot of the incline opposite the front of Mereruka's tomb, one can make an interesting observation on its position. It is built against the western face of the mastaba of Kagemni (but stretching a little further southwards) probably indicating a family relationship between Mereruka and the earlier holder of the office of vizier. To allow space for his predecessors' storerooms to be completed, Mereruka began his mastaba by orientating the entrance to the south instead of the customary eastern access, as in the case of Kagemni and Ankhmahor. At the same time, this practical consideration meant that the exterior carvings of Mereruka could view the pyramid of Teti whom he had served as premier. So, cleverly, the façade of the mastaba and its low inscribed boundary wall are not obscured in a small alley against Kagemni's tomb but attract the eye as having the most impressive approach among the courtiers' monuments near Teti's pyramid. On the door jambs Mereruka, whose 'good name' was Meri, stands with his sceptre, and his wife breathes in the scent of the lotus flower.

Mereruka was promoted by the pharaoh to important secular and religious offices – including chief justice and vizier, inspector of priests attached to the pyramid of Teti (of Dynasty VI), scribe of the Divine Books, chief lector priest and overseer of the royal record scribes. From the ten decorated chambers of his section of the mastaba one gets to know members of his family not depicted in his wife's or son's rooms (fig. 46). There is his mother Nedjetempet whose title 'royal acquaintance' may possibly indicate that she was one of a king's doubtlessly numerous granddaughters. Mereruka therefore probably had royal blood flowing in his veins. His son Meryteti, who was given the northeast corner of this mastaba, is on one occasion called, in Mereruka's tomb where he appears six times, 'his eldest son of his body'. Mereruka had five other sons, but not by his wife Waetetkhethor – who possessed the 'good name' of 'Seshseshat', by which we will now refer to her (82). Her major title is 'King's eldest daughter of his body' – the pharaoh concerned is Teti. Out of forty-six principal scenes in Mereruka's tomb the status of Seshsehat demands that she be included in thirty-nine of them. Her three decorated rooms in this mastaba show only her own two children – one daughter and her 'eldest son her beloved' Meryteti who appears there eleven times. The stage is now set for the friction between

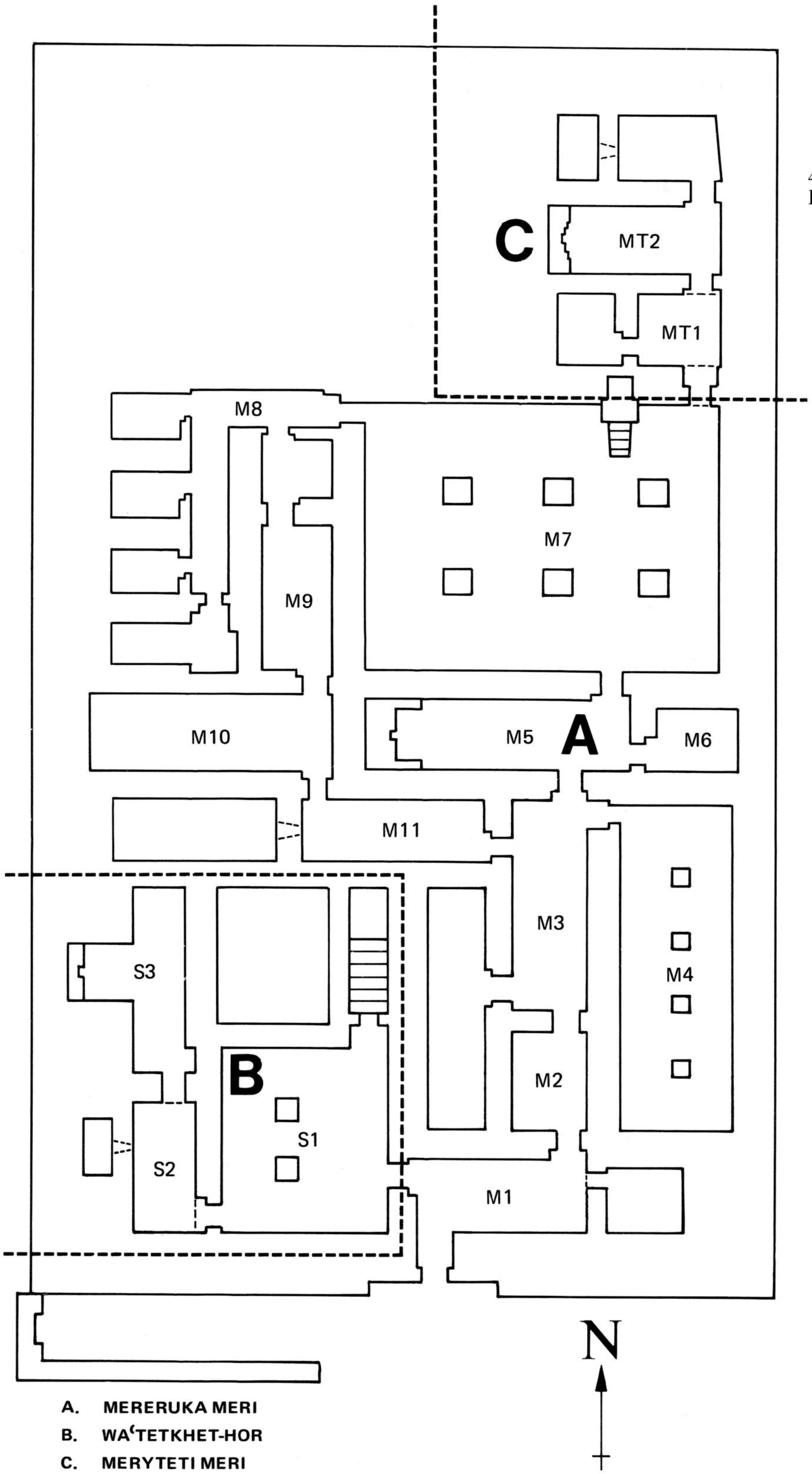

45. Mastaba of Mereruka, Dynasty VI, Saqqara

C

MT2

MT1

M8

M7

M9

M10

M5

A

M6

M11

M3

M4

S3

M2

B

S1

S2

M1

N

A. MERERUKA MERI
B. WA'TETKHET-HOR
C. MERYTETI MERI

Memi and his half-brother Meryteti to erupt into a struggle for possession of the northeast chambers of the mastaba.

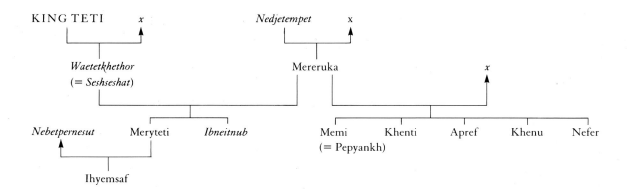

46. The Family of Mereruka

KEY

TETI = monarch
Nebetpernesut = female
x = unknown
        female
↑ = married to
| = child of
x = unknown
        male

On the eastern thickness of the small entrance vestibule a scene quite static ought to bring you to a stop with a jolt. Mereruka is seated holding a paintbrush in his hand before an easel supporting a panel. For company he has his son Khenu 'Lector priest and scribe of the Divine Books'. In this representation, Mereruka's desire to participate in the yearly cycle of agrarian activities forevermore is given a pronounced position at the start of his tomb. He has just finished painting personifications of the three seasons of the farmer's calendar, each holding oval shapes inside which four crescent moons symbolize the twelve 30-day months of the Ancient Egyptian year. From right to left the seasons are labelled *Akhet* (inundation) *Peret* (winter sowing) and *Shemu* (summer harvest). At this point it will be best to turn left through the western doorway to make a rapid excursion into the section of the mastaba dedicated to Seshseshat. Three rooms bear reliefs, a few of which rival the quality of the best carvings in Mereruka's tomb. To the north of the pillared hall (fig. 45:s1) a staircase, now closed off, led to a storechamber. Just west of this stairway lies the shaft down to the burial chamber. There in an uninscribed sarcophagus were found the bones of a large woman, middle aged at the time of her death – an unwelcome correction to the slender image of young-looking Seshseshat carved on the walls of the mastaba above. Returning to the hall with its two pillars, among the personified estates of Upper and Lower Egypt bringing mortuary offerings, the main point of interest is on the western wall beyond the fishermen and cattle: Seshseshat is depicted with her son Meryteti, and her daughter Ibneitnub who only appears here, and whose life must remain a closed book to us. Through the doorway into the inner rooms we face the west wall (fig. 45:s2) behind which was built the *serdab* for the now-lost statue of Seshseshat. Around the north door she watches girls dancing and beating time to the music. The innermost chamber (fig. 45:s3) has a recess in the west wall containing a well-cut false door while the north wall displays Seshseshat and her son being carried on an official 'progress' in a palanquin decorated with a lion –

their pathway kept clear by the escort, which includes three dogs and a monkey.

Now it is time to survey the nucleus of this grandiose mastaba – the apartments of Mereruka himself. One glance at the south wall of the first room beyond the entrance vestibule (fig. 45:M1) and one is transported back to the papyrus marshes that flourished along the Nile in the days of the pharaohs. In a boat constructed from papyrus reeds stands Mereruka, his wig encircled by a ribbon tied in a knot to resemble the umbels of the papyrus plant, together with Seshseshat decked out in a splendid collar and an amuletic necklace. However, one's attention, drawn downwards past the frog and grasshoppers, is soon riveted by the confrontation between a hippopotamus and a crocodile in which the latter lethal reptile is lifted and crushed between the jaws of its rival. Another crocodile risks incurring a similar fate as it creeps up behind a hippopotamus to give it a nasty nip in the rear. In these scenes of actual or imminent struggle a humorous touch is introduced by the artist through a slight modification in the size of a baby hippopotamus and a huge fish: of practically equal dimensions they face each other, mutually bewildered. One of the men on the papyrus canoe which accompanies Mereruka on this marsh expedition has caught an ichneumon by the tail to prevent it reaching the nest of fledglings around which the parent birds are flying and screeching frantically. Nearby, oblivious to this uproar, stands a graceful flamingo. Mereruka's cattle are guided across the marshes past a watchful crocodile and reach the estate-pastures indicated in the upper registers of men roping and grounding bulls for slaughter. Above, men carrying water-pots on yokes plant and water gardens.

Pass by the offering bearers on the doorway thicknesses and turn sharp left to the south wall in room (fig. 45:M2) where upper portions of the structure are missing. In addition to Mereruka and Seshseshat you meet his brother Ihy and Memi his 'eldest son' by another wife. On the west wall there is a hunting scene taking place in a fenced enclosure. Eager greyhounds bite into an antelope, tearing at its body viciously. In rather hieratic iconography a lion confronts a wild bull with the intent of savaging it, even if the relief leaves us more with the impression that it is whispering into its quarry's ear. The east wall displays craftsmen at work. At the top they drill into stone vessels to produce either low bowls or vases with elegantly slender cylindrical necks. Then carpenters manufacture a bed and a door. The scene next shifts to a street between the workshops where statues of Mereruka are dragged along on sledges ready for inclusion in the inventory of his tomb equipment. Then you enter the metal-workers' shop (fig. 47) to find a scribe recording the amount of metal being weighed in the scales by the overseer Ikhi. Seated around a furnace are six men with blowpipes to raise the intensity of the heat for smelting ore. Molten metal is poured out and when cooled is beaten into the shape of a collar called, in the hieroglyphs, 'gold'. Stressing the importance of the finished item for use by Mereruka in the afterlife there follows a row of collars, a headdress and pectoral. Four dwarfs work on low benches to produce jewellery.

Acknowledge the rows of offering bearers on the doorway and walk into the next room (fig. 45:M3) where on the west wall justice can be seen

47. Mastaba of Mereruka: The
metal-workers' shop

to be done. The lawcourt is depicted as a columned hall and into it are
brought village headmen to give an account of their payments before
local tax officials. Facing left, with their brushes for writing documents
stuck behind their ears, are the magistrate Kar and the household
overseer Khnumankh. The mayor of one village has failed to meet the
tax quota. So, to deter such a shortcoming at the next demand, he is held
naked against a whipping-post and cudgelled. The two small heads on
top of the pole are probably artificial and meant to intimidate those being
punished. A lively fishing scene takes place opposite on the east wall.
Fishermen, some naked except for the buoyant vests, use both hand-nets
and basket traps to make their catch. Fish are shown cut up and left to
dry in the sun. You can spot Mereruka's eldest brother Ihy – he is the
smug corpulent man seated on a boat holding his duckling-snack while
drink is held up to his lips by a retainer. At the end of this wall turn right
into the room with four rectangular pillars (fig. 45:M4). A lot of the
carving in here is poor quality workmanship. The male and female
dancers on the east wall are worth looking at for a moment or two if only

to try to imagine the rhythm being beaten out by the people clapping their hands. Otherwise, just concentrate on the scene of domestic bliss on the west wall. Mereruka squats on a long couch holding his fly-whisk of foxtails. Opposite him Seshseshat, relaxing without the encumbrance of a wig, kneels at a harp to accompany herself as she sings. Not only does this give a picture of how an evening or leisure hours could be spent in Ancient Egypt, but also reveals what skills were taught to a daughter of a pharaoh.

In room (fig. 45:M5) an iron grille installed by the Antiquities Organization bars access to the shaft leading down 14.5 metres to the burial chamber. On the west wall above the shaft is a false door on which is carved a bolt keeping it locked until Mereruka's spirit deigns to use it. Robbers in pharaonic times descended into the burial chamber cutting their way through the corner of a stone barrier. The walls around them, devoid of any image of a living creature that might become animated and cause damage to Mereruka's body, displayed an elaborate painted offering list and designs of mat-hangings. A ramp led westward to the

96. (opposite) Statuette of Pepi I
with Horus hawk, Dynasty VI,
?Saqqara. Alabaster, 26.5 cm
high. The Brooklyn Museum,
39.120. Charles Edwin Wilbour
Fund

limestone sarcophagus. The thieves heaved the lid forward to get at the mummified corpse of Mereruka. In their search for valuables on the body they hacked through the linen wrappings with knives, as the gouges on the arm bones of Mereruka's dismembered and scattered skeletal remains showed all too well. Still, from what survived of his bones it was possible to deduce that he was at the time of his death a middle-aged man. Further, the reliefs in his mastaba above give no hint of his short wide head and jutting jaw.

The doorway opposite the false door leads into a small room (fig. 45:M6) where the reliefs again show the workmanship was done by sculptors of inferior ability to those carving elsewhere in the tomb. Yet there is a scene on the north wall that illustrates the working practices of Egyptian winemakers. Two men sit in a circular area clapping sticks together. They are keeping the rhythm for the men nearby to make vigorous twists on the poles which tighten the sacks to squeeze out the grape-juice.

As you enter the most impressive hall (fig. 45:M7) in the mastaba – a six-piered cult chapel – it is clear that a dramatic architectural plan has succeeded. Your eyes catch the broad dimensions of the chamber but are at once drawn to look straight ahead between the pillars to the massive enshrined statue of Mereruka above an alabaster offering table (83). Perhaps to get accustomed to the grand scale of this chapel and the lavishness of its decoration one ought to wander between the six columns. Mereruka was sculpted on the rectangular faces of these pillars in all his dignity as a courtier or a priestly official wearing the panther skin. If the representations seem remarkably even in scale it is because of the set proportional guidelines used by the artists cutting the human figure into six segments at the level of the knees, the base of the buttocks, the elbows, the armpits, the base of the neck and the hairline at the top of the forehead. The stone ring among the pillars could have been for tethering sacrificial cattle. However, it is difficult to prove that it was part of the original architect's plan for this chapel. Anyway, would Mereruka have wanted blood and offal over the floor of this splendid chamber? More likely the slaughter was carried out in the open area in front of the mastaba. Then this intrusive stone-ring could have been inserted into the floor by the tomb robbers in order to secure their ropes for the descent into the burial crypt.

There are all kinds of details sculpted on the walls in this cult chapel that recreate the Nile valley environment for Mereruka and commemorate the last moments of leaving it for his sepulchre. Beginning to the east of the doorway in the south wall a refreshingly naturalistic riverine scene reveals an otter killing a fish to devour – the total preoccupation of the animal with its meal is faultlessly rendered by the artist. Yet another instance of humour comes through in the depiction of a surprise face-to-face encounter between a 'smiling' crocodile and a fish with its mouth open. Moving beyond the doorway to the west the funeral procession of Mereruka occupies the lower surviving section of the original mastaba superstructure. Mourning women, some collapsing on the ground in grief, follow the coffin to its funerary barge. Three rowing boats are about to tow the vessel, once the oarsmen begin their stroke

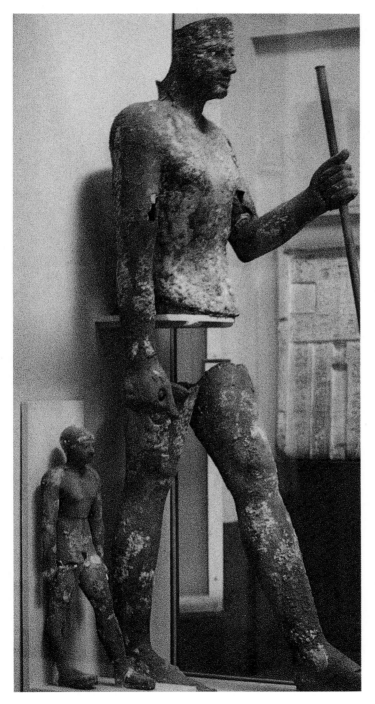

97. (opposite) Statuette of Pepi I
kneeling and holding libation
pots, Dynasty VI, ?Dendera.
Slate, 15.2 cm high. The Brooklyn Museum, 39.121. Charles
Edwin Wilbour Fund

98. (left) Pepi I, possibly with his
son Meryenra, made by hammering sheets of copper over a
wooden frame, Dynasty VI,
Hierakonpolis, Cairo Museum

when the swimmers have pushed it off from the shore. Men then convey
the coffin accompanied by dancers to the tomb where the lector priest
stands facing outwards to conduct the funerary ceremonies. On the west
wall Mereruka's private flotilla is travelling along the Nile. Five of the
boats are under full-sail following, as the text reveals, 'the good route
into the Beautiful West in peace'; Mereruka has his small fleet of boats
for journeys in the afterlife, his bed even appearing on the afterdeck of
one vessel. There is also a boat with its sail furled and its mast lowered
onto pinions. The rowers are at their oars and Mereruka is there on the
foredeck receiving an offering of fowl – the magnate cannot be allowed
to travel hungry either in this life or the next.

On the north wall, despite losses in the upper level, are to be found
some of the finest carved representations of Mereruka and his family and
some intriguing scenes of animal husbandry. From the western end
Mereruka is met carried in his palanquin and two dwarfs in charge of his
pet monkey and guard-dogs. The procession of men below accompanying him comprises six brothers, his sons Nefer and Khenti, three more
brothers and two scribes. Then a large relief shows Mereruka led along
by his two sons Memi and Apref who lovingly cup his hands. Nowhere
in the tomb is there more sensitive and exquisite carving of the human
face than here. The replacing of Memi's name here by another ending in
the element 'ankh' does not mean his identity has been usurped but is all
tied up with the rivalry between him and Meryteti – an imbroglio which
we will soon be resolving. Next follow six magnificent registers of estate
activity. Concentrate on the practice of force-feeding livestock in order to
make them gain excess weight. Herdsmen are thrusting their food-filled
hands down the throats of oxen and semi-domesticated antelopes from
the desert edges supplement the meat supply. But the most surprising
animals shown here being reared for human consumption are the
hyenas. Their hind legs are bound together, their front paws held and
then the creatures are thrown onto their backs. Men then have to carry
out the unenviable task of forcing food past the snapping jaws of the
hyenas. It is not known if it was through the loss of fingers or bitten
limbs that this particular exploitation of a possible food supply was
discontinued in the Old Kingdom. In Mereruka's tomb, however, no
injuries are received and the hyenas' distended bellies are witnesses to the
success of the exercise.

At the foot of the altar you can look up at the statue of Mereruka
dominating this offering hall. Standing as if ready to come down from
the niche to receive the requisite oblations of the funerary cult, the
statue's magisterial presence is, if anything, rendered more ruthless by
the fact that Mereruka's face has been blinded by robbers who have
gouged out the inlaid eyes and the metal overlay of the eyebrows. In the
reliefs beside and above the eastern doorway into Meryteti's apartments
Mereruka with Seshseshat and his mother Nedjetempet view children at
play. Nothing must spoil these images of joy and carefree behaviour so,
'regardless of their doom', the boys and girls are protected by the
obscuring columns and by distance from the funeral ceremonies on the
north wall. The boys' games include making a human vine-trellis, tug of
war, leapfrog and parading a make-believe prisoner. The girls play at

99. (opposite) Pepi II on the lap
of his mother Meryraankhnes,
Dynasty VI, ?Saqqara. Calcite,
39.2 cm high. The Brooklyn
Museum, 39.119. Charles Edwin
Wilbour Fund

215

spin-a-top and perform a dance with mirrors in honour of the goddess Hathor (*84*). Predominating on the east wall are the essential farming scenes securing an eternal supply of grain and flax. They include ploughing, reaping barley, pulling flax, loading donkeys with produce and threshing. Notice peasants trapping quails in the corn fields – it is likely some of these birds will supplement their own basically meatless diet of bread and fish. A pipe player sets a lively mood for the reapers and where the sheep and goats tread the grain, the accompanying hieroglyphs give the shepherd's song:

> 'The shepherd is in the water among the fish.
> He converses with the cat-fish and swaps pleasantries
> With the oxyrhynchus fish.
> O West! Where is the shepherd?
> A shepherd of the West!'

Possibly the meaning of this song lies in the self-mockery of the shepherd spending so much time in marshy areas or wading across canals that he gets on greeting terms with the fish. I prefer to interpret it however as a pseudo-lament: a shepherd falls and nearly drowns in the water almost giving him time to get to know the fish by name. But this rescue in the nick of time deprives the western necropolis of a burial – so the 'West' feels cheated. Watching attentively the agricultural activities are Mereruka with his wife and mother, protected by sunshades and escorted by two patrol-dogs.

It is time to consider the section of the mastaba dedicated to Meryteti, son of Mereruka and Seshseshat. So go into his three decorated apartments off the northeast corner of Mereruka's cult chapel, bearing in mind that the reliefs will not impress with the high standards exhibited elsewhere in the mastaba. The themes are also familiar – the desert hunt, butchery, offering bearers with animals, linen clothing, jewellery and jars of unguent. On the south wall of the first room (fig. 45:MT1) Meryteti is accompanied by his son Ihyemsaf. On the east wall Meryteti and his wife Nebetpernesut are carried in a palanquin around the estate. It is now the occasion to sort out the struggle for ownership of this portion of the mastaba that broke out between Mereruka's two eldest sons by different mothers. So look at the inscribed false door in the next room (fig. 45:MT2) while trying to imagine the frustrations and animosities in the family of Mereruka.

The tomb of Meryteti underwent three modifications in the hieroglyphs writing the name of its owner. The original possessor had his name obliterated, but there are traces of 'Teti' and titles including 'king's son' that are consistent with Mereruka's and Seshseshat's son. Laid over the original name was that of 'Pepi-ankh' and the title 'son of Meri' (Mereruka's 'good name' substituted for 'king's son'). Then the 'ankh' element was erased and the name 'Pepi' used in the titles of Meryteti. Who then was 'Pepi-ankh'? Well, in Mereruka's tomb you met his 'eldest son' Memi, born from a previous marriage. There his name survives intact once, is erased elsewhere and is once replaced by a name ending in 'ankh' i.e. 'Pepi-ankh'. If one assumes that on the accession of Pepi I to the throne of Egypt, Memi celebrated the fact (and perhaps desperately sought royal favour) by changing his own name to 'Pepi-ankh' or 'Pepi is Life itself', then the vicissitudes of this corner of the mastaba all reflect the rivalry between Memi and Meryteti. So on Mereruka's death Memi usurped the tomb of his younger half-brother Meryteti. But what an uproar must have ensued. Meryteti was Mereruka's acknowledged heir by Seshseshat, daughter of King Teti, and hence he was a king's grandson – as the vague generic title 'king's son' can be interpreted. No change of name by Memi could disguise his lesser pedigree and he was forced by protocol to give up his claim to this tomb. Meryteti then regains his rightful inheritance and in addition to possessing forty-one titles of Mereruka, extols his own particular honours in the inscriptions – 'King's eldest son of his body' 'Lector priest of his father' and 'Inspector of the priests attached to the pyramid of King Pepi I'. You will see the cartouche of Pepi I, the king whom Meryteti served, mentioned thirty-three times in this tomb.

The main apartments of the mastaba have now been covered but if you are inclined, and have a torch, there are some side rooms in Mereruka's tomb that you can explore on the way out. Go through the passage in the northwest corner of the main cult chapel (fig. 45:M7) and walk straight ahead to the long corridor on the north-south axis (M8). Off this are four storerooms with brief inscriptions over their doors – some idea of the space allowed for utility goods for the afterlife such as jars of grain and oil and chests of clothing can be gained here. If you retrace your steps and turn right before the entrance back into the cult chamber you pass through another storeroom and into a chamber (fig. 45:M9) decorated with men carrying chests of jewellery and linen and dragging large storage jars on sledges. In the next room (M10) is a damaged false door in the west wall. It is below this room that Mereruka was laid to rest in his sarcophagus about 4,300 years ago. The remaining scenes in room (M11) show cranes receiving scattered seed, fattened livestock and women and men bearing fruits as mortuary offerings from Mereruka's estates, some titled as endowed to him by King Wenis and King Teti. Now re-enter the main tomb complex in room (M3). I admit that I leave the mastaba of Mereruka with some unease about a noticeable gap on the family tree. Was the name of his first wife and mother of his son Memi included in the now missing portions of the superstructure? Or did the ambitious Mereruka heartlessly consign her to oblivion when he made his career-marriage with Seshseshat, daughter of a pharaoh? Possibly the fault is not Mereruka's at all. He is proud to show this unknown lady's legacy of five sons in his tomb. But they are barred from Seshseshat's walls. Perhaps the princess went further and demanded that no other woman should participate in Mereruka's sexual afterlife.

Two mastabas adjacent to the tomb of Mereruka also represent the high-quality craftsmanship found in the early reigns of Dynasty VI. Visits to these courtiers' monuments will not be as time-consuming as the study of the panoramas on the walls of Mereruka's mastaba. Kagemni, who is met first, held the office of vizier (the pharaoh's chief executive) and was also responsible for the administration of the town

Kagemni: Overseer of the pyramid town of King Teti

which grew around the pyramid of Teti opposite this tomb (fig. 48). The doorways extol Kagemni and his titles; some indication of his affluence is noticeable on the thickness of the door jambs where he is carved as a corpulent – and consequently successful – royal official. If you go diagonally left through A into the pillared hall B then on the immediate right (fig. 48:1) a lively display of dancing is being given by female acrobats and male entertainers. On the adjacent wall (2) are remains of scenes showing metal-workers. Turning into C you pass men carrying furniture and vases carved on the thickness of the doorway. To the left on wall (3) men are dragging along a statue while wall (4) shows a procession of female offering-bearers – source of sustenance for Kagemni's spirit. On the adjacent wall (5) are a number of interesting activities being carried out under the watchful eye of Kagemni. Among the scribes and men both tending cattle and trapping birds in nets are scenes of force-feeding hyenas and fowl to obtain every morsel of flesh from the latter, and to experiment with a possible new food supply in the case of the desert canines, as discussed in Mereruka's tomb. Above the doorway Kagemni sits in a stately manner in his palanquin. One of his retainers, a dwarf, looks after a monkey and dogs who would be part of the officious 'clearing-the-way' entourage whenever the vizier journeyed around in his sedan chair. In room D the number of offering-bearers might seem tedious decoration of the mastaba walls but as always you have to remember that these carvings were considered magically to 'activate' and provide food for the afterlife. Turning left into room E the walls (6–7) show Kagemni together with his sons. Minor officials are present while retainers carry chests of his belongings and food and lead along animals. Retracing your steps into room F, wall (8) recreates the earthly dining habits of Kagemni for his spirit to use. The adjacent wall (9) displays the false door – symbolic link for Kagemni's spirit between the tomb chapel and the burial chamber below. Leave wall (10) where Kagemni is at table, eternally supplied by people bringing offerings, and go into room G – men drag oil jars on sledges and carry chests of goods (11) and Kagemni receives linen (12). You can exit back into room F and look at wall (13) where below the ubiquitous offering-bearers, butchers are at work. Now you can get to know Kagemni's wife a little better by proceeding to room C and looking at wall (14). Her name is, again, Seshseshat, also a daughter of the King of Egypt and the probable means of Kagemni's secure career prospects. Surrounding scenes include men fishing with baskets from canoes. Go through the doorway back into room B and turn right. Along this wall (15) are some of the most lively scenes in the tomb. Kagemni is fishing and hunting birds while his retainers spear hippopotomi. On his estate men are manufacturing the buoyant canoes from stalks of papyrus. Cows are milked and a delightful vignette shows a man holding a suckling-piglet to his lips to feed it (85). Cautious herdsmen in boats guide cattle across water, ever watchful for crocodiles. On the end wall (16) Kagemni's scribes compile and hand in inventory lists among boats of grain and animals.

Ankhmahor: Overseer of the Palace

Just to the east of Kagemni's mastaba lies the monument of Ankhmahor (fig. 49), popularly known as the 'Doctor's Tomb' from the surgical

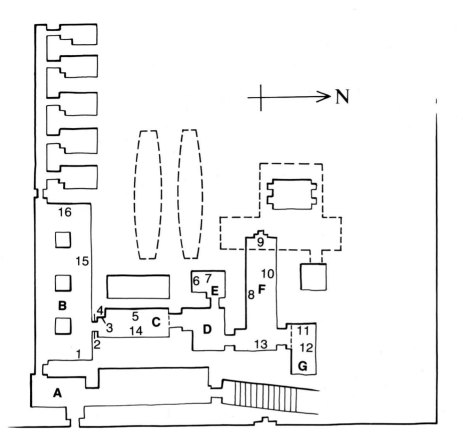

48. Mastaba of Kagemni

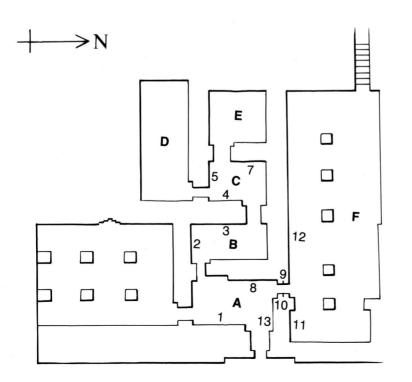

49. Mastaba of Ankhmahor

scenes which it contains. However, this is an erroneous description since it suggests that the tomb's owner was a physician when in fact, like Mereruka and Kagemni, Ankhmahor was a vizier of the pharaoh living around 2300 BC. His close connections with the palace are reflected in his title, the 'Overseer of the Great House'. He was also Inspector of the priests of King Teti whose pyramid lies opposite. Pass the carvings of Ankhmahor decorating the doorway and turn left into room A to look at wall (1). In the upper register are agricultural scenes of men winnowing grain and stacking the stalks. Also present are donkeys, the ubiquitous draught-animals of Ancient Egypt – the camels almost synonymous with the country today did not arrive on a large scale until nearly 2,000 years later. Below, herdsmen in canoes accompany cattle across water, reciting anti-crocodile spells as they do so. Passing by the entrance to a pillared offering-room you can enter room B and regard the left wall (2). Bustling reliefs abound: sculptors, metal-workers, jewellers including dwarfs as in the mastaba of Mereruka, leatherworkers and vase-makers. On the adjacent wall (3) you will see birds in the marshes being trapped by nets which collapse over them when the rope is pulled by men who have been hiding some distance away. On the thickness of the doorway leading into room C a bull is being overthrown for slaughter by butchers. Left on wall (4) Ankhmahor surveys with satisfaction the provisions carried along and more offering-bearers troop along the walls of room D. Back in room C on wall (5) Ankhmahor is receiving his brother and three sons – while all of note in room E is on wall (6) where there are men carrying wooden chests. Go back into room C and turn left to wall (7) to see Ankhmahor greeting rows of offering bearers with two smaller figures near him, one of which is his brother. Nothing new to detain you here so return to room A past the wall (8) where the fragmentary registers remaining indicate scenes originally involving crocodiles, hippopotami and fish. The 'gems' of this tomb are waiting on the thickness of the walls of the doorway. On the left wall (9) are surgical operations on the hand and toe – although here I must admit an element of doubt in my mind since the details are consistent also with massage or manicure techniques. However, a definite medical scene can be seen on wall (10) where circumcision is being performed by the priest-surgeon on two boys of about twelve years of age. Some of the accompanying hieroglyphs can be translated 'Hold him well so that he does not fall' and others may possibly contain a reference to a local anaesthetic. One of these 'surgical' reliefs includes a fairly rare depiction of a pregnant woman.

In room F there are five pillars in the centre and on wall (11) there are two registers to note: the upper represents priests and the lower indicates mourners before the house of Ankhmahor. On the other side of the doorway on wall (12) two girls clapping their hands are the accompanying percussion for five acrobats. On your way out of the tomb you can see on wall (13) the bakers and brewers hard at work.

III · SUNSET

CHAPTER II

'KING OF THE HORIZON, OLDEST OF GODS'

The Pyramid of Wenis

The ancient quayside and valley (reception) temple of King Wenis form the ruins which the visitor to Saqqara observes diagonally opposite the Antiquities Department ticket office on the road to the necropolis (*86*). From here the causeway (*87*) began a 660-metre-long, upward-sloping route to reach the mortuary temple on the eastern face of his pyramid. Along the way, it had been necessary to fill in depressions in the desert plateau – often, it seems, 'borrowing' blocks from Djoser's funerary monument. The undulations of the Western Desert also demanded that the causeway change the angle of its approach to the pyramid at two points. Except for one short stretch, the causeway today is open to the sky and elements. In antiquity it was protected by 3.15-metre-high walls and roofing blocks decorated with stars. The limestone walls are amazingly thick – over 2 metres – which the roof covered for most of the 2.60-metre-wide passageway, apart from a central gap which admitted light for the ceremonial approach.

You will find evidence for the decoration of the causeway walls in the existing covered section and at several points further west. Among the scenes you can see are reliefs showing the transport of columns by boat and metal-workers. But the whole journey along this causeway was originally a rich panorama of which only the meagre reliefs in situ are a hint. The most important blocks have been removed to storerooms. As you walk along the causeway, recreate for yourself some of the following themes which decorated the walls, as well as studying those still on view.

On the southern wall of the covered passage you will find the depiction of columns and architraves transported by boat to the valley temple of King Wenis' pyramid complex. You can see two columns with palm-leaf capitals, exactly the same as the real ones discovered in the valley and mortuary temples. The columns lie on sledges which in turn rest on wooden blocks on the boat deck. Scaffolding ensures that the columns remain fixed in the middle of the cargo vessel. Propitiatory offerings of bread, beer and a calf's head accompany the columns on their long journey. In fact the hieroglyphs above the boat tell where the boats have sailed from: 'Coming from Aswan loaded with granite columns'. The destination is given as well: 'The pyramid of Wenis-Beautiful-of-Places'. It is useful to note that the columns appear to be in a finished state, indicating that most of the dressing of the stone was done near the quarries of Aswan. This relief is the sole extant representation of the transport of granite monoliths hundreds of miles along the Nile in the art of the pyramid age. Yet the valley temple of Rakhaef and the lower courses of stone in Menkaura's pyramid are just two examples of the regular exploitation of the granite quarries. Not until nearly a thousand years later does one find cargo boats shown with similar colossal granite monuments – that is the obelisk reliefs in the temple of Queen Hatshepsut at Deir el-Bahari.

100. Exterior of the tomb of Harkhuf, Dynasty VI, Aswan

101. The pyramid of Pepi II at South Saqqara

On the opposite wall of the covered stretch of the causeway you can see artisans at work and a market scene. In the upper registers craftsmen are heating the furnace using blowpipes in order to melt silver, and others beat out fine gold. Vessels of gold and stone are polished, a man makes the metal blade for an adze, and a pair of scales is weighing ingots under the careful supervision of a scribe. You then witness all the activity of an Egyptian market. Fish are being gutted and sold, while the keeper of the 'guard baboon' appears to help himself to a lettuce as he passes a basket – an early example of protection money?

Some reliefs from the causeway represented the continuing cycle of the seasons of the year. Figs are gathered, honey stored, barley cut and birds and animals are trapped. A veritable zoo was depicted on some surviving blocks providing a repertoire of animals not found elsewhere in Old Kingdom monuments. Cervids are well represented – mufflon, antelope, gazelle, ibex, oryx and a stag – the great cats are here – lion and leopard – and desert hares, hedgehogs, jerboas and foxes. One animal shown here must have caused great excitement on its arrival in Memphis – a giraffe.

The most startling of the Wenis causeway reliefs concerns an episode difficult to interpret in significance but quite clear in its realism. It was discovered in a trial sondage towards the eastern section of the causeway and, thinking of late-twentieth-century events in East Africa, implies famine has been a recurrent feature of that continent. People are shown starving to death in this relief-fragment (88). A man sinks dying into his wife's arms despite the attempt of a friend to hold him upright, a child with an abdomen swollen by lack of sustenance begs for food, and a woman is driven to the extremity of searching in her hair for lice to eat. This situation is not at all an indication of the prosperity which King Wenis would hope to convey as existing in Egypt during his reign. The emaciated people, however, in some cases appear to be foreigners. Possibly, then, this relief was part of an overall scene where desert Bedu tribes were driven by famine to seek aid from the granaries of the Nile valley. At any rate one can be sure that the solution to their distress was achieved by King Wenis and considered a fitting boast for his causeway reliefs.

To the south of his causeway Wenis ordered two pits, 49 metres long, to be dug in a naviform shape. These boat-pits were lined with limestone blocks. No trace of any vessels inside were discovered, and probably they never existed. The symbolism of the boat pits would have been sufficient for Wenis to travel in the day and night boats used by the sun god. Further along the causeway you pass through a gate inscribed with the cartouche of Wenis into the mortuary temple. This temple was completed for Wenis by King Teti, first king of Dynasty VI, implying a smooth transition of power on Wenis' death to a new royal family. The paving slabs are of fine calcite and there were fourteen red-granite palmiform columns and two made of the mellow sandstone from the Kom el-Ahmar quarries. Fragments of the columns and chapels lie scattered around as you cross the temple to reach the northern face of the pyramid. Examples of these columns in good preservation grace the galleries of the museums of Cairo, Paris, London and New York.

The Wenis pyramid (89), the entrance of which is now before you, has collapsed into an amorphous heap of stones – now only 19 metres high, degenerated from an original 43 metres. Attempts were made in Ancient Egpyt to prevent the deterioration of the pyramid superstructure, caused, as at Abusir, by lack of attention to internal buttress walls. You can see hieroglyphs on the southern face of the pyramid which record the work of the 'antiquarian' prince, Khaemwaset, son of Ramesses II, who, over a thousand years after the reign of Wenis, tried to refit the fallen outer casing of the pyramid.

But the dilapidated state of the pyramid disguises its great importance on another count. In its interior you will find a surprise which reveals an immense amount of information about royal rituals and the afterlife. So go down into the desert rock through the granite-lined passage. After 14.35 metres at an angle of 22° you reach a vestibule leading to an 18-metre-long horizontal stretch. Here you pass easily the three niches which originally were blocked by granite portcullises. Arrived at the antechamber, you will see three recesses to the east, probably for statues, while to the west is the passage to the burial chamber. You are now surrounded by the earliest large-scale religious composition in the world, the hundreds of spells carved out in hieroglyphs (90), known collectively as the Pyramid Texts, many of which were later included in the New Kingdom compilation, *The Book of the Dead*. They make their first appearance here in the pyramid of Wenis and continue in the monuments of Dynasty VI.

Go into the burial chamber so that you can see where Wenis originally lay in his highly polished black-granite sarcophagus. Here the walls are lined with polished calcite on which around the sarcophagus you see the palace-façade design with the distinctive entwined double-lotus motif (91 & 92). The gabled ceiling is decorated with stars (93) carved in relief against a blue background. Now let your eye take in the exquisitely carved hieroglyphs of the Pyramid Texts, coloured blue to hint at the primaeval watery chaos out of which the sun god emerged.

The Pyramid Texts encapsulate centuries of funerary ceremonial performed at the time of a monarch's burial, probably at set stages on the journey of the sarcophagus, as well as ensuring the well being of the king in the hereafter. They are an ornate tapestry of ritual and belief. Egyptologists have argued about nuances in the grammar of these texts and have offered explanations for obscure passages. However, as you survey the walls of Wenis' sepulchral chamber I would like to paraphrase a portion of the 228 spells inscribed here (a complete edition of all the spells found here and in the pyramids of Dynasty VI would number in excess of 700). Many of the spells are designed to restore the dead monarch to life and provide victuals to feast upon. Water, beer, linen, sceptres, crowns and incense are just a few of the commodities and equipment that the texts can magically create for Wenis. Then there are spells whose formulation concerns his ascent into the sky on a ladder, being ferried across the firmament on reed floats, and joining Ra the sun god. It was the priests of Heliopolis who compiled the nucleus of the Pyramid Texts for the king, so it is not surprising that the solar references abound throughout. Yet there are tantilizing spells about the king soaring into the sky to become a star, giving a glimpse of an important astral cult. Perhaps the most fascinating spell of all envisages the king as a hunter preying on other gods. This compilation is occasionally referred to by modern writers as 'The Cannibal Hymn'. Dramatic phraseology enhances the terrifying image of a ruthless predator king:

> The sky is clouded over ... and stars have no light ... the bones of the earth-gods [Akeru] shake ... the king comes as a god living on his fathers and feeding on his mothers ... the king is lord of knowledge, mightier than Atum the god who created him ... the king is the bull of heaven ... the king eats men and lives on the gods ... he eats their magic ... the king is the most ancient of gods ... he breaks backbones and seizes the hearts of the gods ... he is lord of the horizon ... he devours the Red Crown ... he swallows the intellect of every god.

The essence of the imagery is that the monarch has become an indestructible and all-powerful ruler in the next life, whose magical force is substantially magnified by his banquet of deities.

Twilight: The Pyramids of Dynasty VI

For reasons which currently elude our grasp, the ancient compilers of the papyrus known as the Turin Royal Canon considered the reign of King Wenis to mark the end of an era. The accession to the throne of King Teti (94), son of a Queen Seshseshat, in 2323 BC inaugurated Dynasty VI probably, but not indisputably, by a peaceful transition of power. Certainly the title of his Queen Ipwet as 'royal daughter' indicates that Teti is likely to have married into his predecessor's family to strengthen his hold on the throne. The emphasis also seems to be on continuity in Teti's choice of a region of Saqqara contiguous to sepulchres of Dynasty V, and not too distant from the pyramids of Weserkaf (founder of the previous dynasty) for his own royal necropolis. The mastabas of Mereruka, Kagemni and Ankhmahor, the high officials of his reign, opposite his pyramid, have already been surveyed (see pp. 204–20). From the results of the excavations in the 1980s of Macquarie University, Sydney, in the area northwest of Teti's pyramid we can see that his pyramid city and cult flourished into the reigns of his successors. The pyramid-priest Semdent bore the title 'Overseer of the king's breakfast in all his places', while in the tomb-chapel of Iries 'priest of Maat' and 'royal chamberlain' there has been carved a luxurious list of ninety-five ritual offerings. The rule of King Teti continued the momentum of vigorous trade abroad both south of the First Cataract of the Nile and at Byblos. Internally provisions were made at Saqqara for the construction of pyramids for his two queens Khuyet and Ipwet (mother of Pepi I). To date archeology has not been able to substantiate the assertion of Manetho that Teti, called Othoes, was murdered by his bodyguards. If it were true then it has all the hallmarks of a harem conspiracy such as is found in the reign of his successor Pepi I. If a death-mask, now in Cairo Museum, discovered in his pyramid-temple at Saqqara were less poignantly serene, then one might possess some slender 'emotional' evidence for an assassination. However, as it stands there is not even conclusive proof that the mask's features are those of King Teti himself.

As for Teti's funerary monument many visitors to the tomb of

Mereruka opposite are often oblivious to the fact that the sandy-coloured mound devoid of sharp contours is a pyramid at all (95). It is worth taking a few minutes to descend into the sepulchral chamber of Teti's pyramid even though the funerary apartments are not in the same state of preservation as those of Wenis, due to the 'stone fatigue' and the vandalism of tomb robbers. Pyramid texts on the walls of the burial chamber continue to sustain the royal hereafter, although the decoration was not fully completed at the time of Teti's – untimely? – demise. Looking at the sarcophagus of black graywacke makes one aware that its dimensions are such that it must have been introduced into the burial chamber in the first stages of the pyramid's construction, its enormity precluding haulage along the descending corridor. It is not cut into the floor but rests on wood and stone wedges. The hieroglyphs which are carved on the lid and casket of Teti's sarcophagus form religious texts rather than just the royal protocol – an Old Kingdom prototype inaugurating a concept which burgeoned a thousand years later into the immaculate and intricate underworld images on the sarcophagus of Sety I currently suffering in appalling obscurity in the Sir John Soane Museum, London.

The immediate successor of King Teti was Weserkara known only as a name in the king list in Seti I's temple at Abydos. Accordingly, proceed directly to King Teti's effective successor Pepi I, son of Queen Ipwet (96). Now the exploratory trading missions beyond Egypt's frontiers become blatant aggressive expansionism through the subjugation of large tracts of Palestine and Nubia. Possibly the first proponent of 'gun-boat' diplomacy in the Middle East, Pepi I gave Egypt a taste for imperialism that was to reach its zenith in the reign of Tuthmosis III (1479–1425 BC) when pharaoh's troops dominated principalities and tribes from the north Sudan to Syria. Because in Dynasty VI the king's high officers of state became bolder and step unhesitatingly into the limelight one can get a glimpse of Pepi's campaigns through the eyes of Weni, whose boasts were carved on a limestone slab of his Abydos cenotaph which is now in Cairo Museum. In his youth Weni had served King Teti as a storeroom guard. With the accession of Pepi I his career took off and he became 'Overseer of the robing-room'. Concentrating on Weni's military exploits, it is learnt that Pepi I recruited an army of tens of thousands of troops from the Delta, Upper Egypt, Libyan tribes and Nubia. At that time Weni's chief rank was 'Overseer of royal tenants' and he delights in revealing that Pepi I put him as commander-in-chief of the whole army – doubtless to the chagrin of the aristocrats, top bureaucrats, town mayors, intelligence officers, and senior clergy who were also drafted into this campaign. A few telling phrases before the action begins reflects the law-and-order problems of four millennia ago. Weni's moral presence apparently was the reason why no camp fights broke out, no innocent travellers lost their food or sandals, no towns were looted for linen and no families had their livestock stolen. Weni leads the attack against the Bedu of Sinai and South Palestine and his inscription contains a paeon extolling the army's prowess and safe return from the 'land of the sand-dwellers'. But Pepi I sent Weni on a further campaign in order to consolidate Egypt's success in the Levant. In the last campaign it is likely that Weni broke enemy resistance by trapping the Bedu tribes between the army approaching from the south and his own commando force landing on the Palestinian seaboard to the north. The region is left vague in Weni's account but there is a good case for it being in the Mount Carmel range.

The vigour of Pepi I's reign is in the tradition of King Sneferu of Dynasty IV or King Sahura of Dynasty V (97). Like these monarchs Pepi I supervised the construction of an elaborate funerary complex, the richness of which has been revealed more and more in recent years by La Mission Archéologique Française de Saqqara (MAFS). The excursion to South Saqqara to visit the pyramids of Pepi I, Nemtyemsaf I (Meryenra) and Pepi II demands time and stamina but the reward is archeological and emotional – the monuments are there to see and the 'ghosts' of the last pharaohs of the Old Kingdom can almost subvert a rationalist, healthily sceptical concerning the paranormal. Apart from the admittedly undistinguished pyramid of Pepi I his funerary complex is impressive: pyramid town (for which Weni was an inspector of priests), quayside and canal, valley temple, ceremonial boats, causeway, satellite pyramid and mortuary temple. This survey of pyramid architecture has tried to elucidate the symbolism of the orientation of the monuments. Perhaps then, before considering Pepi I's complex in detail, the following schematic synthesis of concepts and cardinal points will provide a summary of pyramid symbolism.

THE AXES

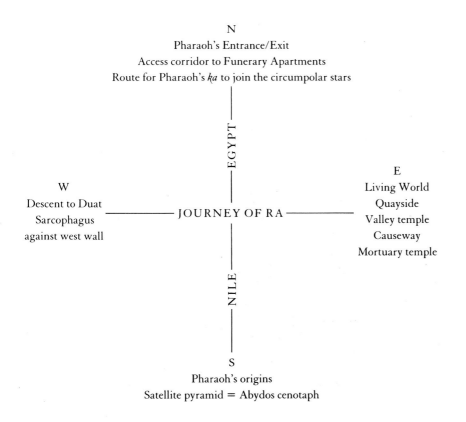

N
Pharaoh's Entrance/Exit
Access corridor to Funerary Apartments
Route for Pharaoh's *ka* to join the circumpolar stars

EGYPT

W
Descent to Duat
Sarcophagus
against west wall

—————— JOURNEY OF RA ——————

E
Living World
Quayside
Valley temple
Causeway
Mortuary temple

NILE

S
Pharaoh's origins
Satellite pyramid = Abydos cenotaph

The pyramid of Pepi I measures 78.6 metres wide and 52.4 metres high. Its internal apartments contain his sarcophagus on which the hieroglyphs were originally highlighted with attached gold leaf. The Pyramid Texts of Pepi I were carved with precision although some were then deliberately smudged with plaster. This was done to neutralize any magical force potentially hostile hieroglyphs might possess. For example, the rear parts of the signs of oxen, a giraffe, lions and elephants were plastered so that the creatures remained effective in the script but immobile. Similarly, horned vipers were sliced in half by a layer of plaster to prevent them attacking the king. The cult of the pharaoh was celebrated in a mortuary temple against the pyramid's eastern face which had a sanctuary protected by rooms and corridors, statues receiving ritual robing and Opening of the Month ceremonies every month and an assembly hall for dignitaries of state both at the time of the funeral of the king and at subsequent festivals.

In the late 1980s MAFS made some exciting new discoveries relating to royal women with scientific probes south of Pepi I's pyramid. It was known that Pepi I had three queens of the first rank. The autobiography of Weni tells of the unfortunate fate of the earliest queen. As 'senior warden of Nekhen' Weni was privileged to sit in with the Chief Justice on sensitive trials. On one occasion Queen Weret-Yamtes was put on trial for crimes which Weni does not divulge. One can assume a 'harem conspiracy' probably involving an attempt to interfere with the succession to the throne and possibly an unsuccessful assassination bid on the life of Pepi I himself. Weni's pride lies in the fact that he alone judged the queen – no other official being present on royal orders. It can be assumed that Queen Weret-Yamtes paid the penalty for treason and was discretely executed. Pepi I's other two queens seem to have been chosen to secure the loyalty of a powerful Upper Egyptian family from the reign of Abydos. Both take the same throne-name so we have Queen Ankhsenmerira I (mother of King Nemtyemsaf I) and Queen Ankhsenmerira II (mother of King Pepi II). Incidentally their brother Djau became vizier.

At South Saqqara MAFS decided to explore the area of sand and rubble south of Pepi I's pyramid. Electromagnetic techniques could simplify the problem of discovering monuments that might be buried 6 metres below ground. Help was enlisted from L'Electricité de France and La Compagnie de Prospection Géophysique Française to study variations in the magnetic field and resistance of different materials in the ground. Because of the small difference of resistance between rubble and dressed stone thousands of measurements were taken and results analysed. Subsequently pillaged and ruined, three funerary complexes gradually emerged, originally built to impressive dimensions for queens of Pepi I – though one cannot imagine the disgraced Weret-Yamtes being one of the honoured recipients. As yet no inscriptions have enabled any of Pepi I's queens to step out of anonymity and claim her pyramid complex and one is left wondering whose foot graced the gilded sandal discovered in the MAFS excavation.

From the reign of Pepi I come two masterpieces of metallurgy originally set up in the temple of Hierakonpolis and subsequently in

antiquity buried below the floor of a chapel either for protection or as
votive offerings. They represent a life-size copper statue of Pepi I and a
smaller copper figure which stood on the same base and is usually
considered to be his son Meryenra (Nemtyemsaf I) (98). The copper was
hammered into shape over a wooden core and despite the severe
corrosion we still get the impression of the pristine majesty of the dyad.
Armed with a torch you should seek out the statues in the ground-floor
galleries of Cairo Museum and shine it into the eyes which consist of
inlay of limestone and obsidian. Pepi I will be seen to wake into life and
defy you to stare for long into his regal eyes. Finally, perhaps fittingly for
the ambitions of this monarch, it was from the description of his pyramid
at South Saqqara as 'Men-nefer' or 'enduring and beautiful' that the
sprawling city to the east took its name to become the Memphis of Greek
writers.

The son of Queen Ankhsenmerira I, Nemtyemsaf, succeeded his
father as pharaoh in 2255 BC. In a move foreshadowing the diminution
of royal authority at the end of the dynasty, Nemtyemsaf appointed the
smug Weni as 'Governor of Upper Egypt'. The boasts of the autobiography continue unsullied by modesty to document Weni's unstinting
efforts on behalf of the King. I suppose one ought to be grateful for the
information it gives concerning the furbishing of a royal pyramid
complex. Nemtyemsaf sent Weni to the First Cataract of the Nile at
Aswan to cut five canals to facilitate the transport of granite from the
quarries. In addition Nubian chiefs organized the felling of acacia trees
to supply timber for three barges and four towing vessels. By this means
granite casing blocks were transported to the pyramid called 'Meryenra
[Nemtyemsaf] shines in splendour' at South Saqqara. In the heat of
summer Weni constructed another barge about 25 metres long by 12
metres wide in seventeen days in Middle Egypt to transport an altar
carved out of translucent Hatnub calcite to Nemtyemsaf's pyramid.
Other expeditions involving a large flotilla resulted in granite door-
jambs and lintels from Aswan and the sarcophagus of Wadi Hammamat
greywacke which rests below the vaulted star-spangled ceiling of
Nemtyemsaf's pyramid. The funerary chamber is quietly polychrome in
appearance with delicate pigments such as crushed green malachite
mixed with acacia gum used as colouring for the hieroglyphs of the
Pyramid Texts. Probably the body discovered in 1881 in the sarcophagus
(and now in Cairo Museum) is that of King Nemtyemsaf himself and
thus the oldest royal mummy to have survived reasonably intact.

We now come to the last effective reign of the sixth Dynasty, that of
Neferkara Pepi II (99). Traditionally he is held to have ruled Egypt from
his accession to the throne in 2246 BC at the age of six until his death in
2152 BC aged 100. Even if we follow the most sceptical view of
misreading in Hieratic giving ninety years instead of sixty years, Pepi II's
rule lasted a sufficient length of time for him to witness the fragmentation of central pharaonic government into influential principalities in the
Delta, along the Nile valley and in Dakhla Oasis in the Western Desert.

In his early years Egypt must have been governed in his name through
his mother Queen Ankhsenmerira II and her brother the vizier Djau.
During Pepi II's minority the governors of Aswan were accruing more

and more wealth from the lucrative trade with southern lands. Their rock-cut sepulchres with steep ascents from the river bank can be seen in the western cliffs of Qubbet el-Hawwa north of the island of Elephantine. One governor, Pepynakht, even became deified in the Middle Kingdom (*c.*1900 BC) and a cult was dedicated to him in his name of Hekayib near the temple of Khnum. In the reign of Pepi II their prestige was immense and no governor exemplifies the honoured status devolved on him by the monarch more than Harkhuf (*100*). His weathered autobiography carved on the façade of his tomb is a mine of information about trade routes to the south and the goods sought from Nile-and-desert dwelling tribes. Harkhuf had made three exploratory trading journeys to remote lands during the reign of Nemtyemsaf, two of them to Yam via el-Kharga oasis which lay on the Darb el-Arabayin route to Darfur. One mission saw him leave Yam with 300 donkeys carrying elephant tusks, panther skins, ebony and incense. However, it was the journey to Yam made in Year 2 of the reign of Pepi II when the monarch was 8-years-old that Harkhuf seems most proud of. The dispatch which Harkhuf received from the excited young king was carved verbatim into his tomb inscription. Pepi II was eager to see the 'pygmy of the god's dances from the land of the horizon-dwellers' whom Harkhuf had acquired. Only once before in the reign of King Izezi of Dynasty V had a pygmy from the land of Punt (a region in the vicinity of the river Atbara inland from the Red Sea coast in eastern Sudan) been the star attraction at the royal court. The king's instructions to Harkhuf were to keep the pygmy closely guarded in a pavilion in the boat on which he was travelling, and for a check to be made ten times a night to ensure that he had not fallen overboard into the Nile.

Elsewhere in Upper Egypt local governors (or nomarchs) were cutting themselves rock tombs, preferring burial near their residence-cities rather than a mastaba in the royal necropolis of South Saqqara. A thorough epigraphic survey by Macquarie University, Sydney, under Naguib Kanawati in the early 1980s was made of a group of such rock-cut sepulchres ranging in date from Dynasties V and VI through to the Middle Kingdom at el-Hawawish near Akhmim in Sohag province. The vivid daily-life scenes in the Old Kingdom range are painted with a freedom not found in Memphite tomb chapels and are reminiscent of some of the scenes on the walls of the later rock-cut sepulchres of the governors of the Oryx district at Beni Hasan. At Edfu the excavations of L'Institut Français d'Archéologie Orientale du Caire (IFAO) in the 1930s discovered the mastaba of the vizier and governor Isi who lived through the reigns of Kings Izezi, Wenis and Teti. His status was a foretaste of the decentralization that characterizes the late sixth dynasty. Like Hekayib, Isi was deified in the Middle Kingdom and his tomb became a local pilgrimage centre. The delightful dyad now in the Louvre Museum, of a couple with distinctive broad 'country' features, discovered in his mastaba is regrettably uninscribed but is likely to represent Isi and his wife.

For many of these district governors the royal court at Memphis had become irrelevant and remote. While paying perfunctory lip service to convention the nomarchs of Upper Egypt were establishing their own dynasties. I believe that this decentralization was accelerated by a loss of respect for the institution of kingship. At Memphis there was, no doubt, superficially expressed loyalty, but it is difficult to escape the feeling that the image of Pepi II had become tarnished. The fragments of a scandalous story survive from a composition committed to writing around 1400 BC but probably reflecting an oral tradition dating back to the Old Kingdom. In this ribald tale there must be a kernel of historical fact. King Neferkara (i.e. Pepi II) is observed making unscheduled nightly assignations with General Sisene. It is the lack of regal dignity in the idea of a pharaoh scurrying furtively in and out of his staff-officer's quarters that is degrading rather than the monarch's sexual predilections. Returning to inscriptional evidence Pepi II married his half-sister Neith, eldest daughter of Pepi I and Ankhsenmerira I. He also married the 'King's eldest daughter' Ipwet, probably a child of Nemtyemsaf, and had at least two other first-rank queens.

Pepi II prepared a grandiose funerary complex at South Saqqara (*101*). Its condition today is ruinous. His pyramid has a coat of rubble masonry revetted with dressed limestone casing blocks. From his mortuary temple a number of well-carved reliefs have been retrieved. Around were pyramids for his queens and painted tomb chapels with small superstructures for his minor officials who had no roots in Middle and Upper Egypt where the truly powerful dignitaries were buried. Pepi II's death and burial closes the Old Kingdom. Ephemeral monarchs survived briefly at Memphis and it is not even possible to console oneself that one of these successors, Queen Nitokrety, is the Queen Nitokris of legend, whom Manetho described as the 'noblest and loveliest of the women of her time' and whose thirst for vengeance Herodotus describes as being sated only when she had drowned the murderers of her brother and committed suicide to avoid retribution.

In a general review of the late Old Kingdom it is possible to isolate some major factors which brought about its demise. Politically, royal authority was severely undermined by the uncurbed license of provincial governors to set up independent courts with, in the words of an American Egyptologist, 'only a perfunctory nod in the direction of Memphis'. Economically the programme of constructing pyramid complexes drained vast resources from the royal treasury. In addition, an almost flamboyant extravagance existed in terms of endowments for private funerary monuments and a reckless granting of tax exemptions for religious bodies and mortuary cults. A good example of this is the exemption decree that King Pepi I promulgated on behalf of his mother Queen Ipwet concerning her chapel in the Temple of Min at Koptos (p. 1). Basically none of its personnel were liable for state service such as the pyramid-corvée, its property was inviolate and untaxable and no royal official on a mission that took him past the chapel could claim any travel expenses against it. Also, events abroad weakened the royal revenue in that around 2200 BC disturbances in Palestine and Syria seriously curtailed the valuable trade routes to the north. Moreover if, as is thought likely, the late Old Kingdom suffered from the failure of rains all over the Nile sources, then the spectre of famine and drought would stalk Egypt, and grain resources would be at a premium.

Faced with a build up of calamities the government at Memphis ran out of ideas and momentum and pharaonic authority dwindled: the king became merely a pious nomenclature carved on necropolis monuments. The sombre words of the reactionary Ipuwer who lived in the period immediately following the collapse of the Old Kingdom are preserved a thousand years later on a New Kingdom papyrus in Leiden Museum. Ipuwer's world is changing and his political and social values are no longer those under which his contemporaries operate. But even allowing for his cynical exaggerations there is no denying that the grandeur of the pyramid age is over:

> The land spins round like a potter's wheel ...
> No one sails north to Byblos ...
> The land is deprived of kingship
> by a few who do not believe in tradition ...
> Men rebel against the Uraeus ...
> The poor have become wealthy
> but the property owner is now a pauper ...
> The state has gone to rack and ruin.

Ipuwer is inconsolable so leave him indulging in his sustained catalogue of miseries. In 2040 BC Egypt's problems were to be overcome when a Theban ruler restored the unity of the kingdom. However, that lies beyond the scope of this volume. In retrospect, reviewing this eclectic survey of the first thousand years of dynastic Egypt from the nadir of royal fortunes at the close of the Old Kingdom, it is possible to isolate the one factor that made its downfall inevitable. Quintessentially, the pyramid era was the age when the realm of Ra flourished under the rule of god-kings who were remote and jealous of their authority: it collapsed when pharaohs shed prerogatives and powers which were picked up by ambitious courtiers. The domain of Ra had splintered into loose confederations and autonomous principalities – Egypt a thousand years after King Narmer was once more in need of a uniter of the Two Lands.

Photographic Credits

Thanks are due to the following for the appearance in this book of pieces from their public collections.

THE VISITORS OF THE ASHMOLEAN MUSEUM, OXFORD
BRITISH MUSEUM, LONDON
BROOKLYN MUSEUM, NEW YORK
CAIRO MUSEUM
EGYPTIAN MUSEUM, BERLIN
FITZWILLIAM MUSEUM, CAMBRIDGE
LEIDEN MUSEUM OF ANTIQUITIES, LEIDEN
LOUVRE MUSEUMS, PARIS

The photographs were supplied by the following:

MICHAEL DUIGAN: half-title, frontispiece, 1, 5, 13, 14, 18, 24, 35, 41, 47, 48, 50, 52, 54, 76, 82, 88, 94, 95, 100

MRS M. HACKFORTH-JONES: 6, 10

AYESHAH HALEEM: 12, 17, 21, 25, 27, 29, 31, 34, 36, 37, 42, 46, 51, 53, 55, 59, 63, 65, 66, 68, 70, 72, 73, 74, 75, 80, 81, 90, 91, 92, 93, 98, 101

GEORGE HART: 7, 8, 9, 15, 16, 19, 20, 22, 26, 28, 30, 32, 33, 38, 39, 56, 57, 58, 60, 64, 67, 69, 71, 77, 79, 83, 85, 86, 87, 89

DAVID MILLAR: 23, 30, 61, 71, 78, 84

ASHMOLEAN MUSEUM: 2

BRITISH MUSEUM: 3, 4, 11, 40, 43, 44, 45, 62

BROOKLYN MUSEUM: 96, 97, 99

Further Reading

ALDRED, C., *Old Kingdom Art in Ancient Egypt*, London, 1949

ALDRED, C., *Egypt to the End of the Old Kingdom*, London, 1965

BADAWY, A., *A History of Egyptian Architecture*, Vol. I, Giza, 1954

BAER, K. *Rank and Title in the Old Kingdom, The structure of the Egyptian Administration in the Fifth and Sixth Dynasties*, Chicago, 1960

BAINES, J., & MALEK, J., *Atlas of Ancient Egypt*, London, 1980

VON BISSING, F. ET AL., *Das Re-Heiligtum des Konigs Ne-Woser-re* (3 vols), Berlin, 1905–28

BORCHARDT, L., *Das Grabdenkmal des Konigs Sahu-Re* (2 vols), Leipzig, 1910–13

BOURRIAU, J. *Umm el-Ga'ab, Pottery from the Nile valley before the Arab Conquest*, Cambridge, 1981

BROOKLYN MUSEUM, *Africa in Antiquity, The Arts of Ancient Nubia and the Sudan* (2 vols), Brooklyn, 1978

BRUNTON, G. AND CATON-THOMPSON, G., *The Badarian Civilization*, London, 1928

BUTZER, K. W., *Early Hydraulic Civilization in Egypt*, Chicago, 1976

DAVIES, N. DE G., *The Mastaba of Ptahetep and Akethetep*, London, 1900/1901

DUELL, P. *The Mastaba of Mereruka* (2 vols), Chicago, 1938

DUNHAM, D., AND SIMPSON, W. K., *The Mastaba of Queen Mersyankh III*, Boston, 1974

EDWARDS, I. E. S., *The Pyramids of Egypt*, London, 1961

EDWARDS, I. E. S., *The Early Dynastic Period in Egypt*, London, 1964 (fasc. 25 of *The Cambridge Ancient History*)

EMERY, W. B., *The Tomb of Hemaka*, Cairo, 1938

EMERY, W. B., *Great Tombs of the First Dynasty* (2 vols), Cairo and London, 1949–58

EMERY, W. B., *Archaic Egypt*, London, 1961

FAKHRY, A., *The Monuments of Sneferu at Dahshur*, Cairo, 1959

FAKHRY, A., *The Pyramids*, Chicago, 1961

FAULKNER, R. O. *The Ancient Egyptian Pyramid Texts*, Oxford, 1969

FAULKNER, R. O. *The Ancient Egyptian Book of the Dead*, London, 1985

FIRTH, C. M. AND QUIBELL, J. E., *The Step Pyramid* (2 vols), Cairo, 1935–6

FRANKFORT, H., *Kingship and the Gods*, Chicago, 1948

FRANKFORT, H., *The Birth of Civilisation in the Near East*, London, 1951

GARDNER, E., *Egypt of the Pharaohs*, Oxford, 1961

GOEDICKE, H., *Reused blocks from the Pyramid of Amenemhet I at Lisht*, New York, 1971

GONEIM, M. Z., *The Buried Pyramid*, London, New York & Toronto, 1956

HART, G., *A Dictionary of Egyptian Gods and Goddesses*, London, 1986

HART, G., *Egyptian Myths*, London, 1990

HAYES, W. C., *The Scepter of Egypt* I, New York, 1953

HOFFMAN, A., *Egypt Before the Pharaohs*, London, 1979

HOLSCHER, U., *Das Grabdenkmal des Konigs Chephren*, Leipzig, 1912

KANAWATI, N. *Excavations at El-Hawawish, Cemetery of Akhmim*, Sydney, 1980

KANAWATI, N. *Governmental Reforms in Old Kingdom Egypt*, Warminster, 1980

KANAWATI, N. *Excavations at Saqqara, N.W. of Teti's, Pyramid*, Sydney, 1984

LAUER, J. P., *La Pyramide a degres* (4 vols), Cairo, 1936–59

LAUER, J. P., *Saqqara: The Royal Cemetery of Memphis*, London, 1976

LES DOSSIERS D'ARCHÉOLOGIE, *Saqqara: aux origines de l'Egypte pharaonique*, Numéro 146–147, 1990

LICHTHEIM, M., *Ancient Egyptian Literature* I, Berkeley, Los Angeles and London, 1975

MOKHTAR, G. (ed.), *General History of Africa*, Vol II, Paris and London, 1981

MONTET, P., *Les scenes de la vie privée dans les tombeaux egyptiens del'ancient empire*, Strasbourg, 1925

MURNANE, W., *The Penguin Guide to Ancient Egypt*, Harmondsworth, 1983

PETRIE, W. M. F., *The Pyramids and Temples of Gizeh*, London, 1883

PETRIE, W. M. F., *Meidum*, London, 1892

PETRIE, W. M. F., *The Great Pyramid*, London, 1893

PETRIE, W. M. F., *The Royal Tombs of the First Dynasty* (2 parts), London, 1900–1

PETRIE, W. M. F. *Prehistoric Egypt*, London, 1920

PETRIE, W. M. F. AND QUIBELL, J. E., *Nagada and Ballas*, London, 1896

POSENER-KRIÉGER, P., *Les archives du temple funéraire de néferirkarî-Kakai* (2 vols), Cairo, 1976

QUIBELL, J. E., *Hierakonpolis* (2 parts), London, 1900–2

QUIRKE, S., *Who were the Pharaohs?* (A history of their names, with a list of cartouches), London, 1990

REISNER, G. A. AND SMITH, W. S., *A History of the Giza Necropolis* II, Cambridge, Mass., 1955

REISNER, G. A. AND SMITH, W. S., *The Tomb of Hetepheres*, Cambridge, Mass., 1955

SALEH, M., AND SOUROUZIAN, H., *Official Catalogue of the Egyptian Museum, Cairo*, Munich, 1987

SIMPSON, W. K., *The Mastabas of Qar and Idu*, Boston, 1976

SIMPSON, W. K., *The Mastabas of Kawab, Khafkhufu*, Boston, 1978

SMITH, W. S., *A History of Egyptian Sculpture and Painting in the Old Kingdom*, Boston, 1949

SMITH, W. S., *The Art and Architecture of Ancient Egypt*, London, 1958

SMITH, W. S., *The Old Kingdom in Egypt*, London, 1962

STADELMANN, R. *Die Ägyptischen Pyramiden vom Ziegelban zum Weltwander*, Mainz am Rhein, 1985

STEINDORF, G., *Das Grab des Ti*, Leipzig, 1913

TRIGGER, B., *Nubia under the Pharaohs*, London, 1976

VERDERSLEYEN, C., *Das alte Egypten*, Propylaenkunstgeschichte Vol. XVII, Berlin, 1985

VANDIER, J., *Manuel d'Archeologie Egyptienne* (2 vols), Paris, 1952–5

WARD, W. A., *Egypt and the East Mediterranean World*, 2200–1900 BC, Beirut, 1971

WILLIAMS, C. R., *The Decoration of the Tomb of Per-Neb*, New York, 1932 (A good account of materials and techniques used in tomb decoration.)

NB: Many of the older publications will only be available in National and University Libraries.

Index

Figures in italics refer to captions